THE JOY

FEARING

GOD

THE FEAR OF THE LORD IS A LIFE-
GIVING FOUNTAIN ⌐ PROVERBS 14:27

JERRY
BRIDGES

WATERBROOK
PRESS

THE JOY OF FEARING GOD
PUBLISHED BY WATERBROOK PRESS
5446 North Academy Boulevard, Suite 200
Colorado Springs, Colorado 80918
A division of Random House, Inc.

ISBN 1-57856-254-6

Printed in the United States of America
1999—First Trade Paperback Edition
10 9 8 7 6 5 4 3 2 1

To
JEFF AND KATHY
DAN AND LISA

These are the commands, decrees and laws
the LORD your God directed me to teach you to observe
in the land that you are crossing the Jordan to possess,
so that you, your children and their children after them
may fear the LORD your God as long as you live
by keeping all his decrees and commands
that I give you, and so that you may
enjoy long life.

DEUTERONOMY 6:1–2

CONTENTS

From A Fellow Pilgrim

PROVERBS 31:30 reads, "Charm is deceptive, and beauty is fleeting; but a woman who fears the LORD is to be praised." I memorized that verse (in the King James Version) more than forty years ago to give myself, as a young single man, an important guideline in looking for a wife.

But what does it mean *to fear the Lord?* Looking back now, I realize I had only the foggiest notion. I suggest this is true for most Christians.

Fast-forward my life almost thirty years to 1982. While doing research for a book on godliness I came across the statement that "the fear of God is the soul of godliness." My attention was arrested, and I began a small study on the fear of God. Ten or so years later, my friend Dan Rich asked me to consider writing a book on the subject. This book is the response to that request.

A man who is himself a nationally known Bible teacher has said that people who teach the Bible are hypocrites because none of them live up to their teaching. I agree with the intent of his statement, but not his choice of words. In my mind a hypocrite is someone who pretends to be something he isn't. At the same time, though, I agree that none of us live up to the truths we teach. I don't want to be a hypocrite—so let me say right up front that I don't fully live up to the standard of truth presented in this book. I want to and I seek to, but I'm not there yet, nor will I ever be completely, in this life.

So as you read this book, think of me as a fellow pilgrim walking alongside you. I'm not on top of the peak calling you to climb up where I am. Rather I'm standing with you as we both look to the summit of this great mountain called the fear of God. It's a challenging climb upward, but also a joyous climb. My prayer is that this book will help us both in our journey.

MY THANKS

I'm grateful to several people who have contributed significantly to this book. My pastor friends Larry McCall and Steve Martin brought to my attention, or supplied me with, valuable resource material. Thomas Womack, my editor, contributed far beyond an editor's usual responsibilities. And the entire team at WaterBrook Press has been supportive and encouraging. A few friends have taken a special interest in this project and have prayed regularly for me in it. To all of you, thank you so much.

THE JOY

of

FEARING
GOD

PART I

What Is This Fear?

GLORIOUS TRUTH

Joy, Wisdom, and the Fear of God

THE *JOY* OF FEARING GOD? It sounds like a contradiction in terms. One of the first times I used the expression, my listener (a Christian leader) gave a puzzled look and responded, "That's an interesting combination of words." I suspect he was being polite as he really thought, "How can anyone enjoy fear? And more to the point, how can you enjoy fearing God? Christianity means a relationship with God—but how can you have a relationship with someone you fear?"

The fact that a Christian leader would respond to this concept with a puzzled look tells us something about the current state of Christianity. There was a time when committed Christians were known as God-fearing people. This was a badge of honor. But somewhere along the way we lost it. Now the idea of fearing God, if thought of at all, seems like a relic from the past. That's to our detriment. The fear of God is actually as relevant today as it was in bygone generations.

And strange as it may seem, there *is* joy in fearing God. The Bible says God delights in those who fear Him and holds out to them the promise of blessing. Surely then, this is a subject that deserves our attention.

But what *is* the fear of God?

When we mention this concept, one proverb from the Bible seems particularly to come to mind: "The fear of the LORD is the beginning of wisdom." I'm not sure why that one sticks in our memory, but it seems to be almost as universally recognized as "Do unto others as you would have them do unto you." Unfortunately, while both statements are widely recognized, few people seek to apply them in their daily lives.

So let's begin our study by looking at this verse, "The fear of the LORD is the beginning of wisdom" (Proverbs 9:10). As we do, let's first consider its corollary, "The fear of the LORD is the beginning of knowledge" (Proverbs 1:7). *Knowledge* and *wisdom* are not the same, though they're closely related. We might describe wisdom as the best application and use of the knowledge we have. So we need to consider the beginning of knowledge before we look at the beginning of wisdom.

FOUNDATION FOR RIGHT PERSPECTIVES

Proverbs 1:7 reads in full, "The fear of the LORD is the beginning of knowledge, but fools despise wisdom and discipline." *Knowledge* as used here is more than an accumulation of information. It involves the ability to view that information with the right perspective and to use it for its proper end. Paul, for example, speaks of a knowledge that "puffs up" (1 Corinthians 8:1) as well as a knowledge that "leads to godliness" (Titus 1:1). Only the latter has the right perspective and proper end in mind.

Two people may possess essentially the same knowledge in the sense of a body of facts. One person views this knowledge as a means of acquiring position, power, or possessions, and uses it to that end. The other person sees it as a gift from God and as a stewardship to be used to serve Him.

Contrast two physicians, both with approximately the same training and skill. One fears God and earnestly seeks to use his expertise to serve Him by serving people. The other has no fear of God and uses his skill as an abortionist. Both doctors have the same information but not the same knowledge. Only the one who fears God has the right perspective, which leads him to use his information for the proper end.

Solomon says that knowledge begins not in learning a body of information or in acquiring various skills, but in the fear of the Lord. He is saying that the fear of God must be the foundation upon which knowledge is built. It is the fear of the Lord that gives us the right perspective and prompts us to use it for the right end. It is the fear of the Lord that should determine our fundamental outlook on life.

Our main goal in life should be to glorify God. That is the ultimate goal to which all knowledge should be directed. Regardless of how helpful an item or body of knowledge may be to society, if it does not have as its final purpose the glory of God, it remains defective. It is at best partial and to a degree distorted. It is like a structure without a foundation, a plant without a root.

Of course since our fear of God is always imperfect, our knowledge will always be defective and incomplete—not only factually, but also in its use. But the person who does not fear God doesn't even have the right foundation on which to build. He may be a decent person and generally beneficial to society, but in the end he falls short because he neither knows nor fears God. Let me give you an example.

Several years ago I read *Evolution: A Theory in Crisis* by Michael Denton, an Australian physician who does research in microbiology. In my opinion his book is one of the most brilliant and devastating critiques of the theory of evolution available today. Dr. Denton did his homework well. From a number of perspectives he makes a convincing case that animal life as we see it today, and particularly the human body and brain, must be the product of specific design by an infinitely intelligent designer rather than the result of mere time and chance.

As you read through the book, you keep waiting for Dr. Denton to make a seemingly obvious statement that this intelligent designer must be God. Instead the book ends with this remarkable sentence: "The 'mystery of mysteries'—the origin of new beings on earth—is still largely as enigmatic as when Darwin set sail on the *Beagle.*"[1] After thoroughly debunking the Darwinian theory of evolution, Dr. Denton throws up his hands. "We don't know," he essentially says. We didn't know before Charles Darwin made his observations about plants and animals on the Galapagos Islands, and we still don't know today.

Why would a brilliant scientist come to such a conclusion? The reason is found in Solomon's words that the fear of the Lord is the beginning of knowledge. Dr. Denton has amassed a formidable amount of information and makes a strong case against evolution, but he is unable to bring his reasoning to a successful conclusion because his knowledge is incomplete. It does not take account of God.

I found Dr. Denton's book highly fascinating. In pursuing his objective to show the fallacy of evolution, he unwittingly gave us a book through which to marvel at the unfathomable wisdom of God in creation. On numerous occasions I found myself pausing to worship as I read. What a pity, I thought, that this man who knows a thousand times more than I about his subject could not use it to glorify God because he did not know or fear the One about whom he was writing.

People who fear God can use their knowledge both to glorify God and enjoy Him. One day I was waiting in the examining room of an ear, nose, and throat doctor. On the wall opposite my chair was a drawing of a greatly enlarged cross section of the human ear. As I looked at the tiny bones commonly called the hammer, anvil, and stirrup, I marveled at the perfection of the human ear and the ingenuity of God in designing it. I enjoyed a few moments of worship while waiting there and transformed a routine doctor's appointment into a delightful time of fellowship with God. I know very little about the ear, but I can thoroughly enjoy the knowledge I have because it is built upon the foundation of fearing the One who created it.

My experience should be true of the believer in every field of knowledge. The student of history can enjoy the subject much more if he or she believes that history is not merely a "tale told by an idiot" but rather the outworking of God's sovereign plan and purpose for this world. The Christian astronomer should worship as he observes through his telescope the vast handiwork of God in the heavens. The godly farmer growing crops rejoices in the awareness that his agricultural skill comes ultimately from God, because he reads in the Bible that "God instructs him and teaches him the right way" of planting and harvesting (Isaiah 28:26). Any sphere of knowledge you're engaged in—every aspect of your workaday world—should be to you as a believer a source of wonder and worship and should be used as a means of glorifying God. And it will be if you enjoy the fear of God.

Finally, we must consider the most important knowledge of all. Jesus said, "Now this is eternal life: that they may know you, the only true God, and Jesus Christ, whom you have sent" (John 17:3). In reality this is where true knowledge begins. The person who knows God and fears Him possesses something more valuable than all the combined knowledge of philosophy and science put together. The scientist and the philosopher may discover ways to improve this life; the Christian has found the way to eternal life. That the Christian's knowledge is more valuable was attested by Jesus when He said, "What good is it for a man to gain the whole world, yet forfeit his soul? Or what can a man give in exchange for his soul?" (Mark 8:36–37).

WHERE WISDOM BEGINS

Now we come to wisdom. Proverbs 9:10 says, "The fear of the LORD is the beginning of wisdom, and knowledge of the Holy One is understanding." Again observe the close connection between wisdom and knowledge. Both Proverbs 1:7 and 9:10 use both words. Since wisdom is knowledge applied to the right end, knowledge realizes its purpose only in conjunction with wisdom.

Wisdom is commonly defined as good judgment or the ability to develop the best course of action in response to a given situation. In the Bible, however, wisdom has a strong ethical content. For example, James 3:17 says, "But the wisdom that comes from heaven is first of all pure; then peaceloving, considerate, submissive, full of mercy and good fruit, impartial and sincere."

The ethical emphasis in wisdom is particularly strong in Proverbs. This doesn't exclude what we might call the practical dimension, such as the wise use of time or money. In fact the book of Proverbs is filled with instructions for day-to-day living. But this practical wisdom always has an ethical tone to it. Wisdom in Proverbs is more concerned with righteous living than with shrewd judgment. The practical is never divorced from the ethical.

It is with this ethical-practical relationship in mind that we should understand how the fear of the Lord is the beginning of wisdom. Just as the fear of God is the foundation of knowledge, so it's also the foundation of wisdom.

Consider for example Proverbs 11:1—"The LORD abhors dishonest scales, but accurate weights are his delight." Society says, "Honesty is the best policy." Why? The world's answer is, it's good for business. The honest auto repair shop gets a good reputation and presumably more cars to repair. Biblical wisdom, however, recognizes that God—even more than the customer—is concerned about honesty. Biblical wisdom always factors God into the equation. Society might cut corners when it isn't apt to hurt business, but the person who fears the Lord strives to be honest all the time. He's more concerned about pleasing God than about what's good for his business.

The fact is, honesty *is* the best policy. That's practical wisdom. That's what the world says (though too often it doesn't practice it). But this kind of wisdom has the wrong foundation. It is essentially self-serving. It leads us in the wrong direction and ultimately ends in futility and frustration. By contrast, wisdom based on the fear of God recognizes the supremacy of

God over every area of life and realizes that it is God who sends poverty and wealth, who humbles and exalts (1 Samuel 2:7). And in this wisdom rests, and it rejoices in the fear of God.

This principle that wisdom based on the fear of God ultimately leads to joyful living is taught over and over in the book of Proverbs, and throughout the Bible for that matter. One of its most meaningful illustrations for me is found in Proverbs 15:16–17—"Better a little with the fear of the LORD than great wealth with turmoil. Better a meal of vegetables where there is love than a fattened calf with hatred."

The particular principle set forth here is that love is more valuable than wealth. A "meal of vegetables" is descriptive of a poor-to-moderate living standard. In Solomon's day, ordinary people rarely had meat. On the other hand, "a fattened calf" connotes a wealthy family. With this background we can understand Solomon as saying that it's better to live in a poor family with love than in a wealthy family with hatred. This kind of wisdom can come only from the Lord.

The truth that love is more valuable than wealth ought to be self-evident. Yet throughout history, and especially in our culture today, it's obvious that wealth is deemed more valuable than love. People might deny that, but their actions speak louder than their words. Our society literally chases after wealth and possessions. This is true in inner-city ghettos as well as in upscale suburbs. All levels of our society base their supposed happiness on their ability to acquire the possessions they want.

This drive to acquire money and possessions has wide-ranging social implications. To name one, many parents place their professions or jobs above their children. It often results in a "swinging door" syndrome at home whereby families seldom sit down together to a meal, let alone spend extended time together. Parents become alienated from each other, and children from their parents, all in the interest of acquiring more things.

Families who base their wisdom for living on the fear of God, however, recognize that "a man's life does not consist in the abundance of his possessions" (Luke 12:15). They esteem love far more than material things.

Some of these families may indeed be blessed by God with wealth, but that isn't the defining characteristic of their lives.

The priority of love over possessions was brought home to me deeply and poignantly some ten years ago. My wife of twenty-five years was dying of cancer. We had been on the staff of a Christian organization all our married lives, and our income had usually hovered around barely adequate. If we went out to eat, it was to Burger King or the local cafeteria. We seldom had discretionary income.

Two things we did have lots of, though, were love and fun. My wife had elected to be a full-time, stay-at-home mom. She spent hours with the children when they were small, and after they were in school she never missed a game or scholastic event in which they participated. When I left for the office each morning, she always stood at the door to wave a loving good-bye. Our standard of living could have been described by Solomon's expression as "a meal of vegetables." But we had lots of love, and we enjoyed life.

With this history of twenty-five years of love and the realization that my wife was probably dying, I came across Proverbs 15:16–17 one day in my Bible reading. As I read, I wept for joy. I wrote in the margin of my Bible, "Thank you, Father, for a home with love."

My wife has now been with the Lord for ten years, but still today "her children arise and call her blessed" (Proverbs 31:28). There is joy in fearing God and in the wisdom that comes from it.

GOD'S TRUST FUND

Before we end this chapter, let me give you one more reason, from my own experience, why there is joy in fearing God.

Psalm 31:19 reads, "How great is your goodness, which you have stored up for those who fear you, which you bestow in the sight of men on those who take refuge in you." God is pictured here like a wealthy person who establishes trust funds for his children to be used after they reach maturity. The money is on hand, it has been set aside—but it isn't available to the children until they reach the prescribed age.

That is what God does for those who fear Him. He sets aside or stores up goodness for His children, to be given at appropriate times in the future. What this goodness is, and when it will be bestowed, is unique to each individual according to God's plan and purpose for that person.

I came across Psalm 31:19 during one of the more difficult periods of my life. I desperately needed encouragement at the time, and God gave it to me through that Scripture. What caught my attention was the thought that God *stores up* goodness, which He bestows at some time in the future. Even though things may be dark today, God is still storing up goodness for us.

As I prayed over Psalm 31:19 during those discouraging days, God gave hope that at some point in the future He would once again bestow His goodness, the goodness that He was then storing up for me. That's exactly what happened. In due time God opened up ministry opportunities far beyond anything I had ever imagined. Ironically, the very circumstances that brought about those discouraging days were used by God to both equip me and set me free for the ministry He had stored up to bestow in His good time.

Notice, though, that God stores up His goodness not for everyone, but for *those who fear Him.* How are we to understand this condition? Why did I think I qualified and had a right to gather confidence from that Scripture? This verse is an example of parallelism; that is, where a single idea may be stated again in another form. In this case, fearing God and taking refuge in Him are the parallel thoughts. We have not yet discussed what it means to fear God, but I can anticipate that discussion by saying that taking refuge in God is one expression or outworking of fearing Him.

Though the circumstances leading to that discouraging period occurred years ago, I still remember how the Holy Spirit enabled me to respond. While kneeling at our living room couch early one morning, the words of Job 1:21 came to mind: "The LORD gave and the LORD has taken away; may the name of the LORD be praised." As I prayed over that verse, I was able to trust in the sovereignty of God, to believe He was in control of my future, and to submit myself to whatever He was doing. To use the words of 1 Peter 5:7, I humbled myself under His mighty hand and trusted Him for the outcome. This is what it meant for me to fear the Lord in that situation. The *joy* of fearing Him did not come immediately, but it certainly did in His good time.

The assurance of future good, however, is not limited just to the difficult periods of life. The Holy Spirit no doubt brought Psalm 31:19 to my attention at that particular time to encourage and give me hope. The wonderful truth, though, is that God is always storing up good for those who take refuge in Him, and He bestows it at the proper time. That's another reason why there's joy in fearing God.

What *Is* the Fear of God?

We've come this far, and I still haven't defined the fear of God. That's because it's better described than defined. I've planted clues in this chapter which you've probably picked up, and they'll get more explicit as we go along. In the next chapter I'll give a concise definition, and a more expanded one follows in chapter three, but that's just to get us started. Actually the whole book is an attempt to describe the biblical concept of the fear of God and its outworking in our lives.

So join me in our journey to discover that there's joy in the fear of God; that the title of this book is not an oxymoron, but a glorious truth. We'll start with a brief story about a young marine whose experiences will help us begin to see what it means to fear God. I realize that some who read this book may not be able to identify with the experiences I describe of Marine Corps life. But I believe the truths illustrated in the story will be clear and you'll have no difficulty understanding them. So let's go now to this parable.

***

Notes

1. Michael Denton, *Evolution: A Theory in Crisis* (Bethesda, Md.: Adler & Adler, 1985), 358–9.

2

A PARABLE OF AWE

How the Right Fear Grows

THIS STORY BEGAN years ago, when Butch McGregor was only eighteen. He stood trembling as the drill instructor screamed in his face, calling him "a stupid imbecile" and a few other choice abusive terms. Butch hadn't done anything seriously wrong; he had just somehow managed to get out of step with the rest of his platoon as they marched across the drill field. But the slightest infraction, the most insignificant mistake, could cost Butch fifty push-ups or ten laps around the drill field in full combat gear. Only a few days earlier, he'd stood at attention, holding his rifle straight out in front of his chest until his arms could stand it no longer, while the drill instructor chewed him out for being such a weakling.

This wasn't exactly what Butch had in mind when he talked to the recruiting sergeant just after graduating from high school. He'd heard the marines were "looking for a few good men," and at six feet two inches and 200 pounds of solid muscle, he thought he qualified. Butch was intelligent enough and had fairly decent grades in school, but his real love was football. He played inside linebacker on his high school team and he loved physical contact, so the Marine Corps with its reputation for physical toughness appealed to him.

What Butch hadn't expected was how much mental and emotional abuse he would experience in basic training. He wasn't prepared for the verbal intimidation and humiliation he and his fellow recruits suffered every day. He was four inches taller and forty pounds heavier than the sergeant now screaming at him, but he dared not move a muscle or blink an eye. A humble but distinct "yes sir" or "no sir" was the only acceptable response.

Such is life at Marine Corps boot camp, where merciless drill instructors try to mold undisciplined young Americans into men and women who obey orders without hesitancy or questioning, a trait absolutely vital in combat. In this atmosphere the drill instructor takes on an aura of being just less than God. His every word is law; the slightest mistake or infraction is caught and punished. Very quickly the new recruit learns to stand in awe of this man who wields such authority and power over him.

Butch was no dummy. He soon learned to respect authority and to promptly and correctly carry out commands. Near the end of his basic training he was actually beginning to enjoy the challenge of this tough, disciplined life. Then something completely out of the ordinary happened, something that doesn't normally occur during basic training. The commanding general of the recruit training base decided to conduct an inspection of all recruit platoons nearing the end of their training.

A sort of disciplined pandemonium broke out among the drill instructors. Standards were pushed to even higher levels. Rifles were meticulously cleaned, boots were polished to a mirrorlike sheen, barracks were well-scrubbed, and beds were tightly made.

When General Collins and his entourage entered the barracks, Butch stood stiffly at attention. The confidence he had gained while adjusting to marine life quickly drained away as the general paused in front of him. Fear gripped him as the general carefully looked him over with cold, steely eyes and asked him a question. Butch's mouth was as dry as cotton as he sought to answer respectfully. He experienced a profound sense of awe as he, a lowly, humble recruit, stood in the presence of this Marine Corps general.

MIXED EMOTIONS

Following basic training, Butch was assigned to a divisional motor pool where he soon became recognized as a skillful and responsible driver and was rewarded with promotion to corporal. Meanwhile General Collins was promoted to major general and became the commanding officer of Butch's division. Because of his reputation, Butch was eventually selected to be the general's driver. Butch had mixed emotions about this new assignment. He relished the confidence shown in him; on the other hand he remembered those cold, steely eyes on that memorable inspection day back in boot camp. Awe once again gripped him as he reported for duty the first day.

Sergeant McGregor, as Butch now was called, soon discovered that behind those steely blue eyes was a no-nonsense general who was tough but fair. As he listened to the general's conversations with other officers riding in the car, Butch was often amazed at the general's evident wisdom and military skill. He also noted the increased morale and esprit de corps that the general's leadership gave to the entire division. His awe for the general actually increased, though its dominant aspect was no longer fear but respect and admiration. He could easily envision General Collins one day being commandant of the entire Marine Corps.

Of course Butch had always *shown* respect toward the general. That was absolutely essential to his job. But now he *felt* respect. He genuinely admired the general for both his personal character and his military leadership. One day he realized he had even begun to like the general, and he was fairly certain the general liked him. Despite this growing personal relationship though, Butch never lost his sense of awe toward the general. He was always conscious of the vast difference in rank between them. Even in casual conversation he always addressed the general as "Sir."

In the course of time war broke out, and Butch's division was shipped overseas. As the general's driver, Butch was never involved in actual combat, though they often traveled in dangerous territory.

Then one day the car struck a land mine. General Collins was thrown clear of the car, but was seriously hurt when his body slammed to the ground. Butch, meanwhile, remained trapped in the front seat of the burning vehicle. Despite the general's own injuries, and at the risk of his life, he managed to pull Butch out of the car to safety. Both men were quickly evacuated to the field hospital.

General Collins soon recovered sufficiently to resume his duties, but Butch remained in the hospital for weeks. Despite the pressures of commanding a division in battle, the general often stopped by to see Butch and check on his progress. Butch was surprised at the general's obvious concern, but what really astounded him was the realization that at the scene of the accident, the general had literally risked his life to save him.

As he lay in bed over the weeks, Butch frequently recalled with amazement the day General Collins had rescued him from a fiery death. And the general's continued visits made him realize the rescue was not simply a spur-of-the-moment heroic act, but was prompted by the general's heartfelt concern for him.

Butch often pondered the question, "Why would a two-star general, in command of a marine division in battle, risk his own life to save a mere sergeant?" He could readily understand one enlisted marine risking his life for his buddy on the battlefield—but a general for a sergeant? How could this be? He slowly came to the conclusion that, despite their vast difference in rank, the general genuinely loved him.

Now, in addition to his sense of awe, respect, and admiration, Butch began to experience love and gratitude toward the general. He longed for the day when he could once again be the general's driver. He determined that he would be the best driver any marine general ever had. But he also realized that however much he and the general loved each other, they would never be buddies. It would always be a "yes sir" and "no sir" relationship.

That's how both General Collins and Sergeant McGregor would want it.

THE PARABLE EXPLAINED

Jesus often taught by means of parables, fictional stories recounted as if they had once happened. The purpose of such stories was to give vivid, concrete expression to a more abstract religious concept. For example, He used the parable of the unmerciful servant (Matthew 18:21–35) to teach the concept of forgiveness, and the parable of the workers in the vineyard (Matthew 20:1–16) to teach the concept of grace. In some parables, particularly the two just mentioned, Jesus stretched the story's details to the point of the incredible or improbable in order to make His point more forcefully.

Parables are useful today when the subject matter being taught is abstract or little understood by an audience or reader. The account of the young marine Butch McGregor is intended to be such a story, illustrating the complex set of emotions that the Bible calls *the fear of God*.

Recall the various emotions this young marine faced as he moved through successive stages of his Marine Corps life. There was the initial awe of his drill instructor, an awe which in that setting was an emotion of pure fear, a dread of being punished or humiliated for the slightest infraction. Later, in the presence of the general, he experienced an even greater sense of awe. It was a sense not only of fear, but also of self-abasement as he realized that he, a mere recruit, stood in the presence of an officer whose rank and authority were vastly superior even to that of his drill instructor.

Next Butch McGregor was thrown into day-to-day contact with the general and had opportunity to observe both his personal character and leadership skills. He began to experience a different kind of awe—not of fear, but of respect and admiration. Yet even now he was always conscious of the vast difference between his and the general's respective ranks. He knew that although the general was cordial in their relationship, he would tolerate no unseemly familiarity. Butch was careful to maintain a respectful demeanor at all times.

Finally, after the rescue from the burning car, Butch came to realize how much the general cared for him personally. His sense of awe toward the general grew to include the amazement that this commanding general of a marine division would risk his own life to save him. And while he would thereafter continue to maintain a respectful distance in deference to the general's rank, he would feel a special bond of love and gratitude inspiring him to strive even harder to please the general.

What is awe? Like many words in our language, it has several related definitions. The dictionary I have defines *awe* as:

- An emotion in which dread, veneration, and wonder are variously mingled.
- Submissive and admiring fear inspired by authority.
- A fearful reverence inspired by deity.

You can easily see that, depending on the situation and the object of awe, it could include the emotions of fear (or dread), respect (or reverence), admiration, and amazement. We could see each of these as we traced the experiences of the young marine Butch McGregor.

SPECIFICALLY FOR GOD

Why this detailed analysis of a sense of awe? It is because *a profound sense of awe toward God is undoubtedly the dominant element in the attitude or set of emotions that the Bible calls "the fear of God."* A popular definition of the fear of God is "reverential awe," and I've concluded that this is indeed a good definition.

Why do we say *reverential* awe? It's to indicate that this sense of awe is specifically directed toward God. Imagine yourself driving across one of our central states on a sultry, overcast day. Suddenly you catch sight of a violent tornado spinning across the plains toward you, lifting houses and barns in the air and leaving wholesale destruction in its path. Immediately you feel a gripping sense of awe that includes not only fear for your own safety, but also amazement at the storm's overwhelming power.

Obviously you're experiencing awe in a very real sense. But it is not reverential awe.

Finally the tornado passes beyond, leaving you safe. You begin to think of the hand of God behind the tornado. You reflect on the fact that the roaring twister was a visible manifestation of His mighty power. Now your awe is focused not on the tornado, but on God. It has become a reverential awe—a mixture of fear, veneration, wonder, and admiration, all directed toward God Himself.

There are indeed many facets to the fear of God and many outworkings of its presence in a believer's life, so to restrict its meaning only to reverential awe would fail to do justice to the biblical concept. But underneath all these many facets and outworkings is this profound sense of awe toward God that provides the motivation and driving force for all the other elements that together make up the biblical portrait of fearing God.

One problem we face in using the term *awe*—even *reverential awe*—is that the true meaning of the word is so little understood in our culture today. Its meaning has been essentially debased through frequent flippant usage. It isn't uncommon, for example, to hear someone speak of the awesome chocolate sundae she enjoyed at an ice cream shop. Compare such a statement with the true meaning of awe as "an emotion in which dread, veneration, and wonder are variously mingled." The ice cream sundae was undoubtedly tasty, but it hardly qualified as awesome. Even the popular chorus "Our God Is an Awesome God" is too often sung with the gusto and enthusiasm of a pep rally rather than with the sober realization that God is indeed awesome.

Remember again the dictionary meaning of *awe* and how all three definitions contain the idea of *dread* or *fear*. We can easily see then that it's appropriate to use the word *awesome* to describe a tornado but not an ice cream sundae. We should be afraid of a tornado; we should enjoy an ice cream sundae.

REASON TO FEAR

Should we be afraid of God? Let's explore this topic first in light of the general situation we've inherited just by being a part of mankind.

As the "only proper answer" to this question, John Murray wrote:

it is the essence of impiety [i.e., ungodliness] not to be afraid of God when there is *reason* to be afraid. . . . The Scripture throughout prescribes the necessity of this fear of God under all the circumstances in which our sinful situation makes us liable to God's righteous judgment.[1]

After Adam sinned he was afraid (Genesis 3:10). In fact, in his situation it would have been the height of presumption *not* to be afraid. Likewise when the apostle Paul was describing the abject depravity to which the human race had fallen, he climaxed his descriptive terms with the statement, "There is no fear of God before their eyes" (Romans 3:18). People were neither in awe of God nor afraid of His judgments. They acted as if there were no God, no One to whom they were accountable for their conduct, no One who had the power and authority to bring them into judgment for their sins. They essentially thumbed their noses at God.

This lack of fear toward God, in the sense of being afraid of His judgments, is actually the very root of wickedness. John Calvin wrote,

All wickedness flows from a disregard of God. . . . Since the fear of God is the bridle by which our wickedness is held in check, its removal frees us to indulge in every kind of licentious [i.e., without moral restraint] conduct.[2]

Pharaoh is a classic example. He said to Moses, "Who is the LORD, that I should obey him and let Israel go? I do not know the LORD and I will not let Israel go" (Exodus 5:2). Pharaoh was neither in awe of God, nor afraid of His judgments. Even after the Egyptians had suffered through seven of ten plagues, Moses said to Pharaoh, "But I know that you and your officials still do not fear the LORD God" (Exodus 9:30).

In spite of overwhelming evidence of God's power as shown in the plagues, Pharaoh still was not convinced of God's ability to bring disaster on his land. He still was not afraid of God, so he persisted in his pride and presumption.

The Bible often links a lack of the fear of God with sinful conduct.[3] In fact, the first use of the expression *the fear of God* makes this association. Genesis 20 gives us the account. The patriarch Abraham had moved into the region of a local king, Abimelech, where for the second time Abraham lied about Sarah his wife, saying she was his sister. As a result Abimelech sent for Sarah to make her one of his wives. Fortunately God supernaturally intervened to keep that from happening.

When Abimelech confronted Abraham about his terrible deceitfulness, he asked,

> "What was your reason for doing this?"
>
> Abraham replied, "I said to myself, 'There is surely no fear of God in this place, and they will kill me because of my wife.'" (Genesis 20:10–11)

Abimelech apparently had more integrity than Abraham expected. But Abraham was correct in linking a presumed absence of the fear of God with a lack of moral integrity.

IS GOD SAFE?

There is no fear of God before their eyes. What could be more descriptive of our own society today? Our denial of any objective moral standards, or even our basing of morality upon society's consensus instead of God's Word, is tantamount to saying, "Who is God that we should obey Him?" Like Pharaoh of old, our society today is neither in awe of God nor afraid of His judgments.

Can you imagine a new class of marine recruits making up their own training rules by consensus—or even denying the necessity for any objective training standards? Such a thought is preposterous. It is too absurd even to think of what might happen, since we know that in the very nature of recruit training it couldn't happen. Yet this is the situation in our society today—and yes, even in our churches.

"In our churches?" you might ask. "Do you mean even Christians should be afraid of God? Haven't we been delivered from the prospect of God's wrath? Doesn't perfect love drive out fear?" We'll explore these questions in future chapters, but for now, think of visiting the lion pit at the zoo. The lions are safely separated from you by a large moat and a high fence, so you don't experience the dread or terror that would overtake you if you encountered a lion in the savannas of Africa. Yet even at the zoo you notice a certain caution, a respect, even a nagging fear of the *potential* danger of the lions that makes you glad you're safely separated from them.

Although we've been delivered from the ultimate wrath of God, we are not guaranteed deliverance from His temporal judgments. Aaron's sons Nadab and Abihu were killed instantly for offering unauthorized fire before the Lord (Leviticus 10:1–2). Uzzah was struck down by the Lord for touching the ark of God (2 Samuel 6:6–7), and Ananias and Sapphira died for lying to the apostles and the Holy Spirit (Acts 5:1–11).

It is vain for us to say such judgments from God happened only in biblical times. We have the advantage of divine commentary on those events. We simply don't know today the extent, if any, to which tragic and traumatic events may be the expression of God's judgment against those who do not fear Him. Certainly we should not automatically assume that people, either individuals or groups, who are overtaken by disaster are being punished for their sins. The story of Job refutes that notion. My point is that we should not dismiss the prospect of God's judgment today simply because we don't have clear proof of it. We do know that the apostle Paul warns us to consider *both* the kindness and the severity of God (Romans 11:22, NASB).

In C. S. Lewis's book *The Lion, the Witch, and the Wardrobe,* one of the children asks Mr. and Mrs. Beaver about Aslan the Lion.

"Is he—quite safe? I shall feel rather nervous about meeting a lion."

"That you will, dearie, and no mistake," said Mrs. Beaver. "If there's anyone who can appear before Aslan without their knees knocking, they're either braver than most or just plain silly."

"Then he isn't safe?" said Lucy.

"Safe?" said Mr. Beaver; "don't you hear what Mrs. Beaver tells you? Who said anything about safe? 'Course he isn't safe. But he's good. He's the king, I tell you."[4]

Is God safe? The Scriptures teach us that in His grace and mercy God allows Himself to be our place of refuge. However, there's a larger sense in which God definitely is *not* safe. Yet in our thinking about Him we've tried to make Him exclusively safe. It's no longer in good taste in most quarters to speak of the judgment of God or His impending wrath. When we talk about God's "unconditional love" we often mean He simply overlooks or ignores our sinful behavior and would never judge anyone.

But God isn't that way at all. Scripture tells us that "our God is a consuming fire," and cautions us therefore to worship Him "with reverence and awe" (Hebrews 12:28–29).

No, God isn't safe—but He's good. And we must keep both these truths in mind if we are to understand and practice the fear of God. And, as we'll discover, even His goodness leads us to a proper fear of God when we truly understand it.

Notes

1. John Murray, *Principles of Conduct* (Grand Rapids: Eerdmans, 1957), 233.

2. John Calvin, *The Epistles of Paul to the Romans and Thessalonians*, vol. 8 of *New Testament Commentaries* (Grand Rapids: Eerdmans, 1980), 67.

3. For example, see Deuteronomy 25:17–18, Ecclesiastes 8:13, Jeremiah 5:23–24, Malachi 3:5, and Luke 18:1–5.

4. C. S. Lewis, *The Lion, the Witch, and the Wardrobe* (Hammondsworth, Middlesex, England: Penguin Books, 1950), 75.

SOUL OF GODLINESS

Should Christians Fear God?

SHOULD CHRISTIANS fear God? And if you and I *should* fear Him, *why* should we?

John Murray offers a compelling reason: "The fear of God is the soul of godliness."[1] That is, the fear of God is the animating and invigorating principle of a godly life. It is the wellspring of all godly desires and aspirations. Do you desire to be a godly person? Then you must understand and grow in the fear of God.

To appreciate that last statement we need to move beyond equating the fear of God only with being afraid of Him. We must not drop that aspect altogether, since even for the Christian it remains an element in the overall concept of fearing God. But it is by no means the dominant element.

What then is that fear of God which is "the soul of godliness"? Note carefully the elements in John Murray's description:

The fear of God in which godliness consists is the fear which constrains [compels or powerfully produces] adoration and love. It is the fear which consists in awe, reverence, honor, and worship, and all of these on the highest level of exercise. It is the reflex in our consciousness of the transcendent majesty and holiness of God.[2]

This kind of fear obviously goes beyond simply being afraid of God, for it yields within us such glad responses as adoration, love, honor, and worship. And I would add that these responses are a conscious "reflex" not only to God's "transcendent majesty and holiness," as Murray says, but also to His amazing grace and unfathomable love for us in Christ. We stand in awe not only of God's fiery splendor and absolute purity, but also of His grace and mercy to us.

Butch McGregor's awe of General Collins was complete only when he reflected with amazement on the fact that the general had risked his own life to save his. His respect for the general's vastly superior rank and his admiration for his character and leadership were joined by amazement at the general's love. *Respect, admiration,* and *amazement* all mingled together to create the complete sense of awe that the young sergeant felt.

Likewise the lack of any one of those attitudes will result in something less than the awe which is the fear of God. In our understanding of this biblical concept we need to include all three elements: respect (which toward God means *reverence)* in recognition of His infinite worth and dignity; admiration of His glorious attributes; and amazement at His infinite love.

HIS SLAVE OR HIS SON?

Even that aspect of the fear of God which respects His righteous judgments should not be a slavish or servile fear. Sinclair Ferguson has made a helpful distinction between "servile fear" and "filial fear." The word *servile,* by the way, comes from the Latin *servus,* which means "slave," while *filial* is from *filius,* meaning "son." Ferguson explains servile fear as "the kind of fear which a slave would feel towards a harsh and unyielding master."[3] It's the kind of fear that young recruit McGregor felt toward his drill instructor, at least initially.

Servile fear is illustrated by the third servant in Christ's parable of the talents. The servant said to his master, "I knew that you are a hard man, harvesting where you have not sown and gathering where you have not scattered seed. So I was afraid and went out and hid your talent in the ground" (Matthew 25:24–25).

We believers are apt to fall into a servile fear if we don't fully understand the grace of God and His acceptance of us through Christ. If we believe we're in a performance relationship with God, then He can seem to be a hard taskmaster whom we can never please. We'll see Him as the divine ogre ready to judge us for even our least failure to live up to His rules. We might never express our fear in such bald terms, but such a feeling lurks deep within the hearts of many Christians.

John Bunyan, in his treatise on the fear of God, points to the devil as the author of this servile fear. Bunyan said the devil uses it to haunt and disturb Christians and to make our lives uncomfortable. But we are heirs of God and His kingdom, and Bunyan reproves us for not resisting this slavish fear as we ought. He says we actually rather cherish and entertain this wrong view and thus weaken the filial fear which we instead ought to strengthen.[4]

In contrast to servile fear, filial fear is the loving fear of a child toward his father. Ferguson describes it as "that indefinable mixture of reverence, fear, pleasure, joy and awe which fills our hearts when we realize who God is and what He has done for us."[5] *This is the only true fear of God,* and it's the concept we'll focus on in the remainder of this book. We'll see how a focus on the holiness and greatness of God tends to create that reverence and fear which Ferguson speaks about. We'll exult in the infinite wisdom of God. Most of all, though, I hope our hearts will be filled with pleasure and joy as we gaze upon the breadth and length and height and depth of the love of God revealed to us through Christ Jesus.

There are more than 150 references to the fear of God in the Bible.[6] While the majority of these occur in the Old Testament, there are a sufficient number in the New Testament to convince us that fearing God is indeed an attitude of heart we should cultivate today.

Fearing God involves both the most common and the most exalted endeavors in our life. John Murray observes that even "the most practical of mundane duties derive their inspiration and impetus from the fear of God." Then he immediately adds, "The highest reaches of sanctification are realized only in the fear of God."[7] In support of this Murray cites Colossians 3:22 and 2 Corinthians 7:1. The first passage, addressed to "slaves" or "bondservants," prescribes a level of work that is performed "not with external service . . . but with sincerity of heart, *fearing the Lord*" (NASB). Even the work of slaves is to be done in the fear of God. The same goes for the high pursuit of holiness. In the second passage we're encouraged to "cleanse ourselves from all defilement of flesh and spirit, perfecting holiness *in the fear of God*" (NASB). Note that both these Scriptures occur in the New Testament.

Here are two more: We're given an explicit command to fear God in 1 Peter 2:17—"Show proper respect to everyone: Love the brotherhood of believers, *fear God,* honor the king." And Luke records that after the conversion of Saul the persecutor, the church "was strengthened; and encouraged by the Holy Spirit, it grew in numbers, *living in the fear of the Lord*" (Acts 9:31). God tells us to fear Him, and living that way is the mark of a spiritually healthy body of believers.

One of the most compelling reasons for us to cultivate the fear of God is the example of our Lord Jesus Himself. Consider Isaiah 11:1–3, one of the many messianic prophecies in Isaiah.

> [1]A shoot will come up from the stump of Jesse;
>> from his roots a Branch will bear fruit.
> [2]The Spirit of the LORD will rest on him—
>> the Spirit of wisdom and of understanding,
>> the Spirit of counsel and of power,
>> the Spirit of knowledge and *of the fear of the LORD*—
> [3]and *he will delight in the fear of the LORD.*

As the Spirit of God rested on the Messiah, one of His endowments would be the fear of the Lord (verse 2). As a result, this prophecy says, "He will delight in the fear of the LORD" (verse 3). This is undoubtedly a reference to Jesus in His humanity. He who was born of a woman, born under law (Galatians 4:4), feared God His Father. His heart was completely filled with reverence, awe, honor, adoration, and obedience. And not only was His heart filled, but Scripture adds that He *delighted* in the fear of the Lord. If we would be like the Lord Jesus, we also should delight in fearing God.

IT DETERMINES HOW WE LIVE

To cultivate this fear, as God's people should, let's analyze it further. Is this fear of God a mix of various emotions, or is it an attitude? Emotions are feelings that come and go, depending on external stimuli, while an attitude is a more or less settled state of mind. Into which category does fearing God belong?

The answer is both. Emotional feelings of awe, reverence, honor, and adoration will definitely be stimulated within us as we have great thoughts about God—as we encounter His majesty, splendor, holiness, and love. Psalm 47 is an example of how thinking great thoughts about God stirs our emotions to fear Him:

> [1]Clap your hands, all you nations;
>> shout to God with cries of joy.
> [2]How awesome is the LORD Most High,
>> the great King over all the earth!
> [3]He subdued nations under us,
>> peoples under our feet.
> [4]He chose our inheritance for us,
>> the pride of Jacob, whom he loved.
> [5]God has ascended amid shouts of joy,
>> the LORD amid the sounding of trumpets.
> [6]Sing praises to God, sing praises;
>> sing praises to our King, sing praises.

⁷For God is the King of all the earth;
   sing to him a psalm of praise.
⁸God reigns over the nations;
   God is seated on his holy throne.
⁹The nobles of the nations assemble
   as the people of the God of Abraham,
for the kings of the earth belong to God;
   he is greatly exalted.

Notice the expressions here that convey the psalmist's heightened emotions: "Clap your hands" and "shout to God with cries of joy" (verse 1), and "shouts of joy . . . amid the sounding of trumpets" (verse 5). The command to sing praises is given four times in verse 6 and again in verse 7. Obviously the psalmist is excited about God and wants us to join him in his exuberance.

What is it that awakens such strong emotion in his heart? It is the recognition of God's awesomeness (verse 2) and the confident realization that He is indeed the great King of all the earth (verses 2, 7, 8, 9). We'll learn more about the significance of God's incomparable kingship in the next chapter, but for now notice in this passage how great thoughts about God have stimulated emotions that we can rightly call the fear of God. The psalmist is not only deeply stirred in his own heart, but also wants us to join him in his joyous experience of fearing the Lord.

At the same time our fear of God must be a settled state of mind—an attitude of awe, reverence, honor, and adoration, a fixed mental outlook that isn't dependent on feelings that come and go. The right feelings over time will of course shape our attitude. If we make it a practice to think great thoughts about God (we'll learn more about this later), we will develop a sustained attitude of the fear of God.

Whether we think of a complex set of emotions or an attitude, however, the important thing is that this mix is to be *determinative*. The emotions and attitude should determine the way we relate to God—the way we obey Him, trust Him, and worship Him. Properly fearing God is more than just a feeling or attitude—it's a feeling or attitude *that changes our lives.*

Without this proper fear, for example, our view of God may tend toward the servile or slavish type of fear, and our obedience will be somewhat reluctant and driven more by the fear of consequences than by a desire to please a loving Father. On the other hand, if our approach to God lacks the proper dimension of awe that has regard to His majesty, splendor, power, and dignity, we'll tend to be overly familiar with God and lacking in reverence toward Him.

So the right fear of God is not just a concept to be entertained in our minds. Rather, it's an invigorating and guiding principle that deeply affects every area of our lives and determines the way we live, as we'll see more extensively in future chapters. Meanwhile, stay with me as a fuller picture continues to unfold.

A Healthy Respect for His Discipline

For a number of months prior to writing this book, I prepared by studying many passages of Scripture as well as reading what other authors have written on the subject. As I answered people's questions about what I was working on now, I was quite interested in their responses. Most were encouraging, but some were a bit disturbing. People often said something to this effect: "Make sure you emphasize that to fear God really means to *FEAR* Him!" I got the impression they wanted me to make people afraid of God.

I suspect that those who responded in this way were acutely concerned about the pervasive lack of reverence and awe of God and the consequent disregard of His moral laws that abounds in our Christian circles today. I share their concern but I question this emphasis on being afraid of God.

In Exodus 20:20 we see Moses telling God's people, "Do not be afraid. God has come to test you, so that the fear of God will be with you to keep you from sinning." Here Moses draws a contrast between being afraid of God and fearing God. Note that this fear of God was to keep them from sinning. *Simply being afraid of God will lead to distrust and disobedience of Him. But fearing God—in the biblical sense we've seen in this chapter—will keep us from sinning.*

Someone may object and refer to 1 Peter 1:17, which tells us, "Since you call on a Father who judges each man's work impartially, live your lives as strangers here in reverent fear." Isn't the fear of God in this verse meant to be a deterrent to disobedience? The Greek word *phobos,* usually translated as "fear," can mean to be afraid in the normal sense of the word, but it can also mean the reverential awe that we call the fear of God. The New International Version translates it as "reverent fear," and this is the way we should understand it—as the fear of God in the sense of reverential awe.

However, Peter is setting before us a particular application of this reverent fear. It is meant to be a motivator for our conduct. This fear is intended to stimulate us to holy living. In the verses immediately preceding this one, Peter calls us to be holy because God is holy. In this context of a challenge to holy living, he then reminds us that God judges impartially, that He has no favorite children whom He will allow to get away with disobedience. God is no indulgent grandfather who overlooks our sin.

The particular aspect of the fear of God that Peter has in mind, then, is a healthy respect for God's fatherly discipline. Such a fear is entirely consistent with our assurance of the Father's love for us and with our desire to please Him because of our love for Him.

We can easily see this principle at work in a well-ordered family. The children have a healthy respect for their father's discipline but are not afraid of him. They don't live in dread of either physical or emotional abuse (in fact, they may not even be aware there is such a thing), but they know that willful disobedience will bring punishment.

I grew up in a home where I never questioned my father's love for me. At the same time I never questioned his commitment to discipline me (read that as "spank me") when he felt I needed it. My mother's most fearsome words to me were, "I'm going to tell your father when he gets home."

When I was small—four or five years old—my father led the congregational singing in our small church. While the pastor was preaching, my father sat on the platform facing the congregation. Sometimes when I would get unusually wiggly, I would suddenly "feel" his eyes on me. I would look up and see him staring at me with a stern look, and I would immediately stop my wiggling. The prospect of an after-church spanking was all the deterrent I needed. Yet I never doubted my father's love.

That's a small human illustration of what Peter meant when he said, "Live your lives as strangers here in reverent fear." Remember, God disciplines those He loves (Hebrews 12:6). Although the word *discipline* in that passage denotes a wider meaning of overall child training, we know that it includes the "spiritual spankings" we all need from time to time. And while God desires that we obey Him because we love Him rather than because we're afraid of Him, He does resort to the punishment aspect of discipline when necessary. We see this clearly in the case of the Corinthian believers who were blatantly abusing the Lord's supper (1 Corinthians 11:27–32).

Many Christians seem to disregard the prospect of God's discipline. They apparently don't believe that stubborn and persistent continuance in sin will invoke God's fatherly displeasure. They mistake God's grace for a license to live as they please, on the assumption that God's forgiveness is automatic and unconditional. I recall an acquaintance of mine who in the midst of leaving his wife for another woman said, "I know this is wrong, but God will forgive me." Unfortunately pastors hear this kind of statement all too frequently.

These people apparently have no fear of God's discipline. They're strangers to the idea of living their lives in reverent fear.

And what about us? Though our disobedience may not be as crass and obvious as that of the man leaving his wife, we can have this same attitude in a more subtle way. Anytime we sin with the thought lurking in the back of our minds that God will forgive us, we aren't living in the fear of God.

It's true, in a judicial sense, that God has already forgiven us all our sins, past, present, and future. As Paul said in Colossians 2:13, "He forgave us all our sins." Christ fully paid for each and every one of our sins on the cross so God no longer counts them against us (see Romans 4:7–8).

However, though God will never judge true believers for their sin, He will discipline us if we persist in an unrepentant attitude toward sin. Lest this last sentence cause anxiety in the mind of someone who struggles with some persistent sinful habit, let me emphasize that God's discipline occurs because of an unrepentant and irreverent attitude— not because of failures in a sincere struggle with sin. There's a vast difference between the attitude of a person who is struggling to put away some sin and the attitude of one who thinks, "I know it's sin, but God will forgive me."

SIMPLY BECAUSE HE IS GOD

In the next four chapters we'll see other reasons why we should fear God. We'll look at His majesty and power, His holiness and wisdom, and His love expressed in His grace and mercy to us. We'll come to admire His attributes and stand amazed at His love. Then we'll examine how the fear of God should express itself in our character and daily conduct.

But before we move on to consider those attributes of God that should elicit our fear of Him, there's one other dimension we want to look at: the awe of His person, being in awe of God *simply because He is God.* We see this dimension of the fear of God in the lives of several people in Scripture, including Gideon, Job, Isaiah, and Ezekiel (Judges 6:22–23, Job 42:5–6, Isaiah 6:1–5, Ezekiel 1:25–28). There are three other men whose encounters with God we want to examine more closely to help us understand what it means to be in awe of God's person. They are Jacob and the apostles Peter and John.

Jacob was running for his life. He had deceived his father and stolen from his brother both the birthright and the eldest son's blessing. His brother, Esau, held a grudge against Jacob and purposed to kill him. Jacob was fleeing to his uncle's home in faraway Haran.

The first night of his journey, Jacob had a dream. Notice carefully the five promises God made to him in this dream, as recorded for us in Genesis 28:12–15.

> He had a dream in which he saw a stairway resting on the earth, with its top reaching to heaven, and the angels of God were ascending and descending on it. There above it stood the LORD, and he said, "I am the LORD, the God of your father Abraham and the God of Isaac. I will give you and your descendants the land on which you are lying. Your descendants will be like the dust of the earth, and you will spread out to the west and to the east, to the north and to the south. All peoples on earth will be blessed through you and your offspring. I am with you and will watch over you wherever you go, and I will bring you back to this land. I will not leave you until I have done what I have promised you."

God said nothing in the dream about Jacob's deceitful character or actions. God did not reprimand him or threaten to punish him. Instead He gave Jacob five astounding promises related to possession of the land of Israel, a multitude of descendants, being a blessing to everyone on the earth, and enjoying God's protective guidance and His continual presence.

What was Jacob's reaction to such a wealth of promised blessings? Did he wake up rejoicing and praising God as we might have expected? Here is Jacob's response:

> When Jacob awoke from his sleep, he thought, "Surely the LORD is in this place, and I was not aware of it." He was afraid and said, "How

awesome is this place! This is none other than the house of God; this is the gate of heaven."

Instead of exaltation, Jacob was afraid. Instead of counting his blessings, he said, "How awesome is this place!" What was it that created such a solemn sense of awe in Jacob and made him afraid? We've already seen that God did not reprimand or threaten him in any way. He only gave him promises. Still, Jacob was awestruck and afraid. Why?

The reason for Jacob's fear was the realization that he had somehow been in the very presence of God. It was not the consciousness of his sin but the consciousness of his creaturehood in the presence of deity that created his sense of awe. In the words of Rudolph Otto, Jacob's response was "the emotion of a creature, submerged and overwhelmed by its own nothingness in contrast to that which is supreme above all creatures."[8]

Think back to Butch McGregor's first experience of standing before General Collins. He had no reason to believe the general would harm him in any way. He had gained competence and confidence as a basic trainee. His personal appearance, his rifle, and his barracks space had already passed the eagle-eye inspection of his drill instructor and company commander, so he had no reason to be afraid in those areas.

Why then was the marine so in awe? It was because he was in the presence of one who, at least to his mind, possessed unlimited authority and power, one who towered tremendously above him in rank and dignity. During the course of basic training Butch had been made to feel he was the lowliest of the low, and now he stood in the presence of one who was near the very top. No wonder he experienced such awe.

A CREATURE IN THE CREATOR'S PRESENCE

If we can enter into the emotions of the young marine as he stood before the general, we can begin to understand something of what Jacob felt when he realized he had been in God's presence. The vast difference in rank and dignity between the recruit and the general, though very great, was nothing compared to the infinite difference between the creature and the Creator. It was nothing more than the realization that he had been in the very presence of God that caused Jacob to be afraid. Jacob experienced an overwhelming awe of God simply because of who God is — infinitely above the most powerful human beings who have ever lived.

The apostle Peter had a reaction similar to Jacob's. His story in Luke 5:1–11 is a familiar one. Jesus had used Peter's boat as a seat from which to teach people crowding around Him on the shore. When He finished, He told Peter to move out into the deep water and let down his nets.

Peter and his partners had been up all night fishing and caught absolutely nothing, so they weren't at all eager to launch out again. In fact they were already washing their nets when Jesus got into their boat. You can almost hear the skepticism and resignation in Peter's voice: "Master, we've worked hard all night and haven't caught anything. But because you say so, I will let down the nets" (verse 5). In addition to being tired and discouraged from a fruitless night's work, Peter was perhaps a bit peeved that this carpenter-turned-teacher would presume to tell him when and where to fish. He knew the worst time for fishing was when the sun was on the water. But perhaps to humor Jesus, Peter did as instructed.

You know what happened. They caught such a large number of fish that their nets began to break and their boats began to sink. What was Peter's reaction? Was he elated at such a monumental catch of fish? Did he immediately try to recruit Jesus as a new partner and fishing guide?

Instead of elation there was fear (verse 10). Instead of trying to recruit Jesus, he fell at His feet and said, "Go away from me, Lord; I am a sinful man!" (verse 8).

Peter had already seen at least one other miracle, when Jesus healed his mother-in-law (Luke 4:38–39). But this one was different. This revelation of Jesus' power over the fish in the lake spoke to him in a special way, because it was in the field of his own trade. He well knew how humanly impossible it was to catch fish in these daylight hours. That's why he fell down before Jesus. He recognized that he was somehow in the presence of God.

Note again that Jesus said nothing about Peter's sin. Everything was positive. In their nets Peter could see what must have been the equivalent of what it took days or weeks to catch. He should have been excited and rejoicing—except for one thing: He now saw who Jesus really was.[9] Peter was awestruck to realize that he was in God's very presence.

Peter became acutely and painfully aware of his sinfulness. But what made him fall down before Jesus was not his sin, but Jesus' deity. It was the reaction of the creature to his Creator. It was the profound awe of recognizing the vast difference between himself and the infinite, eternal God. It was like the awe of Butch McGregor before the general, but multiplied to the nth degree.

INESCAPABLY AWESTRUCK

John Calvin speaks of "that dread and wonder with which Scripture commonly represents the saints as stricken and overcome whenever they felt the presence of God." Then Calvin concludes, "As a consequence, we must infer that man is never sufficiently touched and affected by the awareness of his lowly state until he has compared himself with God's majesty."[10] Over and over again we see this phenomenon in Scripture—men awestruck in the presence of God.

One of the more striking illustrations of this profound awe occurred in the life of the aged apostle John. Revelation 1 recounts John's experience of seeing the ascended, glorified Christ in His infinite majesty, power, authority, omniscience, and holiness (1:12–16). John records his reaction: "When I saw him, I fell at his feet as though dead" (verse 17).

Remember, this is the same John who had lived with Jesus for three years, who was part of His inner circle, and who was even called "the disciple whom Jesus loved." Yet when he saw Jesus in the unveiled glory of His deity, he was awestruck in the most profound way.

This was not the first time John had fallen down before Jesus. The first occasion is recorded in Matthew 17:1–8 when Jesus took Peter, James, and John up a high mountain and was transfigured before them. There they heard the voice of God saying, "This is my Son, whom I love; with him I am well pleased. Listen to him!" (verse 5). At this the three disciples fell facedown to the ground, terrified (verse 6). In Revelation, though, John's awestruckness was highly intensified. The text says, "I fell at his feet *as though dead.*"

Peter had fallen at Jesus' knees (Luke 5:8), and the prophet Ezekiel had fallen facedown before the glory of the Lord (Ezekiel 1:28), but only John fell at His feet as though dead. Why did John experience such a life-draining response to Christ's magnificent glory—a response seemingly more profound than anyone had ever experienced?

John was about to receive the most awesome revelation of God ever granted to man. In a series of vivid and striking visions he was to see pictorial representations of God's sovereign rule over all of history, of the final victory of Jesus Christ the "KING OF KINGS AND LORD OF LORDS" (Revelation 19:16), and finally of the ushering in of the new heavens and the new earth. It seems that such grand exaltation of John required this severe humbling to prepare him to receive these revelations. Paul had been given his thorn in the flesh *after* his revelations (2 Corinthians 12:1–9). John was humbled in the dust *before* receiving his. In each instance it was to show both them and us that we are at best only "jars of clay" (2 Corinthians 4:7) in which God is pleased to deposit the excellency of His glory.

Neither Jacob, nor Peter, nor John could have helped themselves. They had no choice but to respond in deepest awe. Each of them was afraid because each realized he was (or had been, in Jacob's case) in the very presence of God.

Will we then have "no choice" but to fall down in awe before God as did Jacob, Peter, and John? That might happen to us on occasion. There have been a few times in my life when the Holy Spirit gave me such an overwhelming realization of God's glorious splendor that I had no choice. I was simply impelled by a spontaneous reaction. Our normal experience, however, will be to quietly and slowly grow in our apprehension of the infinite majesty of God. As this happens we will choose to bow before Him in worship and adoration.

THE INFINITE DISTANCE

The comparison of the marine recruit to the commanding general is a feeble analogy of our status before God. The difference in status and dignity between the recruit and the general is vast, but it is still finite. Theoretically, in fact, the recruit could one day be a general. But the difference between God and ourselves, even apart from our sin, is an infinite distance. Even if we succeeded in becoming the most powerful human being in all of history, the difference between us and God would still be infinite.

The God who revealed Himself to Jacob, Peter, and John is the same omnipotent and holy God today. He has revealed to us in His Word all that we need to know of Him to properly fear Him. Though we may not have the same kind of direct encounter with God as did those men, we can encounter Him in His Word as the Holy Spirit opens it to our minds and hearts.

The next four chapters are designed to help us see some of the glorious awesomeness of God in His greatness, holiness, wisdom, and love. As we turn to these attributes, may His Spirit create in each of our hearts something of the awe that those men of old experienced when they realized God is indeed God.

Before moving ahead, however, it would be good for each of us to pause and prayerfully assess our present experience of the fear of God. The following questions may be helpful to you in this exercise:

1. Do I experience, at least to some degree, the fear of God as it has been described so far?

2. Does my fear of God tend to be "slavish" so that I view God as a stern taskmaster who's never pleased with me?

3. Is my fear of God so shallow that I tend to be overly familiar with God and fail to show the reverential awe that is due Him?

4. Do I sometimes indulge in known sinful actions (or thoughts or words) because I do not have a proper regard for God's fatherly discipline?

Perhaps the Holy Spirit has brought other questions or applications to your mind. If so, heed them. Remember, the truths of God's Word are not to be simply admired. They are to be applied in specific ways in our lives.

Notes

1. John Murray, *Principles of Conduct* (Grand Rapids: Eerdmans, 1957), 229.

2. Murray, *Principles of Conduct*, 236–7.

3. Sinclair Ferguson, *Grow in Grace* (Colorado Springs: NavPress, 1984), 35.

4. John Bunyan, "A Treatise on the Fear of God," *The Works of John Bunyan*, vol. 1 (1875, reprint, Grand Rapids: Baker, 1977), 483. I have tried to capture the essence of Bunyan's statements rather than quoting him, so as to make his thoughts more understandable for today's readers.

5. Ferguson, *Grow in Grace*, 36.

6. The New International Version sometimes uses the word "reverence" where most other translations have "fear of God." Examples of such usage are 2 Corinthians 7:1 and Colossians 3:22. My count of more than 150 includes instances where the NIV uses "reverence." Both the Hebrew word *yare* and the Greek word *phobos* carry the full range of meaning of *fear*, from dread or terror to reverence and awe. Both words are sometimes rendered as "reverence" by the NIV translators.

7. Murray, *Principles of Conduct*, 231.

8. Rudolph Otto, *The Idea of the Holy* (New York: Oxford University Press, 1958), 10.

9. The title "Lord" with which Peter addressed Jesus is used again and again as an equivalent of God in the Greek translation of the Old Testament that Peter would have known. See William Hendriksen's *New Testament Commentary, Exposition of the Gospel according to Luke* (Grand Rapids: Baker, 1978), 284.

10. John Calvin, *Institutes of the Christian Religion*, Book 1, *The Knowledge of God the Creator*, ed. John T. McNeill, trans. Ford Lewis Battles (Philadelphia: Westminster, 1960), 38–9.

PART II

—————

The God We Fear

4

BEYOND MEASURE, BEYOND COMPARE

The Greatness of God

THE NARRATIVE PARTS of the Old Testament often read like an adventure novel. Many of the stories really are high drama. What could be more suspenseful than Daniel in the lions' den or his three friends in the blazing furnace? What could be more romantic than the aggrieved Gentile woman Ruth meeting her future husband, Boaz, while gleaning in his grainfield, and ultimately becoming an ancestor of both Israel's King David and Jesus the Messiah?

These and numerous other classic stories can lull us into the attitude that what we're reading is hardly more than good fiction.

Reinforcing that tendency is the abundance in these stories of miraculous events that seem so unreal today. We don't read in our newspapers of someone killing a thousand men with a donkey's jawbone, as Samson did. We don't hear about floating axheads, or a family living for months on only a handful of flour and a little jug of oil.

Though entertaining, these events can seem so far back and foreign that we unconsciously view them as having no practical value today. Yet if the Bible is indeed God's Word, we know these amazing stories are authentic accounts of real events happening to real people like you and me.

HE PLAYS FOR KEEPS

Of all the astonishing miracles recorded in the Old Testament, the most momentous for the Jews was their crossing of the Red Sea. To display His glory and destroy Pharaoh's army, God directed the Israelites to a location where they were penned in between the sea and the Egyptians. The Scriptures tell us that when the Israelites looked up and saw Pharaoh's elite forces marching after them, they were terrified and complained bitterly against Moses for bringing them out into the desert to die (Exodus 14).

To appreciate their predicament, imagine being finally delivered from slavery in Egypt, only to see your former masters in hot pursuit and no way of escape. What emotions would surge through you as you faced this extreme danger—and later as you experienced miraculous deliverance?

Imagine seeing the Red Sea waters divided, opening a way for you and two million others to walk through on dry ground. You step down into the sea bottom with those walls of water towering above. Could they at any moment come crashing down?

At last you reach the far side, only to look back and see that the Egyptians have followed. Suddenly you watch those walls of water collapse; you witness an entire army drowning in the sea. In only a few hours you've experienced the highest degrees of fear, apprehension, dismay, excitement, and overwhelming relief.

However, the Israelites experienced something more than relief and elation following the climax of that day's events: "And when the Israelites saw the great power the LORD displayed against the Egyptians, the people feared the LORD and put their trust in him and in Moses his servant" (Exodus 14:31).

The people feared the Lord. Obviously this wasn't the same fear or dread they felt upon seeing the fast-approaching Egyptian army. Rather it was the reverential awe produced by the awesome display of God's might. While they rejoiced that this power had been exercised in their behalf, they could not escape the sober realization that this God was not only an almighty deliverer, but also a righteous judge of those who opposed Him. As a friend of mine put it, they realized that God plays for keeps.

To Fear Him Is to Trust Him

The text says that the Israelites both feared the Lord *and* put their trust in Him. Fearing God and trusting Him are not mutually exclusive. In fact, the Israelites were able to trust God *because* they experienced firsthand His awesome power to deliver them. It was not just the display of raw power—the Egyptians also saw that—but the exercise of it *in their behalf* that caused the Hebrews to trust God. Power without love is terrifying. Love without power is pitiable. In God the Jews saw both working together.

It's apparent that God's aim in the events of the Exodus was not only to gain glory to Himself, but also to stimulate and increase the faith of the Israelites. He deliberately maneuvered them into a situation where they could be saved only by His mighty power, and through that experience come to trust Him.

A similar relationship between the fear of the Lord and trust in Him is expressed in Psalm 33:16–19.

> No king is saved by the size of his army;
>> no warrior escapes by his great strength.
> A horse is a vain hope for deliverance;
>> despite all its great strength it cannot save.
> But the eyes of the LORD are on those who fear him,
>> on those whose hope is in his unfailing love,

to deliver them from death
and keep them alive in famine.

Note that the passage begins by expressing the vanity of trust in such earthly things as an army, one's own strength, or even the strength of a horse (the equivalent of a modern army's tank). Instead we're encouraged to fear the Lord and to hope in His unfailing love—that is, to trust Him.

But why should we fear and trust Him? What basis do we have for doing so? The answer has already been given in the preceding verses:

By the word of the LORD were the heavens made,
their starry host by the breath of his mouth.
He gathers the waters of the sea into jars;
he puts the deep into storehouses.
Let all the earth fear the LORD;
let all the people of the world revere him.
For he spoke, and it came to be;
he commanded, and it stood firm.
The LORD foils the plans of the nations;
he thwarts the purposes of the peoples.
But the plans of the LORD stand firm forever,
the purposes of his heart through all generations.

This passage extols first God's power in creation and later His sovereignty over the nations. Right in the middle we're exhorted to fear the Lord and revere Him, or as other translations say, "Fear the LORD and stand in awe of him." And what will cause us to do so? It is recognizing His greatness as displayed in His mighty power in creation and His absolute sovereignty over the nations. As we become convinced of His greatness, we will fear Him—stand in awe of Him—and also trust Him. We cannot separate trust in God from the fear of God. We will trust Him only to the extent that we genuinely stand in awe of Him.

Sadly enough, we have only to read the ensuing history of the

Hebrews to realize how poorly they had learned to fear Him. Psalm 78 is a dismal account of how Israel continually sinned against God by failing to trust Him. Verse 32 says that "in spite of his wonders, they did not believe." They did not trust God because they did not stand in awe of Him and of the wonders He often performed in their behalf.

Like the Jewish nation, we too need to grow in the fear of God, lest we also sin against Him by failing to trust Him. One problem we have, however, is that God seldom displays His mighty power in such spectacular ways as He did for Israel. This isn't to say God isn't powerfully at work today, but most often He has chosen to carry out His purposes and to work in behalf of His people through seemingly ordinary events.

How then can we grow in the fear of God when we don't see Him performing miracles? One way is by regularly reading through the Old Testament (particularly the historical sections and the Psalms), reminding ourselves that the same God who performed those mighty acts still reigns and rules over His creation and is still working on behalf of His people.

When I was in high school my parents struggled to make ends meet, and there was no way they could have helped me with the expenses of a college education. After graduation I planned to go to the local junior college for two years and see what might happen from there. One evening during my senior year I discovered inside our newspaper a single-column article no more than four inches long. It mentioned a navy scholarship program that provided a college education and an officer's commission upon graduation. I applied, passed the examination, and was accepted.

The seemingly "chance" reading of that article buried in our newspaper was literally a life-changing event. My education, my contact with the Navigators while on active duty, and my subsequent Christian ministry all hinged upon it. Why did I "happen" to see it? Because God was at work on my behalf carrying out His plan for me.

My little experience was certainly not as dramatic as the Israelites crossing the Red Sea, but in some respects it was as life-changing. It also demonstrated that God is just as much at work now on behalf of His people as He was in Old Testament times.

UNFATHOMABLY GREAT

The Scriptures often use the word *great* or *greatness* for the awesomeness God displays in His mighty acts. In the song Moses composed immediately after the Red Sea crossing, he says, "In the *greatness* of your majesty you threw down those who opposed you" (Exodus 15:7). Moses also refers to the Lord as "a *great* and awesome God" and as "the *great* God, mighty and awesome" (Deuteronomy 7:21, 10:17).

The Psalms also use this term as a synonym for God's awesomeness: "For *great* is the LORD and most worthy of praise; he is to be feared above all gods" (Psalm 96:4). Psalm 104, an account of God's rule over all His natural creation, begins with the exclamation, "O LORD my God, you are very *great."* In Psalm 150:2 we're commanded, "Praise him for his acts of power; praise him for his surpassing *greatness."*

Yet however great we may perceive God to be, we still have not fully grasped it: *"Great* is the LORD and most worthy of praise; his *greatness* no one can fathom" (Psalm 145:3). In a word, God's greatness is *infinite.*

One Old Testament passage especially emphasizes the greatness of God, and is thus designed to stimulate our fear of Him. Isaiah 40:12–31 contains a number of rhetorical questions and figures of speech describing God's immense greatness in creation and history. In doing so Isaiah uses several expressions that ascribe human characteristics to God. We see Him measuring with His hand, for example, though we know God doesn't have a physical body. Such anthropomorphic expressions are examples of how God condescends to reveal Himself in words we can understand.[1]

INFINITELY GREATER THAN NATURE

Isaiah's questioning begins: "Who has measured the waters in the hollow of his hand?" (40:12). God is so great that all the waters of the seas could be measured, as it were, in the hollow of His hand. One day I borrowed one of my wife's measuring spoons to see how much water I could hold in the hollow of my hand. It was barely more than a tablespoonful.

By contrast, we know that slightly more than two-thirds of the earth's surface is covered with water, in places six miles deep. The total volume is incalculable. Even if we could estimate it in gallons (our largest unit of liquid measure), the number would be beyond our comprehension. Yet God says He holds all those waters in the hollow of His hand.

We see here the unfathomable distance between God and man—the infinitely vast chasm that yawns between Creator and creature. The dramatic contrast between the entire waters of the oceans and a mere tablespoonful in our hand shows us not just how small we are, but how great God is.

Next from Isaiah comes a second rhetorical question: "Who has . . . with the breadth of his hand marked off the heavens?" A hand breadth is the distance from the tip of the thumb to the tip of the little finger when the fingers are completely spread apart. This was a natural and universal measure of length in Bible times. Again to get an idea of what God is saying to us, I measured the breadth of my hand and found it to be just over eight inches.

God, by contrast, is so great that He marked off the heavens by the breadth of His hand. We can't really calculate the distance across the universe. We do know that the nearest star, other than the sun, is about four and a half light years away. Since light travels at the speed of 186,000 miles per second, that nearest star is over twenty-six trillion miles away. Expressed numerically it looks like this:

26,000,000,000,000

And that's just to the nearest star! The distance across the entire universe, whatever it is, would simply be an incomprehensible figure to us. Yet God tells us He merely marks off that distance with the breadth of His hand.

The smallness of these two measures—the hollow and the breadth of the human hand—are intended to show us the immensity of God Himself, who can deal with the entire universe as we might deal with the most trivial objects. "And these are but the outer fringes of his works," we read in Job 26:14 about God's wonders in nature; "how faint the whisper we hear of him." When we've surveyed to our utmost all of creation, we've seen only the outer fringes of what God has done, we've heard only a whisper. Even the greatest conceivable measurements in creation are but an imperfect picture of how great God is. Truly our God is awesome. He is very great.

Isaiah continues: "Who has held the dust of the earth in a basket, or weighed the mountains on the scales and the hills in a balance?" The word translated "basket" is literally a "one-third measure," such as we might say "quart" to mean one-fourth of a gallon. It was undoubtedly a small amount. Yet God is so great He holds the dust of the earth in such a container, and weighs the mountains on a set of scales.

I've visited Switzerland several times and am always awed by the rugged, majestic mountains there. Though I've never seen the Himalayas, I know they're higher and even more rugged and awesome. Whether it's the Alps or the Himalayas or our own Rocky Mountains, they always impress us with their grandeur and size. And yet God, as it were, weighs them on a balance scale.

The oceans, the heavens, the mountains—all incalculable to us, but not to God. Their measurements are trivial to Him. The hollow of the hand, the breadth of the hand, and the balance scales all speak of easy competence in relation to the task. Isaiah says in effect, Consider the greatest things in nature—boundless seas, infinitely vast heavens, and majestic peaks. Though they are great, they are nothing in comparison to God.

As we think about these truths we will more and more appreciate God's greatness and grandeur and grow in our awe of Him.

INFINITELY GREATER THAN THE NATIONS

Isaiah also shows us God's greatness as manifested in His superiority over the nations:

> 15Surely the nations are like a drop in a bucket;
>
> they are regarded as dust on the scales;
>
> he weighs the islands as though they were fine dust.
>
> 16Lebanon is not sufficient for altar fires,
>
> nor its animals enough for burnt offerings.
>
> 17Before him all the nations are as nothing;
>
> they are regarded by him as worthless
>
> and less than nothing.

Note that verse 15 begins with *surely*, an intensive word giving emphasis to what Isaiah is about to say. Other Bible translations have the word *behold* here as an imperative verb to get our attention. We might say, "Think of this!" Isaiah wants to arrest our attention; what he will tell us is so incredible that we need to stop and consider and ponder. And his message is this: Before God, the nations are no more than a drop in a bucket.

Think of that! The world's most powerful nations all totaled together are no more to God than a single drop in a bucket, or a drop of moisture falling from a bucket, as it has also been translated. A bucketful of water is something, but a drop is nothing. It is infinitesimal. Such are the nations before God.

The next comparison is even more incredible. God regards the nations as simply dust on the scales. The picture is of a pair of balance scales such as we might use in a science laboratory, and which in Bible times were used in ordinary commerce. We know that any dust on their trays would be immaterial, having no effect on the accuracy of measurement.

Imagine buying fruit and vegetables at your local supermarket, then telling the clerk at the checkout counter, "Please wipe the dust off the scales before weighing my produce—I don't want to pay for the dust." Such a concern is absurd. The weight of the dust is insignificant, irrelevant. And to God, the world's nations are nothing more than that.

It's not that the nations aren't imposing enough on a human level. Some of them down through history have been world empires. But however great they are or were, God is infinitely greater. Before Him all the most powerful states in all of history are no more than a drop in a bucket or dust on scales.

Another picture of the nations is brought before us in verse 16: "Lebanon is not sufficient for altar fires." Here the idea is not the power of the nations but their natural resources. Lebanon is singled out as an example. In Isaiah's day this land was noted for dense forests, and the "cedars of Lebanon" was a well-known expression. Psalm 92:12, for example, says, "The righteous . . . will grow like a cedar of Lebanon."

Solomon used cedars from Lebanon when he built God's temple in Jerusalem. Shifts of ten thousand men at a time were involved in cutting trees and hauling them to the sea where they were then floated in rafts to Israel's coast (see 1 Kings 5:8–14). But Isaiah tells us that all the trees of Lebanon would not be sufficient for an altar fire worthy of the dignity and greatness of God.

In verse 17, Isaiah now strengthens the contrast between God and the power of the nations. The nations are seen "before" God—that is, in comparison with God—as "nothing," "worthless," and "less than nothing." Stronger language could not be used. *Nothing* means nonexistent, and *less than nothing* intensifies that idea. *Worthless* conveys the concept of being entirely empty of meaning or purpose.

Compared with God, the nations are only that. After all, He is the Creator who brought them into being and entirely controls their existence: "From one man he made every nation of men, that they should inhabit the whole earth; and he determined the times set for them and the exact places where they should live" (Acts 17:26).

The purpose of these comparisons is not to disparage the nations, but rather to communicate how great God is. As with nature, Isaiah is saying, so it is with the nations: The sum of all their power is indeed great, but compared with God they are nothing and worthless. Let your mind soar to either the most exalted things in all creation or the most powerful nations in all of history; when you have reached that point, consider that God is infinitely greater, without any limitation whatsoever.

No wonder the Psalmist says, "His greatness no one can fathom" (Psalm 145:3). We can never comprehend Him, but only bow in awe and adoration before Him.

In Control of Earthly Rulers

Isaiah goes on to emphasize that God is not only superior to the nations, but also sovereign over their rulers:

> He brings princes to naught
>> and reduces the rulers of this world to nothing.
> No sooner are they planted,
>> no sooner are they sown,
>> no sooner do they take root in the ground,
> than he blows on them and they wither,
>> and a whirlwind sweeps them away like chaff. (40:23–24)

Not only the nations, but also their kings and emperors are reduced to nothingness before God, completely subject to His sovereign power. As Proverbs 21:1 says, "The king's heart is in the hand of the LORD; he directs it like a watercourse wherever he pleases." In our day of figurehead kings and queens it may be difficult to appreciate what Solomon said. In his time the monarch was absolute. There was no legislature to pass laws he didn't like, no judicial court to restrain him. He was president, Congress, and Supreme Court rolled into one. His authority was unconditional and unrestrained.

But the king's heart, Solomon says, is controlled by God. He directs the stubborn will of the most powerful monarch as easily as a farmer channels the flow of water in his irrigation canals.

God controls the destinies of rulers as well as their actions. They are scarcely in their place of authority before He "blows on them and they wither, and a whirlwind sweeps them away like chaff." Psalm 2 portrays the kings of the earth taking their stand against God, then says, "The One enthroned in heaven laughs; the Lord scoffs at them" (2:4).

Think of the great rulers of history. Nebuchadnezzar, king of the Babylonian Empire, was driven insane in a moment and for seven years ate grass as cattle do, until God restored him. Alexander the Great conquered most of the known world, then died when he was only thirty-two. Napoleon and Hitler tried to conquer all of Europe, yet Napoleon died in exile and Hitler in a besieged bunker. Truly the most powerful rulers of all time have ultimately faded before the sovereign power of the One who rules history.

COUNTLESS STARS, COUNTLESS NAMES

Once again Isaiah draws our attention to creation:

> Lift your eyes and look to the heavens:
>> Who created all these?
> He who brings out the starry host one by one,
>> and calls them each by name.
> Because of his great power and mighty strength,
>> not one of them is missing. (40:26)

God created the stars, calls them each by name, and sustains them in their courses. One day on an airplane flight I found myself seated next to an astrophysicist. With this verse of Scripture in mind, I asked him how many stars are in the universe. His reply staggered me. He said there are about one hundred billion galaxies, each one containing about one hundred billion stars. A hundred billion times a hundred billion! Yet the Bible says, "He determines the number of the stars and calls them each by name" (Psalm 147:4).

There are just under six billion people on the earth today, and many of us have the same names. Let's suppose, then, there are approximately three billion different names for people. Imagine trying to come up with that many. Yet God names a hundred billion times a hundred billion stars. We've given a few names to stars, constellations, and galaxies such as Polaris, Orion, or the Milky Way, but God names them all. Not only that, but because of His great power and mighty strength, not one of them is missing. They're part of the "all things" sustained by the powerful word of God the Son (Hebrews 1:3).

Through these word-pictures of God's immensity, sovereignty, and power, Isaiah is seeking to communicate to us something of the greatness of God. As the Westminster Shorter Catechism says, He is infinite, eternal, and unchangeable. His infinity means He is totally without limits. If the waters of the earth were twice as much as they actually are, He would still hold them in the hollow of His hand. If every nation of the world were to unite against Him, the One enthroned in heaven would still scoff at them; in His time and in His way He would blow on them and they would wither. If there were ten or a hundred times as many stars in the universe, He would still sustain them in their respective courses and call them each by name. Truly God's greatness no one can fathom.

TO TRUST HIM MORE

What's the point of all this? The answer is found in Isaiah 40:18 — "To whom, then, will you compare God?"—and again in verse 25, "'To whom will you compare me? Or who is my equal?' says the Holy One." God wants us to see and understand that He is inconceivably great, that nothing or no one can possibly compare with Him.

The fact is, we do compare God to our circumstances, our problems, and the issues of society around us. We compare—and these circumstances and problems often seem bigger than God. Moses did this when the people of Israel grumbled over their lack of meat. God had promised to give them meat not for a day, but for a month until they loathed it. Moses was incredulous:

> Here I am among six hundred thousand men on foot, and you say, "I will give them meat to eat for a whole month!" Would they have enough if flocks and herds were slaughtered for them? Would they have enough if all the fish in the sea were caught for them? (Numbers 11:21–22)

Moses compared God to their situation—out in the desert with no visible source of meat—and found God wanting. At least for that moment Moses did not believe in God's infinite power, even after seeing the ten plagues in Egypt and experiencing the miraculous crossing of the Red Sea. Note God's answers to him:

> Is the LORD's arm too short? You will now see whether or not what I say will come true for you. (11:23)

"Is the LORD's arm too short?" This is obviously a rhetorical question. The answer is, of course not! God also asked Abraham's wife, Sarah, "Is anything too hard for the LORD?" (Genesis 18:14), and He said through the prophet Jeremiah, "I am the LORD, the God of all mankind. Is anything too hard for me?" (Jeremiah 32:27). Again the answer is an emphatic no. As the angel Gabriel told Mary, "Nothing is impossible with God."

In Psalm 50:21, God says, "You thought I was altogether like you." One of our problems is that we tend to think God is like us—or perhaps like us, only more so. We have some power, but we know God has more. We have some wisdom, but God has more. We can handle some circumstances, but we hope God can handle more. We thus limit God to what we can imagine as possibilities.

Isaiah 40 reminds us that God is far, far greater than anything we can imagine. He is not limited to our most creative ideas. There can be no comparison between God—infinite, eternal, self-sufficient—and man, any man, for we are all only creatures, finite, limited, and mortal. If we're to fear God, the infinitely vast distance between God and ourselves must ever be kept in mind. Isaiah 40 will help us keep this perspective.

Remember the response of the Israelites after crossing the Red Sea? After seeing the Lord's great power displayed, they feared the Lord and put their trust in Him. We, too, will trust God to the extent we fear Him; to the extent we stand in absolute awe and amazement at His great power and sovereign rule over all His creation. Frequent meditation on passages of Scripture such as Isaiah 40 will help us fear the Lord and be able to trust Him more.

AN AWESOMENESS TO CHERISH

Everything about God is fitted to fill our minds with awe and supreme veneration. He is the inexhaustible fountain of all being, all life, all intelligence, all wisdom, all power, all good, and all true happiness in the universe. He "gives all men life and breath and everything else" (Acts 17:25), and "every good and perfect gift" is from Him (James 1:17). Reality is that "in him we live and move and have our being" (Acts 17:28); each of us can confess with David, "My times are in your hands" (Psalm 31:15).

He is "the blessed and only Ruler, the King of kings and Lord of lords, who alone is immortal and who lives in unapproachable light, whom no one has seen or can see" (1 Timothy 6:15–16). He is "sovereign over the kingdoms of men and gives them to anyone he wishes and sets over them the lowliest of men" (Daniel 4:17). It is He who judges: "He brings one down, he exalts another" (Psalm 75:7). "For from him and through him and to him are all things. To him be the glory forever! Amen" (Romans 11:36).

Therefore, to fear God is to cherish an awesome sense of His greatness, grandeur, and excellence as these perfections are revealed to us both in His Word and in His works. Every time we look up into the sky we should reflect on the fact that He measures those heavens by the breadth of His hand. Every time we see the ocean or even a lake, we can remember that He holds these waters in the hollow of His hand. Every time I drive out of our neighborhood and look at Pikes Peak, that 14,000-foot mountain standing above our city, I should remember that He weighs the mountains in a pair of balance scales.

We need both God's Word and His works to stimulate our fear of Him. The Bible interprets creation for us, and creation illustrates the Bible. David's Psalm 19 beautifully brings together these two aspects of God's revelation of Himself. The first part of the psalm declares God's revelation in nature, beginning with the well-known opening verse: "The heavens declare the glory of God; the skies proclaim the work of his hands."

In the center of the psalm, David extols God's revelation of Himself in His Word, beginning with another familiar expression: "The law of the LORD is perfect" (verse 7). Six different synonyms are used to describe the Word of God. It is called the law, the statutes, the precepts, the commands, the fear, and the ordinances of the Lord. "The fear of the LORD" (verse 9) is a strikingly unusual description of God's truth, emphasizing its effect on our hearts—through it, we learn to fear the Lord.

As we learn to see God in both His Word and His works, we'll begin to say with the prophet Jeremiah,

> No one is like you, O LORD;
>> you are great,
>> and your name is mighty in power.
> Who should not revere you,
>> O King of the nations?
>> This is your due.
> Among all the wise men of the nations
>> and in all their kingdoms,
>> there is no one like you. (Jeremiah 10:6–7)

But in all of our meditation on God's greatness and grandeur, we should remember that when we have strained our faculties to the utmost, we are still an immeasurable distance from the reality of who He is. He is truly an infinitely awesome God whom we should fear.

O glorious God! The vast oceans You hold in Your hand and the billions of stars You hold in their courses are but faint pictures of Your infinite greatness. Indeed You spoke the universe into existence in the beginning, and now by Your mighty power You hold it all together from hour to hour. Fill our minds with awe and adoration as we think upon Your greatness. Fill our hearts with gratitude and gladness as we realize that with all Your infinite power and sovereignty, You have condescended to be our God. Through Jesus Your Son we praise You. Amen.

Notes

1. I acknowledge my indebtedness for some of the insights on Isaiah 40 to commentaries on Isaiah by Joseph A. Alexander (Klock & Klock), Edward J. Young (Eerdmans), and J. Alec Motyer (InterVarsity). While I have not used verbatim quotations from any of them, I have gained insights into the text and have occasionally used words or short, apt expressions from all of them.

5

TRANSCENDENT MAJESTY

The Holiness of God

ONE OF THE FAVORITE hymns of the church is the grand and majestic "Holy, Holy, Holy." It seems to be equally appreciated both by people who prefer traditional hymns and by those who favor the contemporary choruses so popular today. "Holy, Holy, Holy" is often sung at conferences where I speak, and every time I hear it I get a tingling down my spine. Sometimes I'm so overcome with a sense of worship that I can't continue singing; I have to just stop and listen to voices lifted in praise to God.

Why would this hymn capture such widespread appreciation and cause a great swelling of emotion in my own heart? It's because the writer (Reginald Heber) addresses the preeminent perfection of God—His holiness. Consider just these two stanzas:

Holy, holy, holy, Lord God Almighty!
Early in the morning our song shall rise to Thee;
Holy, holy, holy! Merciful and mighty!
God in three persons, blessed Trinity!

Holy, holy, holy! Though the darkness hide Thee,
Though the eye of sinful man Thy glory may not see;

Only Thou art holy—there is none beside Thee
Perfect in pow'r, in love and purity.

The threefold ascription "Holy, holy, holy" is taken from the classic passage on the holiness of God, Isaiah 6:1–8. There the prophet Isaiah sees God in His resplendent glory and hears the seraphs (meaning "burning ones") calling to one another, "Holy, holy, holy is the LORD Almighty; the whole earth is full of his glory."

The Hebrew language uses repetition to indicate emphasis, as we do by italics or underlining. Jesus frequently uses this device when He says, "Truly, truly" (as in John 3:3, NASB). To say something three times makes a statement even more emphatic. It expresses a superlative degree or indicates totality. By employing this threefold repetition for His holiness, God is exalting His holiness to the highest possible measure.

GLORIOUS PERFECTION

God is infinitely glorious in all His attributes, but only His holiness is magnified with this threefold ascription. We never read that He is "wise, wise, wise" or "powerful, powerful, powerful," but twice we hear the heavenly throne attendants calling out "Holy, holy, holy is the LORD Almighty" (Isaiah 6:3, Revelation 4:8).

Why is God's holiness so exalted?

Edward J. Young says that *holy*, as used in Isaiah 6:3,

signifies the entirety of the divine perfection which separates God from His creation. God is the Creator who exists in absolute independence of the creature. He is the Lord, and not a man. Although the creation depends upon Him, He Himself is entirely independent thereof.[1]

So holiness represents "the entirety of the divine perfection," a perfection that sets Him totally apart from us. Reading back through the hymn above, we notice the writer encompasses the attributes of mercy, might, power, love, and purity all within the meaning of God's holiness. The holiness of God, in this respect, is not so much one of a number of other attributes, but the sum of them all.

The Puritan Stephen Charnock, in his classic book *The Existence and Attributes of God,* defined holiness as:

> a glorious perfection belonging to the nature of God. Hence he is in Scripture styled often the Holy One, the Holy One of Jacob, the Holy One of Israel; and oftener entitled Holy, than Almighty, and set forth by this part of his dignity more than any other.[2]

Alec Motyer points out that "God's 'name' is qualified by the adjective 'holy' in the Old Testament more often than by all other qualifiers put together."[3]

The first and last songs of the Bible both magnify the holiness of God. Having crossed the Red Sea, Moses and the Israelites sang, "Who among the gods is like you, O LORD? Who is like you—*majestic in holiness,* awesome in glory, working wonders?" (Exodus 15:11). In Revelation 15:4 those who had been victorious over the beast sang, "Who will not fear you, O Lord, and bring glory to your name? For *you alone are holy.*" Note how both songs ascribe holiness to God alone. No creature in heaven or on earth, angelic or human, can share in God's holiness. He alone is holy.

The first petition Jesus told us to pray in the Lord's Prayer is "hallowed be your name." The word *hallow* means to make holy. Obviously we do not make God's name holy. Jesus is telling us to pray that God's name will be recognized and set apart as holy by people here on earth. If we take Jesus' sequence of petitions as indicative of priority, then recognizing God's holiness comes before even the coming of His kingdom or the doing of His will.

I still recall my first encounter with God's holiness, though it occurred almost forty years ago. I had received as a gift Charnock's *The Existence and Attributes of God.* Because I was deeply concerned about personal holiness, I turned immediately to the chapter on the holiness of God. I began reading and soon was driven to my knees before this holy God about whom I was learning. What Charnock wrote triggered in me a profound sense of the majesty and purity of God coupled with a painful awareness of my own creatureliness and sinfulness.

After a while I arose and began to read again. After a few more pages, I once more fell to my knees before Him, not as the result of a conscious decision but as a spontaneous response to what I was discovering about God's holiness. I was utterly in awe of God, and at the same time stricken with a sense of my own unworthiness before Him.

I don't want to suggest that Charnock's book will evoke a similar reaction from everyone. I think God simply used the book at that time to accomplish a particular work in my life. Perhaps it was my own micro-version of Isaiah's encounter with the holiness of God as recorded in Isaiah 6. In any event, since that time I've been captivated by His holiness. I've also learned that progress in personal holiness must be built upon an ever-deepening awareness of God's holiness.

More than Moral Purity

When we think of God's holiness, the first thought that usually comes to mind is moral purity. This is certainly an important aspect of it, as we shall see. But when the seraphs called out "Holy, holy, holy," they meant something far more profound and fundamental.

The Hebrew word for holy is *qadosh,* which generally means "cut off" or "separate." When used of God, the word expresses the idea of separateness or "otherness." God is wholly "other" from all His creation, from angels, from men, and especially from sinful man. He is absolutely distinct from all His creatures and is infinitely exalted above them in incomprehensible glory and majesty.

R. C. Sproul uses the word *transcendence* to describe this holiness:

When we speak of the transcendence of God we are talking about that sense in which God is above and beyond us. It tries to get at His supreme and altogether greatness. . . . Transcendence describes God in His consuming majesty, His exalted loftiness. It points to the infinite distance that separates Him from every creature.[4]

An earlier writer, A. W. Pink, describes God as "solitary in His majesty, unique in His excellency, peerless in His perfections."[5]

In all I've read on God's holiness I continually notice how authors search for words to adequately express the concept. Scan through the three paragraphs above and notice the superlative adjectives and adverbs: wholly, absolutely, infinitely, incomprehensible, supreme, consuming, exalted, solitary, unique, peerless. When we've exhausted the resources of our language, we still have not described God. He is indeed incomprehensible.

I like Sproul's choice of the word *transcendence*. Most other writers seem to choose *majesty* to denote God's holiness. Majesty refers to sovereign power, authority, or dignity. It speaks of grandeur and splendor. It can be a relative term, however, when we use it of human rulers—some are more sovereign or powerful than others; some have more grandeur and splendor. When we speak of God's majesty, we have to mean absolute, unequaled majesty. Since transcendence means over and above, I propose the expression *transcendent majesty* to enable us to come closest to an understanding of the holiness of God.

But perhaps when we've done all our explaining, we can't improve upon that threefold ascription of the seraphs who cried out, "Holy, holy, holy is the LORD Almighty." This is the heart response of all who fear God.

No Darkness at All

Since God is holy, He is separate not only from His creation but also—in fact especially so—from sin. This leads us to the ethical aspect of God's holiness: the attribute of God commonly called His moral purity, the quality most popularly associated with the concept of His holiness.

We aren't wrong to think this way, since God Himself obviously had this dimension in mind when He said, "Be holy, because I am holy" (Leviticus 11:44–45; 1 Peter 1:16). Because of our creaturehood, we can never be like God in His transcendent majesty. But as people indwelt by His Holy Spirit we should progressively become more like Him in His moral purity.

It would be wrong, however, to think of God's holiness exclusively in terms of moral purity. The majesty of God's holiness cannot be separated from its ethical aspects. They each give luster and brilliance to the other. The transcendent majesty of God gives weight to His moral purity. The ethical holiness of God gives beauty to His majesty.

Try to imagine a God who is infinite in His majesty, but not absolutely perfect in moral purity—with even just a fraction of a tendency toward abuse or contempt. Such a thought is terrifying. Stephen Charnock described this possibility well:

> Though we conceive him infinite in majesty, infinite in essence, eternal in duration, mighty in power, and wise and immutable in his counsels, . . . yet if we conceive him destitute of this excellent perfection [of holiness], and imagine him possessed with the least contagion of evil, we make him but an infinite monster, and sully all those perfections we ascribed to him before. . . . It is a less injury to him to deny his being, than to deny the purity of it; the one makes him no god, the other a deformed, unlovely, and a detestable god.[6]

Thankfully, God is infinitely holy in His moral purity. "God is light," Scripture declares; "in him there is no darkness at all" (1 John 1:5). Light and darkness here have moral qualities standing for purity and impurity. John says there is no impurity at all in God. He is only and totally pure. A famous old slogan for Ivory Soap was "ninety-nine and forty-four one-hundredths percent pure." Apparently that's quite an achievement for soap. To say, however, that God is 99.44 percent morally pure would be utter blasphemy. The only appropriate expression for God is *infinitely pure.*

Louis Berkhof points out that "the idea of ethical holiness is not merely negative (separation from sin); it also has a positive content, namely, that of moral excellence, or ethical perfection."[7] Alec Motyer gets at the same idea when he speaks of God's "total and unique moral majesty."[8] Once again we see writers searching for words adequate to express a concept beyond us.

Perhaps we can gain an idea of God's infinite moral perfection by going back to the comparisons we saw in Isaiah 40. If a tablespoonful of water in the hollow of my hand represents my holiness, then the waters covering the earth represent God's. If the eight-inch breadth of my hand is a picture of my moral excellence, then the entire span of the universe is a picture of God's. Only by ascribing to it the same infiniteness that Isaiah attributes to His immensity and power can we do justice to the holiness of God.

THE ONLY APPROPRIATE RESPONSE

As indicated earlier, Isaiah 6:1–8 is universally recognized as the classic passage on God's holiness. All the books I've read on the subject, without exception, refer to it in some degree, and I can't recall ever hearing a sermon on the topic that didn't use it as a primary text.

What makes Isaiah 6 so important to our subject is that it sets forth both the holiness of God and our only appropriate response to it. We not only see God's holiness magnified by the threefold call of the seraphs, "Holy, holy, holy," but we see Isaiah's deep humiliation in his cry of "Woe to me! I am ruined!"

For your convenience I include the passage here in its entirety. If you're already familiar with it, I urge you to read it once again, slowly and prayerfully, to fully appreciate Isaiah's encounter with the holiness of God.

> [1]In the year that King Uzziah died, I saw the Lord seated on a throne, high and exalted, and the train of his robe filled the temple. [2]Above

him were seraphs, each with six wings: With two wings they covered their faces, with two they covered their feet, and with two they were flying. 3And they were calling to one another:

"Holy, holy, holy is the LORD Almighty;
the whole earth is full of his glory."

4At the sound of their voices the doorposts and thresholds shook and the temple was filled with smoke.

5"Woe to me!" I cried. "I am ruined! For I am a man of unclean lips, and I live among a people of unclean lips, and my eyes have seen the King, the LORD Almighty."

6Then one of the seraphs flew to me with a live coal in his hand, which he had taken with tongs from the altar. 7With it he touched my mouth and said, "See, this has touched your lips; your guilt is taken away and your sin atoned for."

8Then I heard the voice of the Lord saying, "Whom shall I send? And who will go for us?"

And I said, "Here am I. Send me!" (Isaiah 6:1–8)

One of the first questions coming to mind from this passage might be this: Which aspect of God's holiness is in view here? Is it His transcendent majesty or His moral purity? The answer is both.

The vision of God seated on a throne, high and exalted, with the train of His robe filling the temple, is an inescapable picture of His majesty. The words *throne, high,* and *exalted* first draw our attention to this aspect. The train of His robe filling the temple deepens our impression of His supreme royalty. The sinless seraphs covering their faces before Him are a sign of reverence and awe before this unspeakably exalted One, as they cry, "Holy, holy, holy. . . ."

It was not just God's transcendent majesty, however, that caused Isaiah's deep cry of dismay. It was also the awareness of His blazing moral purity, revealing as it did Isaiah's own sinfulness. H. H. Rowley gives this reason for Isaiah's response: "It is not the consciousness of humanity in the presence of divine power, but the consciousness of sin in the presence of moral purity."[9]

So it is with us: Our reaction to God's majestic holiness is a realization of our own insignificance; our response to His ethical holiness is an awareness of our sinfulness and impurity.

The seraphs, having sinless natures, see the holiness of God and react to it with awe and adoration. Isaiah experiences the same thing, but feels it as a sinner. That is the reason he cries out in woe and ruin.

Isaiah was a righteous man, in fact a prophet of God. Yet he now describes himself as "a man of unclean lips." Seeing God in His holiness, he views himself as morally impure. His own holiness has suddenly become to him no more than a tablespoonful of water in the hollow of his hand.

This word *unclean* is significant. It's the word that was to be uttered by lepers who, as they walked along, must cry out "Unclean! Unclean!" (Leviticus 13:45). Isaiah uses it again in Isaiah 64:6 when he says, "All of us have become like one who is *unclean,* and all our righteous acts are like filthy rags." Now in this encounter with the holiness of God, Isaiah uses it of himself. If leprosy typified sin, then Isaiah saw his sinfulness as moral leprosy.

Isaiah was completely devastated. He was disintegrated. If we left him at this point there would be no hope for him or for us. But God does not leave Isaiah devastated. The Scripture tells us that one of the seraphs flew with a live coal from the altar and touched it to Isaiah's mouth.

"See," said the seraph, "this has touched your lips; your guilt is taken away and your sin atoned for." Think of the impact of those words upon Isaiah. Here was a prophet, a righteous man, who had just seen how unholy, how morally unclean he really was when confronted with the holiness of God. He had been shattered; he had declared moral bankruptcy. How could he possibly continue as a prophet after becoming so painfully aware of his own sinfulness?

Note that it is his lips Isaiah saw as unclean. Why not his hands or especially his heart? I believe it was because Isaiah's lips were his professional instruments. He spoke on behalf of God. Now he suddenly realizes that the very instruments he had been using for God are unclean. This would be like a surgeon ready to begin a delicate surgery only to discover that his hands were filthy—except that Isaiah could not scrub his lips as the surgeon can his hands.

HOLY JUSTICE, HOLY MERCY

But there *is* someone who can cleanse Isaiah's lips. It is God, who addresses Isaiah through the seraph: "Your guilt is taken away and your sin atoned for." How could God say this to Isaiah? Can God just arbitrarily forgive sin? Can He grant a pardon without full satisfaction of His justice?

The answer is no. God cannot subvert His justice any more than He can sin. God cannot magnify mercy at the expense of justice.

We tend to think of justice in a positive sense—as something that is on our side. A child is murdered in the community and everyone wants to "see justice done." We want the perpetrator tried, convicted, and sentenced to severe punishment. That would be justice in our minds. But the murderer doesn't want justice. If tried and found guilty, he hopes for leniency, not justice. He doesn't want to receive what he deserves. He wants mercy.

Suppose the judge in such a case is overly lenient and pronounces a light sentence. What would be the community's response? There would be a tremendous cry of outrage. People would feel justice had been violated, that the guilty person did not receive the punishment justice required.

In our initial standing before God as guilty sinners, justice is not on our side. It's against us. The sentence has already been handed down. The wages of sin is death. In this case we don't want to "see justice done." We want mercy. But God's justice is a holy justice; a perfect justice. God cannot be lenient like the judge. He cannot violate His own justice.

What is the solution? Isaiah himself would later give us the answer in the beautiful prophecy of chapter 53. The prophet's filthy lips, now cleansed by God, would utter those immortal words: "We all, like sheep, have gone astray, each of us has turned to his own way; *and the LORD has laid on him the iniquity of us all"* (53:6). Isaiah prophesied of One who would satisfy God's justice against us by Himself bearing the awful punishment we deserve.

That's why God could say to Isaiah, "Your guilt is taken away and your sin atoned for." According to God's plan, some seven hundred years later His own Son would pay for Isaiah's guilt and satisfy His justice. Jesus Christ reconciled God's justice and His mercy.

HIS HOLINESS AND OURS

How should we respond to the holiness of God? Above all we should fear Him. In fact, like Jesus Himself we should *delight* to fear God, learning to stand in reverential awe before His transcendent majesty and moral purity. As Marine Butch McGregor was in awe before the general, so we should be before God, but to a far greater degree. The general's rank and dignity are as nothing compared to God's transcendent majesty. As the light of a candle pales before the brightness of the noonday sun, so the splendor of the most powerful monarch on earth pales before the supreme grandeur of God. We must learn to cultivate such an exalted view of God so that we fear Him as we ought.

We must do more, however. The fear of God should work its way out in our lives in the vigorous pursuit of holiness. As Paul says, "Let us cleanse ourselves from all defilement of flesh and spirit, *perfecting holiness in the fear of God"* (2 Corinthians 7:1, NASB). We are to pursue holiness as an expression of our fear of Him. We are to be holy because He is holy (1 Peter 1:16).

The basic meaning of *holy* as "separate" applies to us as well as to God. Of course God *is* holy; He *is* separate from all moral impurity. We are not holy, but we can and must take steps to pursue holiness, to separate ourselves from sinful habits and practices. (We'll explore this more fully later.)

Because God is holy, we also need to practice humility. God is infinite in His transcendent majesty and perfect in His moral purity. By contrast we are dependent, responsible but sinful creatures. On this earth we aren't likely to have a sudden overwhelming encounter with the holiness of God as Isaiah did, but God is no less holy today than He was when Isaiah saw Him in the temple. Deep humility is the only proper response as we see our sin in the light of His holiness.

Nothing produces humility in a Christian as much as an abiding sense of one's own sinfulness. For learning "genuine humility and self-abasement," John Calvin taught that we should be "empty of all opinion of our own virtue, and shorn of all assurance of our own righteousness —in fact, broken and crushed by the awareness of our own utter poverty."[10] As we seriously pursue holiness we'll grow in humility, for we discover, as Calvin said, that "our nature, wicked and deformed, is always opposing his uprightness; and our capacity, weak and feeble to do good, lies far from his perfection."[11]

Consider God's encouragement to those who seek humility:

> For this is what the high and lofty One says—
>> he who lives forever, whose name is holy:
> "I live in a high and holy place,
>> but also with him who is contrite and lowly in spirit,
> to revive the spirit of the lowly
>> and to revive the heart of the contrite." (Isaiah 57:15)

This is an incredible promise. The high and lofty and holy God condescends to dwell with those who are humble, who are of a contrite and lowly spirit because of their sin. Surely this is worth the price of being "shorn of all assurance of our own righteousness" in order to learn humility.

We'll also want to grow in gratitude to God for His mercy to us through Christ. We continually sin against His perfect moral purity, and our sin is aggravated by the greatness of His transcendent majesty. Each of us has committed high treason against the supreme, exalted Ruler of the universe—and we've done it again and again and again.

Yet God has not dealt with us in perfect justice as He could have. Rather He has extended mercy to us at the cost of His own dear Son. Surely such grace calls forth our deepest heartfelt gratitude. As those who have been forgiven much, we should love much (Luke 7:47).

Now we may enter into His presence with adoring reverence. In Old Testament times God dwelt symbolically in the Most Holy Place of the tabernacle or temple. Only the high priest was allowed to enter there, and then only once a year, and never without the blood of atonement. God demonstrated His holiness by maintaining this separation from the sinful people.

But all that has changed. When Jesus died on the cross the temple curtain barring the way into the Most Holy Place was torn in two from top to bottom. Jesus opened the way of access for sinners to come into God's holy presence. In fact He invites us to come. We're all invited (not just the high priest), and we may come continually (not just once a year). "Therefore, brothers," says the writer of Hebrews, "since we have confidence to enter the Most Holy Place by the blood of Jesus . . . let us draw near to God with a sincere heart in full assurance of faith" (10:19,22).

One thing hasn't changed, however—the necessity of blood. In Old Testament times it was the blood of the sacrificial animal; now it is the blood of Jesus. We can come boldly and continually, but we must always come through the blood of Christ. Only He provides entry for sinners into fellowship with a holy God.

Had sin never entered the world it still would be fitting for us to fear God—to bow in reverential awe before Him. We would gladly join the seraphs in calling out, "Holy, holy, holy is the LORD Almighty; the whole earth is full of his glory."

But sin did enter the world—and because of His holiness, God now reveals Himself as the hater of sin and the just punisher of sinners. But He also reveals Himself in the person of His Son as a merciful and gracious Savior. Our awe of His holiness can be joined with amazement at His love.

Reflect on these words from John Brown, a nineteenth-century Scottish pastor and theologian:

Nothing is so well fitted to put the fear of God, which will preserve men from offending him, into the heart, as an enlightened view of the cross of Christ. There shine spotless holiness, inflexible justice, incomprehensible wisdom, omnipotent power, holy love. None of these excellencies darken or eclipse the other, but every one of them rather gives a lustre to the rest. They mingle their beams, and shine with united eternal splendour: the just Judge, the merciful Father, the wise Governor. Nowhere does justice appear so awful, mercy so amiable, or wisdom so profound.[12]

When we understand what John Brown is saying, we'll understand why there is deep joy in the fear of God.

O holy God! The sinless seraphs covered their faces in Your presence. How much more should we who are but sinful creatures bow in reverence before Your throne. You alone are holy. You alone are the transcendent, majestic God. You alone are morally pure. You are perfect light; in You there is no darkness at all. And yet, through Your Son You came to us as our Savior. You came not to pronounce woe but blessing to those who trust in Jesus. Fill our hearts with awe because of Your holiness, and with amazement because of Your love. Through Jesus Christ our Lord we praise You. Amen.

Notes

1. Edward J. Young, *The Book of Isaiah,* 3 vols. (Grand Rapids: Eerdmans, 1965–72), 1:242–3.

2. Stephen Charnock, *The Existence and Attributes of God* (1853, reprint, Grand Rapids: Baker, 1979), 2:110.

3. J. Alec Motyer, *The Prophecy of Isaiah* (Downers Grove, Ill.: InterVarsity, 1993), 77, note 1.

4. R. C. Sproul, *The Holiness of God* (Wheaton, Ill.: Tyndale, 1985), 55.

5. Arthur W. Pink, *The Attributes of God* (Grand Rapids: Guardian Press, 1975), 11.

6. Charnock, *Existence and Attributes of God,* 111.

7. Louis Berkhof, *Systematic Theology* (Edinburgh: Banner of Truth Trust, 1939), 73.

8. Motyer, *Prophecy of Isaiah,* 77.

9. H. H. Rowley, *The Faith of Israel* (SCM, 1956), 66; as quoted in Motyer, *Prophecy of Isaiah,* 77.

10. John Calvin, *Institutes of the Christian Religion,* ed. John T. McNeill; trans. Ford Lewis Battles, 2 vols. (Philadelphia: Westminster, 1960), 1:367.

11. Calvin, *Institutes of the Christian Religion,* 367.

12. John Brown, *Expository Discourses on I Peter,* 2 vols. (Edinburgh: Banner of Truth Trust, 1975), 1:472–3.

6

SKILL AND SPLENDOR ON DISPLAY

The Wisdom of God

DURING MY BRIEF stint as an engineer in the aircraft industry I observed two important truths that weren't stressed in school. First, I learned that the design of a jet airplane is very much a team effort. We had aeronautical, mechanical, electrical, and structural engineers all involved. Some engineers designed, others tested the designs, and still others purchased components from outside suppliers. It was a massive team effort. No one engineer could possibly design a jet airplane.

The second thing I came to realize is that much of engineering design is accomplished by trial and error. Using all their expertise, aeronautical engineers design an airfoil, test it in the wind tunnel, then modify it, test it, and modify it again. Or a computer circuit board is designed only to discover that it too isn't quite right and must be changed, retested, and remodified. The process goes on, again and again. No component, regardless of how insignificant it seems, can be accepted when its design is only "almost right."

I came along as a young engineer at the time our company was building its first jet fighter. We created two prototypes and sent them to the Air Force for a long series of test flights. To the company's dismay the planes failed to perform according to Air Force specifications. It was back to the drawing board to redesign both fuselage and wings to increase the aircraft's speed and maneuverability. Finally the plane met the requirements and served the Air Force well for a number of years. But it took a lot of trial-and-error work to get it right.

DEMONSTRATIONS OF HIS WISDOM

Teamwork, and trial and error—both are required to build a sophisticated jet fighter. But a fighter plane, complicated as it is, is simple compared to the human body. "Numberless are the world's wonders," said the ancient philosopher Sophocles, "but none more wondrous than the body of man."[1]

Consider just the heart. Think what a challenge it would be for a team of engineers to design a pump with these specifications:

- 75-year life expectancy (2,500,000,000 cycles)
- Requiring no maintenance or lubrication
- Output varying between .025 horsepower and short bursts of one horsepower
- Weight not exceeding 10.5 ounces (300 grams)
- Capacity of 2,000 gallons per day
- Valves operating 4,000 to 5,000 times per hour[2]

Or what structural engineer would want to tackle the design of the twenty-six bones of the human foot which, in the case of a soccer player, absorb a cumulative force of over one thousand tons in a single game?[3]

I admit to a fascination with the design of the human body. Though I'm not a scientist, I remember enough of my engineering studies to appreciate all I read about the incredible complexity and ingenious design of our bodies. I referred earlier to Michael Denton's book *Evolution: A*

Theory in Crisis. To help us better understand the "unparalleled complexity and adaptive design" of a single human cell, Dr. Denton suggests we imagine magnifying it "a thousand million times until it is twenty kilometers in diameter and resembles a giant airship large enough to cover a great city like London or New York." On its surface we see what appear to be millions of portholes, opening and closing to allow a continual stream of materials flowing in and out. Entering one of these openings, we discover "a world of supreme technology and bewildering complexity":

> We would see endless highly organized corridors and conduits
> branching in every direction away from the perimeter of the cell, some
> leading to the central memory bank in the nucleus and others to
> assembly plants and processing units.... A huge range of products and
> raw materials would shuttle along all the manifold conduits in a highly
> ordered fashion to and from all the various assembly plants in the outer
> regions of the cell.

"We would wonder," Dr. Denton continues, "at the level of control implicit in the movement of so many objects down so many seemingly endless conduits, all in perfect unison."

It would resemble "an immense automated factory, a factory larger than a city and carrying out almost as many unique functions as all the manufacturing activities of man on earth." In one respect, however, it would differ radically from the most advanced factory or machine known to man—"for it would be capable of replicating its entire structure within a matter of a few hours."[4]

Now consider that there are an estimated 75 trillion of these incredibly sophisticated cells in your body—75 trillion unique representations of this "object of unparalleled complexity and adaptive design." What keeps them all working together? It's the DNA strand locked away inside the nucleus of each cell. Your body's DNA is estimated to contain instructions that, if written out, would fill a thousand six-hundred-page books, yet all of it would fit inside an ice cube.[5]

However, "in terms of complexity," Dr. Denton adds, "an individual cell is nothing when compared with a system like the mammalian brain."

> The human brain consists of about ten thousand million nerve cells. Each nerve cell puts out somewhere in the region of between ten thousand and one hundred thousand connecting fibers by which it makes contact with other nerve cells in the brain. . . .
>
> Despite the enormity of the number of connections, the ramifying forest of fibers is not a chaotic random tangle but a highly organized network in which a high proportion of the fibers are unique adaptive communication channels following their own specially ordained pathway through the brain. Even if only one hundredth of the connections in the brain were specifically organized, this would still represent a system containing a much greater number of specific connections than in the entire communications network on earth.[6]

What does all this fascinating information about the human body have to do with the fear of God? It's simply one illustration of thousands that could be drawn from nature's vast resources to demonstrate God's infinite wisdom.

SKILL AND JUDGMENT TO ADMIRE

Remember how Butch McGregor came to *admire* General Collins's wise leadership and military skill and thus to stand more in awe of him? That's an extremely small and inadequate picture of how we can grow in reverential awe of God: by coming to appreciate and admire His incomprehensible wisdom and skill.

In chapter 1 I defined wisdom, as it pertains to us, as good judgment or the ability to develop the best course of action in response to a given situation. Our human wisdom is always exercised in the context of the situation in which we find ourselves. Even in initiating some new course of action we never start with a "clean sheet of paper." Whatever we plan is always affected by surrounding circumstances.

God did start with a clean sheet of paper. There were no external circumstances to affect His plans. He was free to do whatever He desired with His creation. How then can we define wisdom in that context?

Nineteenth-century theologian J. L. Dagg described God's wisdom as "consisting in the selection of the best end of action, and the adoption of the best means for the accomplishment of this end."[7] The best possible end of all God's actions is His own glory. Everything God does or allows in all His creation must ultimately serve His glory. There is no end higher than that because there's nothing or no one higher than God. "For from him and through him and to him are all things. To him be the glory forever! Amen" (Romans 11:36).

The concept of God's glory embraces much mystery that we cannot fully comprehend. We do know, however, that it includes the exaltation of His person and the display of all His splendor and wondrous perfections, including the perfection of His wisdom as we discover it in His creation, in His providence, and in His redemption of lost men and women.

HIS WONDERS IN CREATION

The psalmist said, "How many are your works, O LORD! In wisdom you made them all; the earth is full of your creatures" (Psalm 104:24). All creation is like an art gallery in which God displays the splendor of His wisdom, and Psalm 104 is like a directory to it. I encourage you to walk leisurely through this psalm, pausing at each display of God's workmanship to admire and worship Him.

Then take time to gaze upon the wonderful works of nature as you see them in real life. Consider the beauty and fragrance of the flowers, the exquisite nature of the butterfly, the stateliness of the horse, the cuddliness of the little puppy. Look up at the stars in their courses and at the sun sending forth its life-giving rays. In all the works of nature let your mind dwell upon the glorious wisdom of God.

Not only do we see God's wisdom in the intricate designs of nature, but also in their endless variety. There are, for example, seven hundred varieties of butterflies and eight thousand varieties of moths in the United States and Canada alone. How many indeed are Your works, O Lord! In commenting on that statement in Psalm 104:24, C. H. Spurgeon teaches us about the meaning behind it: "If the number of the creatures be so exceedingly great, how great, nay, immense, must needs be the power and wisdom of him who formed them all." Spurgeon considers how a craftsman who could produce not only clocks and watches but also pumps and mills and firearms would certainly be considered more skilled than if he could make only one of those types of products. Likewise Almighty God displays more wisdom "in forming such a vast multitude of different sorts of creatures, and all with admirable and irreprovable art, than if he had created but a few; for this declares the greatness and unbounded capacity of his understanding."[8]

What is more, in all His creation God did not need a team of engineers to do His design work. He simply spoke and all the teeming works of nature came into being. Their various designs existed in His infinite mind from all eternity.

Nor did God have to rely on trial and error as we do. "God saw that it was good" is a continual refrain throughout the Genesis 1 account of creation. Even the most skilled craftsman, when he has finished a piece of work, can find some minute flaw in it, but "God saw all that he had made, and it was *very* good" (Genesis 1:31).

Apparently God delights to display for us His wisdom in creation. Doing so was a turning point in the saga of Job, that great man of God. After Job reached the point of saying, "It profits a man nothing when he tries to please God" (Job 34:9), the Lord confronted him directly with a series of questions designed to put Job in his place—to remind him of the vast gulf between himself and God. "Who is this that darkens my counsel with words without knowledge?" the Lord asked. "Brace yourself like a man; I will question you, and you shall answer me" (38:2–3).

What follows (in chapters 38–41) is a most remarkable passage that I commend to you as another "gallery" of God's creative wisdom and power. To overwhelm Job with a sense of His greatness, God used His creation as a vivid demonstration.

What was Job's response? He first says, "I am unworthy—how can I reply to you? I put my hand over my mouth. I spoke once, but I have no answer—twice, but I will say no more" (40:4–5). Job in effect surrenders. He recognizes God's absolute majesty.

But God isn't through. He continues to bombard Job with questions designed to both humble Job and exalt Himself. Finally Job responds,

> I know that you can do all things;
>> no plan of yours can be thwarted. . . .
> Surely I spoke of things I did not understand,
>> things too wonderful for me to know. . . .
> My ears had heard of you
>> but now my eyes have seen you.
> Therefore I despise myself
>> and repent in dust and ashes. (42:2–6)

Job acknowledges God's sovereignty—"no plan of yours can be thwarted"—and His wisdom—"I spoke of things I did not understand, things too wonderful for me to know." But most of all he experiences a sudden and significant growth in his fear of God. Job already had been commended by the Lord Himself as "a man who fears God" (Job 1:8); now, through seeing the Lord's wisdom and power in creation, he comes to fear Him even more. Hopefully you and I will not have to go through trials as intense as Job's. But we can learn from him to fear the Lord as we, too, see God's wisdom and power displayed in His theater of creation.

THE WONDERS OF HIS PROVIDENCE

God's providence is His constant care for and His absolute rule over all His creation, directing all things to their appointed end for His own glory. Note that His providence embraces two activities: caring for His creation and governing it. Both have His glory as their goal, and in both we see His wisdom.

God *cares* for His creation. Psalm 104—which describes many facets of creation and states, "In wisdom you made them all"—goes on to praise God's care over all of nature. We read that "He makes grass grow for the cattle and plants for man to cultivate" (verse 14), and that His creatures "all look to you to give them food at the proper time" (verse 27).

His Fatherly care is mentioned throughout Scripture. Here are a few examples: "He himself gives all men life and breath" (Acts 17:25). "He . . . supplies seed to the sower and bread for food" (2 Corinthians 9:10). He "[endows] the heart with wisdom [and gives] understanding to the mind" (Job 38:36). He teaches the farmer practical wisdom (Isaiah 28:23–28). From these last two passages and others we can reasonably infer that all practical wisdom in every field of endeavor comes from God. It may come by way of parents, teachers, or mentors, but it all originated ultimately with God. He is not only infinite in His own wisdom, but is the source of all the finite wisdom we possess. Endowing mankind with all manner of skills and practical wisdom for living on this earth is all part of God's care for the world.

God also *governs* His universe, not only inanimate creation, but also the actions of both men and animals. He is called "the ruler of all things" (1 Chronicles 29:12). "He does as he pleases with the powers of heaven and the peoples of the earth. No one can hold back his hand or say to him: 'What have you done?'" (Daniel 4:35). Our plans depend entirely on Him: "Who can speak and have it happen if the Lord has not decreed it?" (Lamentations 3:37). James instructs us to say, "If it is the Lord's will, we will live and do this or that" (James 4:15).

God's rule is universal and absolute. No one can act outside of God's will or against it. Nothing is too large or small to escape His governing hand. A sparrow cannot fall to the ground without His will (Matthew 10:29); not one drop of rain falls without His command (Amos 4:7). The mighty Babylonian Empire falls in one night because of God's sovereign judgment against it (Daniel 4:22–30). In all of God's rule, Calvin says, "He directs everything by his incomprehensible wisdom and disposes it to his own end."9

HIS UNSEEN HAND

But God's wisdom is not as apparent to us in providence as it is in creation. He works in providence by an unseen hand. He works through what we call secondary causes—the actions of people and other living creatures, as well as the so-called laws of nature. God governs His universe often through unwitting and even unwilling instruments.

The cry of a baby saved the Jewish nation from destruction and ultimately changed the course of history. The decree of a Roman emperor that a census should be taken caused another baby to be born in Bethlehem, rather than in Nazareth, thus fulfilling God's prophecy. Neither baby Moses nor Caesar Augustus had any intention of carrying out God's providence, but both acted under His sovereign prompting.

God raised up the Assyrian army to punish His people, and calls it "the rod of my anger, in whose hand is the club of my wrath!" Yet Scripture expressly says of the Assyrian ruler, "But this is not what he intends, this is not what he has in mind" (Isaiah 10:5,7). The Assyrian king had no thought of carrying out God's will; his intention was to conquer nations. But God used him to do His bidding.

God even caused two cows to act contrary to natural instincts and return the ark of the covenant from Philistine territory to Israel (1 Samuel 6:1–12). Whether it's a baby, the ruler of an empire, a cow, or the seemingly blind forces of nature, God has a limitless supply of agents and instruments at His disposal and through which He governs His creation by His unseen hand.

A classic example of God's using unwitting instruments to fulfill His purpose is the action of Joseph's brothers in selling him into slavery (Genesis 37:12–36). They intended only to give vent to their jealous hatred against him. Yet Joseph could later assure them, "It was not you who sent me here, but God" (45:8).

Years later, after their father died, Joseph said to his brothers, "You intended to harm me, but God intended it for good to accomplish what is now being done, the saving of many lives" (50:20). The sinful brothers intended one thing; God intended another. Both accomplished their purposes, but God used the brothers' sinful actions to save many lives. God's invisible hand is guided by unerring wisdom and ingenious plans.

A MYSTERY TOO HIGH

One reason we may not recognize God's wisdom in providence is because He often works in ways contrary to how we would. His wisdom and ways are so much higher than ours that we can't understand them. He tells us that our thoughts and ways simply are not His, and adds, "As the heavens are higher than the earth, so are my ways higher than your ways and my thoughts than your thoughts" (Isaiah 55:8–9). The implication in this passage, writes Edward J. Young,

> is that just as the heavens are so high above the earth that by human standards their height cannot be measured, so also are God's ways and thoughts so above those of man that they cannot be grasped by man in their fullness. In other words, the ways and thoughts of God are incomprehensible to man. Even though God reveals them to man, he cannot fully understand them; to him they are incomprehensible.[10]

Imagine a certain family with two sons: Joe, fifteen, and Sammy, only four. Joe plays ball with Sammy, wrestles with him, and takes him on walks. But one summer Joe goes away on a ten-week missions trip. The boys' father has actively promoted the trip, encouraged Joe to go, and helped him raise the necessary funds.

As the summer goes by, Sammy is missing his brother a lot. Finally one day he says to his dad, "Why did you send Joe away?"

To answer, Dad could talk about Joe's gaining a vision for world missions, learning to serve others, trusting God to supply the necessary funds, and being a good team member. But Sammy wouldn't understand. Those concepts, readily apparent to you and me, would pass right over his head. He would have neither the capacity nor the experience to grasp what his dad was explaining.

This is what Edward J. Young is saying about our inability to understand God's ways. My illustration, though, doesn't do full justice. The difference between a four-year-old's understanding and ours, though great, is not infinite. In the normal course of growth he will someday be able to understand with the same insight we have.

God's wisdom, however, is infinite; ours is finite. This absolute difference is one that I think we fail to grasp. We tend to assume we *would* understand if God would just explain. We don't really believe that "his understanding *no one can fathom*" (Isaiah 40:28).

When Jesus walked with the two disciples on the road to Emmaus, they said to Him, "But we had hoped that he was the one who was going to redeem Israel" (Luke 24:21). That is exactly what had happened, but they could not see it. God did not work the way they would have worked, so they failed to understand what He was doing. God had even foretold through Moses and the prophets what He was going to do, but the disciples—all of them, not just these two—simply could not comprehend the wisdom of God.

We like the story of Joseph because it ends well and allows us to see God's hidden purpose as He directed the malicious acts of the brothers to accomplish His end. But other situations bother us a bit.

Jesus gave us the Great Commission to make disciples of all nations

(Matthew 28:18–20). Several years ago leaders of four missionary radio ministries met together to map out a strategy for broadcasting the gospel by radio to all the remaining unreached peoples of the world. Each organization accepted the responsibility to reach out to certain groups. Within a year, however, one of the broadcasters was off the air due to civil war in its country of operation.

What was God doing? Hadn't He given us the Great Commission? Weren't these organizations seeking to obey His command to make disciples of all nations? Why would God allow a civil war to frustrate a major part of their strategy for obedience? We don't know what God was doing. We do know God governs His universe, but in ways infinitely higher than our ways.

It has helped me to consider an unexplained setback in Paul's missionary strategy. Paul had gone to Jerusalem, after which he planned to sail for Rome and then to Spain. In Jerusalem he was illegally arrested at the instigation of the Jews and finally ended up in prison in Caesarea. There he stayed for *two whole years* because Felix, the Roman governor, wanted to grant a favor to the Jews (Acts 24:27). Here was God's leading cross-cultural missionary and church planter languishing in prison when he could have been on his way to Rome and Spain. He finally got to Rome, but as a prisoner. We don't know if he ever made it to Spain.

Why would God do this? Why would He allow His chosen apostle to the Gentiles to sit in prison for two years? God hasn't told us. His ways are higher than ours.

Humility should be a hallmark of those who fear God. To accept that God's ways are often mysterious, that His wisdom is infinite and ours only finite, is an important expression of humility. Anyone who rejoices in fearing God should say with David, "My heart is not proud, O LORD, my eyes are not haughty; I do not concern myself with great matters or things too wonderful for me" (Psalm 131:1).

WISDOM'S CLIMAX

If creation is the theater in which God displays His glorious wisdom, and if the various outworkings of providence represent the drama played out, then the redemptive mission of Christ is the climactic act. God's intention, Paul wrote, "was that now, through the church, the *manifold wisdom* of God should be made known to the rulers and authorities in the heavenly realms, according to his eternal purpose which he accomplished in Christ Jesus our Lord" (Ephesians 3:10–11).

The church, as the object of Christ's redemptive work, is intended to display God's manifold wisdom. This word *manifold* has the idea of multicolored or iridescent, producing a rainbowlike effect. It calls attention to the infinite diversity and sparkling beauty of God's wisdom as displayed in the entire drama of Christ's life, death, and resurrection, and the consequent ingathering of people from all nations and all stations of life into one Body of Christ.

It is only in Christ and His work that we see God's justice reconciled with mercy, His law reconciled with grace, His holiness with His love, and His power with His compassion. It is only in Christ that unworthy people are both humbled and exalted, and that formerly hostile Jews and Gentiles are reconciled and brought together into one body.

In our Lord's crucifixion, the most momentous event in all history, God displayed in a special way His glorious wisdom in using the acts of sinful men to carry out His plan. The disciples acknowledged this in their prayer recorded in Acts 4:27–28.

> Indeed Herod and Pontius Pilate met together with the Gentiles and the people of Israel in this city to conspire against your holy servant Jesus, whom you anointed. They did what your power and will had decided beforehand should happen.

They all did what God decided beforehand should happen. The Roman government and the Jewish leaders conspired together. They thought they were getting rid of a religious troublemaker. Instead they were simply stage-hands in the world's greatest drama: the redemption of a people for God from every tribe and language and people and nation.

But the drama doesn't end at the Cross or even with the Resurrection. Christ's redemptive work must be applied to people's hearts. Throughout the centuries God has been calling them to salvation through an infinite diversity of ways and circumstances, all displaying His wisdom. In my own case I think of a conversation I overheard in which I was not even a participant, but which God used to bring me to Christ.

Now through His Spirit—and in a way we cannot understand—Christ dwells in us and we in Him. All this is from God and the out-working of His wisdom: "It is because of him that you are in Christ Jesus, who has become for us wisdom from God—that is, our righteousness, holiness and redemption" (1 Corinthians 1:30).

EVERYTHING ORCHESTRATED FOR GOOD

Now look again at God's providence as it applies to His people. Earlier I defined God's providence as "His constant care for and His absolute rule over all His creation, directing all things to their appointed end for His own glory." It's appropriate now to add a final phrase: "and for the good of His people." God's providence is both for His glory *and* for the good of His people. He has designed His eternal purpose so that His glory and our good are inextricably bound together.

This grand truth gives substance to that bedrock promise in Romans 8:28—"God causes all things to work together for good to those who love God, to those who are called according to His purpose" (NASB). This takes us back again to the mystery of God's providence. How can God cause *all* things—the good and the bad, the big things and the little things—to work together for our good?

The *good* mentioned in Romans 8:28 is explained in the next verse as conformity to the likeness of Christ. We have our own idea of what good is, and it seldom includes difficulties and heartaches. But the psalmist said, "It was *good* for me to be afflicted so that I might learn your decrees" (Psalm 119:71). And the writer of Hebrews said, "God disciplines us for our *good*, that we may share in his holiness" (12:10). God causes all of life's circumstances and events, including discipline and affliction, to work together for our good—to conform us to Christ.

Consider the sheer breadth of God's wisdom in bringing this about. Every event of your life—everything you do, everything that happens to you—is somehow woven together into a fabric that is making you more Christlike. There are millions of such events in your life each year, and God orchestrates them all for your good.

But you're just one person. No one knows how many true Christians there are in the world, but let's assume about one billion (out of six billion people). Multiply that number by the millions of events occurring in each believer's life every year and you see the sheer magnitude of God's work. Only an infinite mind—and I truly mean *infinite*—is sufficient for such a task.

Consider the depth of God's wisdom in conforming us to Christ. We're all desperately sinful. In the words of the venerable J. C. Ryle, our best deeds are no more than splendid sins. We might say God has a big job to do in each of us. But He who named a hundred billion times a hundred billion stars and keeps them all in their respective courses can also cause everything in my life and in yours to conform each of us to Christ.

WANTING OUR TRUST—NOT OUR ADVICE

In Isaiah 40 we pictured God's infinite greatness in holding the waters in the hollow of His hand and weighing the mountains on scales. In the same passage Isaiah asks these questions about God's wisdom:

> Who has understood the mind of the LORD,
>   or instructed him as his counselor?
> Whom did the LORD consult to enlighten him,
>   and who taught him the right way?
> Who was it that taught him knowledge
>   or showed him the path of understanding? (40:13–14)

Who instructed God? Whom did He consult? Think of what we've learned about the design of the human body—the amazing intricacy and efficiency of a single cell, the sheer magnitude of the connecting fibers between nerve cells in the brain. Who could have served as the Lord's consultant on a design task like that? Could you or I?

It's an absurd question, isn't it? Yet we continually want to be God's adviser in His providential workings. We continually want to tell Him how certain circumstances should be changed. Or worse, we question God's wisdom when we can't understand what He's doing.

God's ways are mysterious. But with Paul we can learn to exult in this with praise:

> How fathomless the depths of God's resources, wisdom, and
> knowledge! How unsearchable His decisions, and how mysterious His
> methods! For who has ever understood the thoughts of the Lord, or
> has ever been His adviser? . . . Glory to Him forever!
> (Romans 11:33–36, Charles B. Williams translation)

To this end may the following words from J. L. Dagg encourage us:

> It should fill us with joy that infinite wisdom guides the affairs of the
> world. Many of its events are shrouded in darkness and mystery, and
> inextricable confusion sometimes seems to reign. Often wickedness
> prevails, and God seems to have forgotten the creatures that he has
> made. Our own path through life is dark and devious, and beset with
> difficulties and dangers. How full of consolation is the doctrine that
> infinite wisdom directs every event, brings . . . light out of darkness,

and, to those who love God, causes all things, whatever be their present aspect and apparent tendency, to work together for good.[11]

So with joy and consolation let us stand in awe of the infinite wisdom of God manifested in creation, providence, and redemption. But let's do more. One of the marks of a God-fearing person is trust in the Lord: "The LORD delights in those who fear him, who put their hope in his unfailing love" (Psalm 147:11). To hope in His unfailing love is to trust Him. As we stand in awe, let us trust Him, even when we don't understand what He is doing.

O infinite God! Who has understood Your mind or instructed You as Your counselor? Before the universe was created it existed in all its intricate complexity in Your vast mind. Even the tiny cells in our bodies testify to the sheer brilliance of Your creative genius. But while we marvel at Your creation, we confess that we often wonder at Your providence. Help us to learn that Your ways truly are higher than our ways, and that You are always working for our good despite the many things we don't understand. May we fear You by trusting You. And may we ever praise You through Jesus our Lord and Savior. Amen.

Notes

1. Paul Brand and Philip Yancey, *In His Image* (Grand Rapids: Zondervan, 1984), 13.

2. Brand and Yancey, *In His Image,* 58.

3. Paul Brand and Philip Yancey, *Fearfully and Wonderfully Made* (Grand Rapids: Zondervan, 1980), 70.

4. Michael Denton, *Evolution: A Theory in Crisis* (Bethesda, Md.: Adler & Adler, 1985), 328–9.

5. Brand and Yancey, *Fearfully and Wonderfully Made,* 45.

6. Denton, *Evolution,* 330–1.

7. J. L. Dagg, *Manual of Theology* (1857, reprint, Harrisonburg, Va.: Gano Books, 1982), 87.

8. C. H. Spurgeon, *The Treasury of David, An Expository and Devotional Commentary on the Psalms* (Grand Rapids: Baker, 1984), 5:29.

9. John Calvin, *Institutes of the Christian Religion,* ed. John T. McNeill; trans. Ford Lewis Battles, 2 vols. (Philadelphia: Westminster, 1960), 1:202.

10. Edward J. Young, *The Book of Isaiah,* 3 vols. (Grand Rapids: Eerdmans, 1965–72), 3:383.

11. Dagg, *Manual of Theology,* 91.

7

OUR AMAZING FATHER

The Love of God

WHAT IS GOD'S greatest attribute? I once listened to a series of conference messages on the attributes of God. The first speaker said, "I know it's wrong to exalt one attribute above another, but if we could, I would exalt the holiness of God." The next speaker said, "I know it's wrong to exalt one of God's attributes above another, but if we could, I would exalt the sovereignty of God." As I listened I thought to myself, *And I would exalt the love of God.*

Of course all three of us would be wrong. As the two speakers said, we should not exalt any of God's attributes above the others. All of them, in their infiniteness, are essential to His being. Take away any one of them—say, His omnipotence—and God ceases to be God. God minus omnipotence is not God, just as God minus holiness is not God.

Having said that, there's something about the love of God that should astound us as sinners. His greatness causes us to stand in awe. His holiness lays us prostrate in the dust. His wisdom calls forth our admiration. But His love, rightly understood, causes us to gasp in amazement. It's not without reason that Charles Wesley penned those memorable words, "Amazing love! How can it be that Thou my God shouldst die for me?" We can understand God's love to a worthy object, but it's the fact that He loves *sinners* that so astonishes us.

A HEALTHY TENSION

In the physical realm there are two opposing forces called *centrifugal* and *centripetal*. Centrifugal force tends to pull away from a center of rotation, while centripetal force pulls toward the center. A stone whirled about on the end of a string exerts centrifugal force on the string, while the string exerts centripetal force on the stone. Each of these forces cannot exist without the other. Take away one and the other immediately disappears.

These two opposing forces can help us understand something of the fear of God. The centrifugal force represents those attributes of God such as His holiness and sovereignty that cause us to bow in awe and self-abasement before Him. They hold us reverently distant from the One who, by the simple power of His word, created the universe out of nothing.

The centripetal force represents the love of God. It surrounds us with grace and mercy and draws us with cords of love into the Father's warm embrace. To exercise a proper fear of God we must understand and respond to both these forces.

The fear of God certainly denotes the only fitting response to His awesome greatness and transcendent majesty. It's also a recognition of our own frailty, weakness, and sinfulness in the presence of His sovereign power and infinite holiness. At the same time, the fear of God also denotes the love and humble gratitude of the person who, conscious of his own sinfulness and exposure to divine wrath, has experienced the grace and mercy of God in the forgiveness of his sins.

This aspect of the fear of God is beautifully expressed in Psalm 130:3–4.

> If you, O LORD, kept a record of sins,
> O Lord, who could stand?

But with you there is forgiveness;
therefore you are feared.

Here it is not the dread of divine wrath, but rather gratitude for divine forgiveness that draws forth from the psalmist the response he calls fear.

Both these attitudes—awe and gratitude—are necessary to a proper expression of the fear of God. Just as the centrifugal and centripetal forces cannot exist independently, so neither awe nor gratitude alone can represent adequately the biblical meaning of the fear of the Lord. Sometimes we will sense one more strongly than the other. We may on occasion experience overwhelming awe as God reveals Himself to our hearts in His majesty, or inexpressible gratitude as we encounter His mercy. Cherish those moments, but seek to maintain a balance between awe and gratitude.

There should always be a healthy tension between the confidence with which we come before God as His children and the reverential awe with which we behold Him as our sovereign Lord. There's a difference between holy and unholy familiarity with God. We have indeed received the Spirit of adoption, the Spirit by whom we cry, *"Abba, Father"* (Romans 8:15). This expression conveys the warmth and confidence with which we may come into His presence. At the same time we should remember that this One whom we're invited to address as our Father is still the sovereign and holy God. He is still the King who is eternal, immortal, and invisible, and who lives in unapproachable light, whom no one has seen or can see (1 Timothy 1:17, 6:16).

To seek this healthy tension myself, I like to begin my private worship each morning with words such as these: "Sovereign God of all creation, I come to You today through Jesus Christ, and through Him I call You Father. I acknowledge that in myself I'm the worst of sinners, but through Christ Jesus I'm Your son." With that opening prayer I seek to capture both the awe and the intimacy with which we should all relate to God.

THE FATHER'S PAIN

We've looked at God's greatness, holiness, and wisdom, attributes that convey the great distance between us and God. Each of them should stimulate a tremendous sense of awe in our hearts. Now to balance this we need to give attention to the force of God's love drawing us near, that our hearts might be lifted up in wondrous adoration.

The apostle John said, "God is love" (1 John 4:8)—just three simple words, yet this is one of the Bible's most profound statements. It says more than that God is loving. We might say that of another person. But only of God can we say, He is love. This statement speaks of God's essential nature.

John makes it clear, however, that love is not simply an abstract quality of God. Rather His love is active, for John goes on to say, "This is how God showed his love among us: He sent his one and only Son into the world that we might live through him. This is love: not that we loved God, but that he loved us and sent his Son as an atoning sacrifice for our sins" (1 John 4:9–10).

God *showed* His love by *sending* His Son. This reminds us immediately of the familiar words of John 3:16, "For God so loved the world that He *gave* his one and only Son." This statement is repeated so often, I fear we tend to take it for granted. It doesn't stir us much anymore. How can we recapture that sense of amazement that Charles Wesley wrote about?

One story in the Bible helps us especially to appreciate more of what God did when He gave His one and only Son to die in our place. In Genesis 22:2, God said to Abraham, "Take your son, your only son, Isaac, whom you love, and go to the region of Moriah. Sacrifice him there as a burnt offering on one of the mountains I will tell you about." Remember that Isaac was a "miracle baby," born when Abraham was a hundred years old and his wife, Sarah, was ninety. Moreover Isaac was the child of promise through whom God had said Abraham would become the father of many nations (17:5).

Try to put yourself in Abraham's place and feel something of his astonishment and pain. Surely he must have felt as if a dagger had been driven into his heart. But God doesn't just drive the dagger in—He twists it by His use of three descriptive terms.

God refers to Isaac as Abraham's *only* son. (In recounting this incident, the writer of Hebrews uses the expression "one and only son" [11:17] to make it more emphatic.) Abraham had waited years for this son, and now God tells him to slay him and burn him upon an altar of sacrifice on some distant mountain.

God also calls the son by name, *Isaac*—the name He Himself had given the boy before he was born.

Then He adds the piercing phrase *whom you love.* God seems to go out of His way to remind Abraham how special this son is. Abraham needed no reminders, but we get the idea God wants him to experience the pain as deeply as possible.

Why did God do this? The opening line to this story tells us that God "tested" Abraham (22:1). He tested both his obedience (22:18) and his faith (Hebrews 11:17). But I believe God also did it to help us understand a little of what it cost Him to send His only Son for us.

The parallels between Isaac and Jesus help us see how remarkably Isaac prefigured Jesus. Jesus is also called God's "one and only Son." He too was named by God before He was born (Matthew 1:21). And twice God's voice comes from heaven saying, "This is my Son, *whom I love;* with him I am well pleased" (Matthew 3:17, 17:5). Abraham's love for Isaac, great as it was, was still imperfect. God's love for His Son is perfect and hence a greater love. Abraham's love for Isaac was only a shadow of the Father's love for Jesus.

Along with the parallels, however, there is one significant difference. As they neared the mountain, Isaac said to his father, "Where is the lamb for the burnt offering?" Abraham answered, "God himself will provide the lamb for the burnt offering." As the scene is played out, God provided a ram to be offered instead of Isaac. But there could be no substitute for Jesus. Only He could die on that cruel cross to pay for our sins. Abraham did not have to go through with such a heart-wrenching deed—but God did.

God Himself laid our sins on Christ (Isaiah 53:6). God Himself made Him who had no sin to be sin for us (2 Corinthians 5:21). But this doesn't mean God did not in some way feel a father's pain. We have to be careful in attributing emotional pain to God. It's certainly true that God, being sovereign, can never experience the same pain we do when we are victimized by the hurtful actions of someone else. God's blessedness is eternally undisturbed. Yet it's difficult to think He observed His own dear Son crucified by wicked men without feeling a father's pain, only far more deeply than what Abraham felt.

There's still another important difference in the stories of Isaac and Jesus. Abraham was prepared to sacrifice his son in obedience to the command of the loving God whom he worshiped. God sacrificed His Son to save an unloving people who by nature are hostile to Him and rebellious against Him. Scripture says that God "did not spare his own Son, but gave him up for us all" (Romans 8:32). God spared Abraham's son, but did not spare His own. What amazing, what unfathomable love, that the eternal, sovereign, holy God should sacrifice His Son for sinners such as you and me! May we never again think of the story of Abraham and Isaac without finding within it a picture of God's great love for us.

TURNING ASIDE GOD'S WRATH

We still have not begun to comprehend God's love, however, until we understand John's statement that "God . . . sent his Son as an atoning sacrifice for our sins" (1 John 4:10). A footnote in the NIV translation explains "atoning sacrifice" as that which turns aside God's wrath, taking away our sins. God gave His only Son to die in our place in order to satisfy His justice and thus turn aside His wrath from us.

It's difficult for us to think about the wrath of God. We prefer to concentrate on His love because this is far more congenial to our thinking. Another reason is that we tend to view wrath in human terms. We think of it as strong and sometimes violent anger or fury. We envision a wrathful person as being out of control with his or her emotions.

Though we should never think of God's wrath as uncontrolled, violent passion, the Bible does use strong words to describe it—such as *anger, fury,* and *indignation.* Jeremiah 32:37 speaks of His "furious anger and great wrath." In Revelation 19:15 we see Jesus treading "the winepress of the fury of the wrath of God Almighty." To avoid a comparison to human wrath, God's wrath has been defined as His settled determination to punish sin. It is more than that; it's a determination to punish sin with a vengeance. Unrepentant people are said to be "storing up wrath against [themselves] for the day of God's wrath, when his righteous judgment will be revealed" (Romans 2:5). We've learned that God stores up goodness for those who fear Him, but the unrepentant store up God's wrath for themselves.

We were all born "by nature objects of wrath" (Ephesians 2:3) because we all came into this world under the condemnation of Adam's sin (Romans 5:18–19). The pretty newborn baby girl weighing seven pounds six ounces and measuring eighteen inches long comes into the world an object of God's wrath—not because of her own sin, but because of her identity with Adam in his. All of us then aggravate our condition by daily adding to it our own personal sin, which by its nature would provoke God's wrath if we were not in Christ.

We don't truly appreciate the seriousness of this until we realize that sin—all sin—provokes the wrath of God. But consider God's love in sending His Son as an atoning sacrifice for our sins: On the cross Jesus suffered God's wrath in our place, thereby turning it aside from us. When He cried out, "My God, my God, why have you forsaken me?" (Matthew 27:46), He was bearing the wrath that was justly due to us.

This is the meaning of the atonement. Only as we come to grips with the fact that we truly were objects of God's wrath do we begin to appreciate this good news of the gospel.

It is not enough, however, to appreciate God's love only in terms of our initial salvation. We should be growing each year in our awareness of the depth of His love for us in Christ—as we become more aware of the reality of our own sin even as believers. An increasing understanding of God's holiness, of one's own sin, and the value of Christ's death will always mark a person who's growing as a Christian.

Lutheran pastor Don Matzat wrote, "If you read about the experiences of Christians who progressed in their relationship with the Lord Jesus beyond the norm, you will note the combination of a deep sense of sin and failure together with a deep appreciation for what God accomplished in Christ Jesus."[1] Then he quotes Paul Tournier's observation of two things that increase by degrees and side by side: the awareness of our guilt, and the awareness of God's love.[2]

Some years ago I prayed that God would show me more of His love. He answered that prayer by showing me more of my sin—not just specific sins I'd committed, but the sinfulness of my heart. Then I began to appreciate more His love to me.

This is when we really start to enjoy fearing God: when we realize in the depth of our being that we justly deserve the wrath of God, then see that wrath poured out on Jesus instead of on ourselves. We're both awed at His wrath and astonished at His love.

JESUS DIED FOR ME

When John said, "This is how God showed his love among us: He sent his one and only Son . . . " he was obviously referring to God the Father. It was the Father who sent the Son. We must not overlook the love of God the Son, however. John also said, "This is how we know what love is: Jesus Christ laid down his life for us" (1 John 3:16). Though the

Father sent the Son, the Son came voluntarily. Though He is indeed God, the second person of the Trinity, He took upon Himself our nature and suffered in our place on the cross because of His love for us.

The apostle Paul personalized Christ's love: "The life I live in the body, I live by faith in the Son of God, who loved *me* and gave himself for *me*" (Galatians 2:20). It isn't enough to know Christ died for sinners; I must believe He died for me. Then as I see more of my sinfulness, I appreciate more the love of Christ as He bore those sins in my place. The hymnwriter Charles Gabriel expressed the awe that leads to this appreciation:

> I stand amazed in the presence
> Of Jesus the Nazarene,
> And wonder how He could love me,
> A sinner condemned, unclean.

When we stand amazed at the Savior's love, we find ourselves motivated to live for Him. "For Christ's love compels us," Paul said in 2 Corinthians 5:14. Compels us to do what? To live no longer for ourselves, but for Him who died for us and was raised again (verse 15). Later we'll see that obedience is closely linked to—in fact is a tangible expression of—our fear of God. But for this obedience to be pleasing to God, it must be motivated by love and gratitude, not by fear of punishment or hope for reward. That's why it's so crucial that our fear of God include a strong element of amazement at His love.

However, we'll be amazed at His love only to the extent we stand in awe of His person. The realization of who He is—Creator and Sustainer of the universe—is what makes Christ's love so amazing.

Suppose you had an urgent need for a person-to-person blood transfusion and your best friend happens to have your blood type. He or she would gladly donate, and it would be a routine matter. Suppose, however, that your blood type was extremely rare, and the president of the United States was one of the few people who happened to have it as well.

If the president flew on Air Force One to your city and donated blood to you, it would be a nationally newsworthy event.

One person gives you blood, and no one notices. Another gives you blood, and it makes the evening news. What's the difference?

The difference is in the dignity of the person's position or office. The dignity and prestige of the presidency sets the second person apart, making his donation of blood to you or me an extraordinary event.

Now take that illustration and apply it to our Lord Jesus Christ. Though He comes in humility, He is in fact no ordinary citizen. His status is something that not even the Roman emperor can match. He's the One who created the universe and sustains it by His powerful word (Hebrews 1:1–3). And He has come all the way from heaven's glory to live and die for you and me because of His love.

All that we've studied so far about God in His greatness, holiness, and wisdom applies as much to the Son as to the Father. In fact, on the basis of John 12:38–41 where we learn that Isaiah "saw Jesus' glory," it seems that the Lord whom Isaiah saw in his vision (Isaiah 6:1–8) was the preincarnate Christ. This is what makes Christ's death so amazing—that this Holy One before whom Isaiah is totally devastated should come and die for sinful men and women who are the very antithesis of holiness.

RICH IN GRACE, RICH IN MERCY

In Ephesians 2:1–3 the apostle Paul presents a dismal picture of us before we trusted Christ as Savior:

> As for you, you were dead in your transgressions and sins, in which
> you used to live when you followed the ways of this world and of the
> ruler of the kingdom of the air, the spirit who is now at work in those
> who are disobedient. All of us also lived among them at one time,
> gratifying the cravings of our sinful nature and following its desires and
> thoughts. Like the rest, we were by nature objects of wrath.

Paul says we were spiritually dead, unable to help ourselves or do anything about our plight. We were not drowning people needing a life ring—we were dead people in need of life. Further, we were slaves to the world, to the devil, and to our own sinful natures. And as we've already seen, we were by nature objects of God's holy wrath. Dead, slaves, objects of wrath—what a desperate condition!

Against this dark backdrop of sin and misery Paul gives the solution:

> But because of his great love for us, God, who is rich in mercy, made us alive with Christ even when we were dead in transgressions—it is by grace you have been saved. (2:4–5)

Three key words stand out in this passage: *love, mercy,* and *grace.* Note Paul's superlative language: *great* love, *rich* in mercy, and in verse 7, the *incomparable* riches of His grace. What a sharp contrast Paul draws between our pitiful condition and God's glorious remedy. God is rich in mercy and rich in grace, and He bountifully bestows both on us because of His great love.

How should we understand the words *grace* and *mercy* as Paul uses them? Think of them as the two arms with which God reaches out in His love to save us. His grace is His arm of love reaching out to us in our guilt, while His mercy is His love reaching out to us in our pitiable condition because of our sin. Both grace and mercy contemplate our sin—grace its guilt, and mercy its misery.

Grace is *God's favor through Christ to people who deserve His wrath.* It is more than the oft-quoted definition of "unmerited favor." God's grace addresses not only our lack of merit, but our positive *de*merit. It is blessing bestowed in the presence of demerit.

When I was a small child, homeless men (then called hobos) would sometimes appear at our front door and ask my mother for a meal. Without receiving any work in return, mother would prepare a plate of food for them to eat on our front porch. She was granting an unmerited or unearned favor, but it was not grace. If, however, a hobo appeared at our door whom my mother recognized as a man who had previously robbed us, a new element is introduced. Now the food is given despite demerit. Not only is the man undeserving of the food in the sense of earning it; he actually deserves punishment instead because of his crime.

We all stand before God with innumerable counts of demerit against us. It isn't an overstatement to use Ezra's words: "Our sins are higher than our heads and our guilt has reached to the heavens" (Ezra 9:6). We deserve God's wrath. Instead we receive favor, bountiful favor—we're blessed with every spiritual blessing in Christ (Ephesians 1:3). Why?

The answer is in the two words *through Christ* in our definition of grace. Through Christ and His atoning death we're delivered from the wrath we deserve. And through Christ and His life of obedience for us we receive the boundless favor we don't deserve.

This favor comes to us in many forms. We're first of all saved by grace (Ephesians 2:8–9), but it doesn't stop there. Grace is God's power enabling us to cope with life's difficulties (2 Corinthians 12:9). It supplies the strength we need to live the Christian life (2 Timothy 2:1). Grace provides the spiritual gifts by which we serve in the body of Christ (Romans 12:6). Every blessing you receive, every answer to prayer you experience, is an expression of God's grace to you.

All these favors come to us because of the sinless life and sin-bearing death of our Lord. A popular definition of grace is the acronym, *God's Riches At Christ's Expense.* Jesus suffered in our place and paid for our sins. He also lived in our place and earned all our blessings.

While grace contemplates our guilt, mercy has regard to our misery, which is the consequence of our sin. God's mercy is more than compassion for someone in need. It is compassion in spite of demerit. If the hobo-robber in the above illustration ended up in a wretched condition in prison, and my mother in various ways sought to relieve his distress, that would begin to picture God's mercy.

But it would be only a faint picture. No misery in this life can begin to compare with the misery of those suffering eternally under the wrath of

God. Even the Nazi Holocaust, awful as it was, pales by comparison to the lake of fire of God's judgment.

God is sovereign in extending His mercy. He said to Moses, "I will have mercy on whom I will have mercy, and I will have compassion on whom I have compassion" (Exodus 33:19, Romans 9:15). *Sovereign* in this sense refers not to God's power but to His right to do as He pleases. Paul is getting at this when he asks, "Does not the potter have the right to make out of the same lump of clay some pottery for noble purposes and some for common use?" (Romans 9:21). We should therefore always be amazed that God extended His mercy to us.

God is likewise sovereign in extending His grace. He was under no obligation to forgive our sins. He could have plunged each of us into hell as He did the angels who sinned (2 Peter 2:4). Instead He sent His Son to turn aside His wrath by satisfying His justice. And He did even more: He also called us by His gospel and through His Spirit to trust in Christ (2 Thessalonians 2:13–14). If you're a believer and your neighbor isn't, this is not due to your superior wisdom or greater insight into the issues of life. It's because of God's grace in calling you to Christ.

The gospel invitation is wide-open to all: *"Everyone* who calls on the name of the Lord will be saved" (Romans 10:13). *"Whoever* is thirsty, let him come; and whoever wishes, let him take of the free gift of the water of life" (Revelation 22:17). And yet when we come, we discover that we were chosen in Christ before the creation of the world (Ephesians 1:4). That is grace.

WE STAND IN GRACE

All true believers acknowledge that we're saved by grace (Ephesians 2:8–9). Paul tells us furthermore that we also *stand* in grace (Romans 5:1–2). On a day-to-day basis we stand accepted by God in the same grace by which we were saved. And the same definition of grace—God's favor through Christ to people who deserve His wrath—applies in our continuing relationship with God as believers. Daily we sin in thought, word, and deed. We never completely love God with all our heart, soul, and mind, and never fully love our neighbor as ourselves. Each day we deserve God's wrath, but each day we stand before Him in grace, accepted by Him only through the merit of our Lord Jesus Christ.

As B. B. Warfield said, "Though blessed with every spiritual blessing in the heavenlies in Christ, we are still in ourselves just 'miserable sinners': 'miserable sinners' saved by grace to be sure, but 'miserable sinners' still, deserving in ourselves nothing but everlasting wrath."[3] Our best deeds are polluted with sin and are made acceptable to God only through Jesus Christ (1 Peter 2:5). Even as Christians we never earn favor with God by our performance. All His favor still comes to us through Christ.

Because of this we can be assured of God's unfailing love to us throughout this life and for eternity. We've done nothing to earn His love and can do nothing to forfeit it. His love in Christ is eternal and unconditional. Nothing can separate us from His love, as the apostle Paul put it so eloquently. Do we really believe what Paul says to us here?

> Who shall separate us from the love of Christ? Shall trouble or
> hardship or persecution or famine or nakedness or danger or sword? As
> it is written:
> > "For your sake we face death all day long;
> > we are considered as sheep to be slaughtered."
> No, in all these things we are more than conquerors through him who
> loved us. For I am convinced that neither death nor life, neither angels
> nor demons, neither the present nor the future, nor any powers,
> neither height nor depth, nor anything else in all creation, will be able
> to separate us from the love of God that is in Christ Jesus our Lord.
> (Romans 8:35–39)

Do we believe that nothing—not even our own sin—can separate us from God's love? This doesn't mean God winks at our sin like the proverbial indulgent grandfather. Rather it means that He has *forgiven* our sins because of the atoning sacrifice of His Son. God proved His love to us by sending Christ to suffer in our place. Therefore to doubt His love because of our sin is an affront to Him. It says in effect that the merit of Christ's death is not sufficient to cover the demerit of our sin. What an insult to God!

OUR RESPONSE

How then should we respond to God's love to us through Christ?

First, we should fear Him. "With you there is forgiveness; therefore you are feared" (Psalm 130:4). Here it is helpful to review Sinclair Ferguson's definition of *filial fear* that we saw in chapter 3: "It is that indefinable mixture of reverence, fear, pleasure, joy and awe which fills our hearts *when we realize who God is and what he has done for us.*" Realizing who God is and what He has done for us will elicit this biblical fear. As we grow in our understanding of God's love for us in Christ, we will more and more delight to fear Him.

Our second response comes directly from the passage we've looked at often in this chapter, 1 John 4. After showing us God's love in sending His Son, John immediately draws the application: "Dear friends, since God so loved us, we also ought to love one another" (verse 11). We've seen that God's love is sacrificial and unconditional. He loved us when we did not love Him. Therefore we have no excuse for not loving one another.

Certainly there are people who are difficult to love. The fact is, we all are to some degree. We don't have the power in ourselves to love the unlovable, but that also is no excuse. We do have the Holy Spirit enabling us to love others as we look to Him.

So we have no excuse not to love one another, and we have the direct command to do so, based on God's love for us. In fact Paul urges us to "live a *life* of love"—our entire life, seven days a week, is to be characterized by love, as we'll explore later. Like John, Paul bases that exhortation on Christ's love for us (Ephesians 5:1–2). Our love is to be a reflection of His love.

Third, we should seek to obey God and serve Him in every area of life. We "should no longer live for [ourselves] but for him who died for [us] and was raised again" (2 Corinthians 5:15). Or as Paul says elsewhere, we should "in view of God's mercy, . . . offer [our] bodies as living sacrifices, holy and pleasing to God" (Romans 12:1).

By using the word *should* I'm not seeking to create a sense of obligation or lay a guilt trip on anyone. My desire is to help you develop such a view of God's love that you can't help but fear Him. I want you to experience the *joy* of fearing God and to grow in that joy more and more as you increase in the knowledge of His love.

My desire is that both you and I will be so overwhelmed by Christ's love that it will indeed compel us to live not for ourselves but for Him. Too often we're compelled not by love but by a sense of duty or obligation. God does not delight in that kind of motive. He delights in our heart response of love. His love to us, and our love to Him in return, work together to produce the joy of fearing God.

In the next chapter we shift our attention from the attributes of God that stir up our fear of Him to practical steps we can take to grow in that fear. But let's not lose our focus on God. No practical step will help us if we do not keep growing in the knowledge of God—of who He is and what He has done for us.

O God our glorious Father! With You there is forgiveness; therefore You are feared. While we were still sinners, objects of Your just and holy wrath, You loved us and sent Your Son to die for us. You reached out in Your mercy to relieve our misery, and in Your grace to forgive our guilt. And now through Jesus we call You "Abba, Father." Create in our hearts that sense of filial fear that will cause us to worship and adore You because of Your love to us. Again we praise You through Jesus our Lord. Amen.

Notes

1. Don Matzat, *Christ Esteem* (Eugene, Ore.: Harvest House, 1990), 41.

2. Matzat, *Christ Esteem*, 42.

3. Benjamin Breckenridge Warfield, *The Works of B. B. Warfield: Perfectionism*, Part 1 (Grand Rapids: Baker), 7:113–4.

PART III

Responding to Our Awesome God

8

FANNING THE FLAMES

Growing in the Fear of God

WHENEVER I'M AT a men's retreat, someone invariably will speak of having had a "mountaintop" experience and lament the fact that we now have to go back down to the valley of real life. This mountain has nothing to do with altitude. It's simply a way of saying we've had a great time with God and other men during the weekend.

As a speaker at some of these retreats I do want the men to have a rich experience with God and other men of like heart. More importantly, though, I want them to go back into their workaday worlds better equipped to glorify God in their daily lives. There's no point having a great spiritual retreat if it doesn't affect our lives back home. I desire the same thing for you as you read this book.

We've been considering some grand and glorious truths about God in the last few chapters. Our minds are stretched by His greatness as presented in Isaiah 40. Then we're brought low with the prophet as we encounter God's absolute holiness and moral purity in Isaiah 6. We gaze with the awe of admiration at His wisdom and gasp with amazement at His love for sinners such as ourselves. Now we can understand why John Murray described the fear of God as consisting in awe, reverence, honor, and worship, and all these on the highest level of exercise. But like the men on the weekend retreat, we can't live on the mountaintop. We need to learn how to grow in fearing God amid the duties and pressures of daily life.

You may be like the man who often wrote the letters "YBH" in the margins of books he was reading. A friend, browsing through the man's library one day, noted the frequency of those letters and asked what they meant. "They stand for *Yes, but how?*" the man replied. "I agree with what the author is saying, but I need to know how to apply it."

Hopefully you agree with me that the fear of God should indeed be a foundational attitude in the life of a Christian. And you agree that God is most worthy to be feared, both because of who He is and what He's done for us. You're also persuaded that this fear, whether viewed as a complex set of emotions or a sustained attitude, should be *determinative* in the way we relate to God and other people. Now you want to know, "How do I grow in fearing God? How can I experience more of that mingled emotion of dread, reverence, veneration, and wonder?"

The remainder of this book is intended to help you do this. We'll look first at specific steps for continuing to grow in the fear of God as a life-long process. Then we'll consider how the fear of God should affect the way we live—how we can make it determinative in our everyday lives.

GOD'S PART AND OURS

The good news is that if you're a believer, God has already implanted in your heart the fear of Him—in principle. In Jeremiah 32:38–41 the Lord gives us a gracious promise:

> They will be my people, and I will be their God. I will give them singleness of heart and action, so that they will always *fear* me for their own good and the good of their children after them. I will make an everlasting covenant with them: I will never stop doing good to them, and I will inspire them to *fear* me, so that they will never turn away

from me. I will rejoice in doing them good and will assuredly plant them in this land with all my heart and soul.[1]

Note the two references here to fearing God. First He says He will give us singleness of heart and action so that we'll always fear Him. Then He adds His promise to *inspire* us to fear Him, or as a more literal translation renders it, "I will put the fear of Me in their hearts." God will do more than simply motivate us, as the word *inspire* might suggest; He will actually implant a principle of the fear of Him in our hearts. This is a part of regeneration when God gives us a new heart and puts His Spirit within us (Ezekiel 36:26–27).

If you've been born again and trust Christ as your Savior, you already have within you a basic foundation of the fear of God. In at least an elementary fashion you already have that sense of awe, reverence, honor, and worship toward God which John Murray describes. If you're a believer it is there, though it may be only a spark. It's only unbelievers who have *"no fear of God before their eyes"* (Romans 3:18).

I've deliberately used a *spark* as a metaphor to picture this basic principle. I think for most of us it *is* only a spark at the beginning. Another reason I chose this word is because Paul told us to "fan into flame the gift of God, which is in you" (2 Timothy 1:6). Paul was actually referring to spiritual gifts, which God has given each of us. He wants us to develop our gifts, improving them so they'll be more useful. They are indeed gifts, but we have the responsibility to fan them into flame—to cause them to develop and mature.

We should also fan into flame the spark of the fear of God that He put within us at our new birth. That doesn't mean we do this on our own apart from the Holy Spirit's help. It does mean that we're responsible to *grow* in fearing God. The initial kindling of the spark is solely the work of God; the flaring up of that spark into a flame is a combined effort: We ourselves work with the Holy Spirit, as enabled by His power.

This basic principle within is also like a seed planted in the ground, which only the planter is aware of at first. It is God who has planted the seed of the fear of Him in our hearts, whether or not we have realized it. In this picture too we see the synergistic effort between God and ourselves. Paul said, "I planted the seed, Apollos watered it, but God made it grow. So neither he who plants nor he who waters is anything, but only God, who makes things grow" (1 Corinthians 3:6–7).

In the agricultural realm God has ordained that mankind be fully involved in the growth of crops, but He has reserved to Himself the principle of life, the ability to make things grow. It's the same way in the spiritual life. God ordains that we mature through personal diligence and effort, but He reserves to Himself the ability to make us grow. We're responsible to fan into flame the spark of the fear of God, but we're dependent on Him to make it happen.

INSPIRATION FROM THE ENERGIZER

This leads naturally to the first requirement for growing in the fear of God. We need to ask God to stimulate this growth within us. We can pray with David, "Give me an undivided heart, that I may fear your name" (Psalm 86:11).

An undivided heart denotes singleness of purpose, aim, and affections. This is what David prayed for. He recognized the tendency of his heart to be divided, to seek to serve two masters—himself and God—so he earnestly sought help from the Lord, that he might fear Him.

A lot of people in various pursuits—business and professional people, athletes, farmers—have a singleness of heart and purpose, some to a fault. We sometimes call them "workaholics." But it's rare to find a Christian with an undivided heart. We're constantly pulled by the subtleties of the world and the desires of our sinful natures. So we need to pray that God will unite our hearts to fear His name.

This is where growth in the fear of God begins. God the Holy Spirit is the energizer of all spiritual motion in our lives. Without His work in our hearts we cannot work. So our first step in growing in the fear of God is to pray for a heart single in purpose to that end.

Go back in Jeremiah 32:40 to God's promise to inspire us to fear Him, and ask Him to do exactly that in your heart—not just plant the seed, but also cause it to grow. This should be a consistent prayer for each of us. I have six or eight verses of Scripture that I pray over almost every day, asking God to work out their truth in my life. One of them is Psalm 86:11b, "Give me an undivided heart that I may fear you." I encourage you to make that Scripture a part of your regular prayer times.

REGULAR EXPOSURE TO HIS TEACHING

After prayer, the next ingredient for growth in fearing God is regular, consistent exposure of our minds and hearts to His Word. This exposure should involve reading it for ourselves, hearing it taught, and studying it for ourselves. All three of these methods of Scripture intake are involved.

In Deuteronomy 4:10 the Lord connects hearing His Word with learning to fear ("revere") Him: "Assemble the people before me to hear my words so that they may learn to revere me as long as they live in the land and may teach them to their children." So as we hear the Scriptures preached and taught we should pray that God will use them to stimulate our fear of Him.

When Saul of Tarsus fell down in fear before the risen, glorified Christ on the road to Damascus, he asked two questions: "Who are you, Lord?" and "What shall I do, Lord?" (Acts 22:8,10). These questions are helpful to ask as we hear God's Word taught: *Who are you, Lord?*— Lord, reveal Yourself to me in some aspect of Your greatness, or holiness, or wisdom, or love. Show me more of who You really are. And *what shall I do, Lord?*—how do You want me to apply and obey Your Word today, in reverence to You?

God's Word is preached not to offer us helpful suggestions for improving our lives or making us feel good, but to teach us more of God,

His person, His works, and His will for our daily lives. To that end, pray and listen attentively. Take notes of thoughts that are especially helpful for understanding or applying the Scripture being expounded.

Another way we grow in the fear of the Lord is through regular reading of the Bible. Notice what each future king of Israel was commanded to do in Deuteronomy 17:18–19.

> When he takes the throne of his kingdom, he is to write for himself on a scroll a copy of this law. . . . It is to be with him, and he is to read it all the days of his life so that he may learn to revere the LORD his God and follow carefully all the words of this law and these decrees.

The king was to be a regular reader of God's law, specifically for the purpose of learning to fear the Lord and obey Him. What was true for Israel's kings should be true of us today. Regular, prayerful, personal exposure to Scripture is the most effective means of growing in the fear of God.

Whatever Bible reading plan you use (and many are available today), I strongly urge you to include regular reading through the Old Testament. Here we see God's holiness and sovereignty portrayed most vividly. Consider such a matter-of-fact report as this one:

> That night the angel of the LORD went out and put to death a hundred and eighty-five thousand men in the Assyrian camp. When the people got up the next morning—there were all the dead bodies! (2 Kings 19:35).

Think of it: 185,000 men killed without ever "firing a shot"! You can hardly read this without being impressed with God's sovereignty over the world.

The Old Testament is filled with such stories. As you read these true accounts, stop and pray over them, asking God to use them to stir within you a deep sense of reverential awe.

Throughout these same Old Testament pages that reveal God's sovereignty, we also discover His unfailing love and faithfulness to His people.

(The Psalms alone contain some twenty-five references to the Lord's "unfailing love.") Even after He had punished them with exile, He still said to the Jews, "'When seventy years are completed for Babylon, I will come to you and fulfill my gracious promise to bring you back to this place. For I know the plans I have for you,' declares the LORD, 'plans to prosper you and not to harm you, plans to give you hope and a future'" (Jeremiah 29:10–11). God's love never failed even though He had to discipline the Jews severely for their persistent disobedience. I find it helpful to make notes in the margins of my Bible or in a separate notebook of what I learn from my reading about God's love and other attributes.

As you move into the New Testament in your reading, pay close attention to the gospel—the mission of Christ in His life and death for us as an atoning sacrifice for our sins. We find this not just in the first four New Testament books commonly called "the Gospels," but throughout the New Testament.

Consider, for example, the message of 2 Corinthians 5:21—"God made him who had no sin to be sin for us, so that in him we might become the righteousness of God." This verse essentially teaches us that God charged our sin to Christ and credited His righteousness to us. That's the gospel in a nutshell. Each time we read a passage such as this, we should stop and ponder God's amazing love for us as manifested in the Atonement.

"Godly fear," wrote John Bunyan,

> flows from a sense of the love and kindness of God to the soul. Where there is no sense of hope of the kindness and mercy of God by Jesus Christ, there can be none of this fear, but rather wrath and despair, which produces a fear that is . . . devilish; . . . but godly fear flows from a sense of hope of mercy from God by Jesus Christ.[2]

Bunyan then quotes Psalm 130:3–4—"If you, O LORD, kept a record of sins, O Lord, who could stand? But with you there is forgiveness; therefore you are feared."

Once again we see the importance of the centripetal aspect of the fear of God: His love that draws us to Him. The editor of Bunyan's works made this editorial comment in a footnote: "The filial fear of God is most prevalent when the heart is impressed with a lively sense of the love of God manifested in Christ."[3]

With this in mind I cannot emphasize too strongly the importance of living our Christian lives each day in the atmosphere of the gospel. The gospel is not just for unbelievers. It is also for us, because we are still sinners—saved sinners to be sure, but still sinners in need of the daily assurance of God's forgiveness through Christ. As we experience His love through His forgiveness, our hearts are drawn to Him in this filial fear, and we stand amazed at His love.

GOING FOR DEPTH

Along with reading the Bible, we also need to *study* it. Bible reading gives us breadth, but Bible study gives us depth. Most people probably wouldn't grasp the message of 2 Corinthians 5:21 merely by reading through 2 Corinthians. Only as we begin to dig down into the meaning of a passage do we start mining Scripture's gold.

If you've never done serious Bible study, the idea may sound intimidating. For one thing, you don't know how to do it. You also don't know where to find regular time for it. A practical solution to both these problems is to get involved in a group Bible study where you can learn how to dig into the Scriptures and also benefit from the insights of others. A group Bible study also provides a measure of accountability that usually helps us to somehow find the time to prepare before meeting with the group.

A word of caution, however: All Bible study groups are not created equal. They vary from highly structured classroom approaches to informal gatherings in homes or restaurants. There's nothing wrong with an informal group, provided it promotes a serious attempt to grapple with the message of Scripture. You'll want to avoid a study where people merely share their subjective impressions of "what the passage says to me" apart from objective study of the text.

Obviously some skills are needed in Bible study, and we'll seek to develop them if we're serious about growing in the fear of God. A number of good books are available today on *hermeneutics*—the principles and processes of biblical interpretation. You might ask your pastor or another mature Christian who is experienced in Bible study for a recommendation. Look for one that teaches objective study skills without promoting a particular doctrinal position.

More important than good study skills, however, is the right mental attitude. Proverbs 2:1–5 explains what it is:

> My son, if you accept my words
>   and store up my commands within you,
> turning your ear to wisdom
>   and applying your heart to understanding,
> and if you call out for insight
>   and cry aloud for understanding,
> and if you look for it as for silver
>   and search for it as for hidden treasure,
> then you will understand the fear of the LORD
>   and find the knowledge of God.

The right attitude here is characterized first by a *teachable* spirit. To "accept" Scripture's words suggests an attitude of openness to learn more and to be corrected. None of us possesses all the truth, and we don't fully understand the truth we have. So we always need to be willing to learn more or have our understanding corrected.

We need to avoid becoming like the Jews to whom Jesus said, "You diligently study the Scriptures because you think that by them you possess eternal life. These are the Scriptures that testify about me, yet you refuse to come to me to have life" (John 5:39–40). They were persistent in Bible study but not teachable. Their preconceived ideas about what Scripture taught kept them from being open to the message of Jesus.

A proper mental attitude is also characterized by a spirit of *dependence*. This is expressed graphically in Proverbs 2 by the instruction to "call out for insight and cry aloud for understanding." There's almost a sense of desperateness conveyed. This isn't simply Jewish hyperbole. It squares with reality. The fact is, we're desperately dependent. Consider the words of Jesus in Luke 10:21—"I praise you, Father, Lord of heaven and earth, because you have hidden these things from the wise and learned, and revealed them to little children. Yes, Father, for this was your good pleasure." The comments of Norval Geldenhuys on this passage help us see what Jesus was rejoicing about:

> God in His wisdom, omnipotence and love has so arranged matters that insight is given into the redeeming truths of the kingdom not to those who are self-exalted and wise in their own esteem (as so many Pharisees and scribes were at that time), but to those (like His faithful disciples) who in childlike simplicity and humility feel their utter dependence on the Lord and accept without intellectual arrogance the truths revealed by God through Him. The contrast pointed by the Saviour is not that between "educated" and "uneducated" but between those who imagine themselves to be wise and sensible and want to test the Gospel truths by their own intellects and to pronounce judgment according to their self-formed ideas, and those who live under the profound impression that by their own insight and their own reasonings they are utterly powerless to understand the truths of God and to accept them.[4]

The attitude of those "who in childlike simplicity and humility feel their utter dependence on the Lord" goes hand-in-hand with a teachable spirit. If we're self-opinionated about what the Bible teaches, we'll be neither dependent nor teachable. Even those of us who want to be dependent and teachable can too often give lip service to those qualities while actually approaching Bible study in the strength of our own intellect.

We need to ask God to help us live, in the words of Geldenhuys, under the profound impression that by our own insight and reasoning we're utterly powerless to understand and accept God's truths.

The third characteristic of a right attitude toward Bible study is diligence. This is expressed in Proverbs 2 by the phrases "applying your heart to understanding," "looking for it as for silver," and "searching for it as for hidden treasure." Prayer cannot take the place of diligence. We depend upon the Holy Spirit, but He answers our prayers and enlightens us as we diligently apply our minds to the text of Scripture. The idea of looking for silver and searching for hidden treasure suggests that Scripture truth is valuable and worth digging out, but the digging is indeed labor.

What is the result of such open-minded, prayerful, and diligent Bible study? Solomon says in Proverbs 2, "You will understand the fear of the LORD and find the knowledge of God." Once again we see that consistent exposure to Scripture is the path to growing in the fear of God. The more we know God, the more we will fear Him. The more we see His majesty, sovereignty, and love, the more we will stand in awe of Him.

Listen again to John Bunyan:

The fear of God flows from . . . a sound impression that the word of God makes on our souls; for without an impress of the Word, there is no fear of God. Hence it is said that God gave to Israel good laws, statutes and judgments that they might learn them, and in learning them, learn to fear the Lord their God. . . . For as [to the extent] a man drinks good doctrine into his soul, so [to that extent] he fears God. If he drinks in much, he fears Him greatly; if he drinks in but little, he fears Him but little; if he drinks it not at all, he fears Him not at all.[5]

GOOD BOOKS

To supplement our intake of Scripture we ought to read some of the good books that stimulate us to fear God more. Let me mention a few.

A. W. Tozer exemplified the fear of God as much as anyone in our century. His book *The Pursuit of God* has been a classic for years. A lesser known work, *Whatever Happened to Worship?* is also excellent for stimulating a sense of the fear of God, as is *The Knowledge of the Holy*, his book on God's attributes.

Among authors of our own day, J. I. Packer, John Piper, and R. C. Sproul have been influential in my life. Packer's *Knowing God* is considered by many to be a classic. In my opinion that same status is deserved by Piper's *Desiring God* and Sproul's *The Holiness of God*.

A book that influenced the direction of my Christian life at a critical time years ago is Arthur W. Pink's *The Sovereignty of God*, written in 1930. It's probably the strongest assertion in print today of God's absolute sovereignty. You may have difficulty with some of Pink's positions, but if you prayerfully read it and carefully consider what he says, you'll grow in fearing God. It's the only book, other than Charnock's *The Existence and Attributes of God*, that has forced me to my knees before God while reading it. Another of Pink's books that would be helpful is a small volume, *The Attributes of God*.

Of course there is Charnock's book. Because of its sheer size I recommend it more as a reference source than a book to read. My personal copy is actually in two volumes, together totaling eleven hundred pages. The chapter on "The Holiness of God," from which I quoted in chapter 5, is one hundred pages alone. It certainly belongs in the library of anyone who wants to make an in-depth study of God's attributes.

I've stated that the gospel must have a prominent place in our biblical concept of the fear of God. What book on this subject would I recommend? If I were marooned on the proverbial desolate island with only one book besides the Bible, I'd choose *The Apostles' Doctrine of the Atonement* by George Smeaton, a nineteenth-century Scottish theologian. The book is exegetical (meaning interpretive) rather than popular in nature, but it is not difficult reading. I found it to be not only the most helpful treatment of the gospel I have read, but also the most inspiring. Reading it one day on an airplane flight, I got so excited about the gospel I was almost ready to stand up in the aisle and start preaching.

All these books are good because they grow out of Scripture and lead us back to Scripture. They certainly should not take the place of God's Word, but serve only as a means to enhance our biblical understanding and appreciation so that we grow in fearing God.

GREAT THOUGHTS ABOUT GOD

If you want the fear of God to be a dominant aspect of your day-to-day mind-set, you must work at it. Paul said to Timothy, "Train yourself to be godly" (1 Timothy 4:7). We've already seen John Murray's assertion that the fear of God is the soul of godliness. So training ourselves to be godly means we must train ourselves to be God-fearing.

This word *train* that Paul used referred to the training regimen of athletes as they prepared to participate in the games of that day. In that context the word carried connotations of commitment, focus, practice, and perseverance. All these characteristics are essential to developing a God-fearing view of life. You won't grow in the fear of God unless you work at it.

Along with prayer and Scripture intake, there's an additional discipline necessary to growing in the fear of God: the habit of thinking great thoughts about Him. It isn't enough to stand in awe of God as we read about Him. The word pictures of His greatness in Isaiah 40 (or those we find elsewhere) should become a part of our daily thinking.

God provides illustrations in everyday life to direct our thoughts in this direction. I think of the common ant, which ordinarily is at best a nuisance to us. When Russian scientists and engineers designed their lunar exploratory machine, they used articulated legs (legs with movable joints) instead of wheels to traverse the moon's uneven terrain. What they had done unwittingly was mimic to a large degree the legs of a simple ant.

Here again we see the technological ingenuity in the mind of God from all eternity, and from which He designed even the body of a common insect. All the most sophisticated scientific discoveries and inventions proliferating in our day are simply human beings thinking God's thoughts after Him. So instead of worshiping at the altar of science as our society does, we should turn our minds to God and see Him as the Master Scientist who first programmed all these things into His universe.

Develop the habit also of thinking great thoughts about God's providence. Become mentally aware of His unseen hand orchestrating all the events and circumstances around you. I mentioned my "chance" reading of a newspaper article about a navy scholarship that literally changed my life. That was only the beginning. Several years later God orchestrated a "chance" encounter with another naval officer who would introduce me to the Navigators. In fact it took two such "chance" meetings with him to get me to my first Navigator Bible study. Years later an off-hand remark from a friend—"Jerry, you ought to try your hand at writing"—prompted me to get started on my first book. Were it not for that remark, which he doesn't remember making, you wouldn't be reading this book today.

My life is filled with such examples of God's unseen hand working out His plan for my life. I'm sure yours is, also. Use these events as the mental fuel for thinking great thoughts about God.

Of course His unseen hand does not always work out events the way we would like. I think of a day a few months ago when my flight sat on the runway for seven hours waiting for a fog to lift. We finally took off at the exact time I should have been arriving at my destination. As a result I missed the opening meeting of a retreat where I was to speak.

Disappointments like these happen every day, not to mention those that are much worse. What do we do in such situations? We could stew and fret, as I confess I have done at times. Or we can bow in awe before God, whose infinite wisdom and sovereign power somehow, in ways we don't understand, cause all these events to work together for His glory and our good. This, too, is included in learning to meditate on God's providence.

Great thoughts about God will lead naturally to realistic thoughts about ourselves. We begin to realize how little we know, how uncertain and unpredictable life is, and consequently how little we're actually in control of anything. We begin to see that we're physically and spiritually frail and vulnerable, and that every second of our lives is lived at the good pleasure of God. As John Calvin wrote, "Man is never sufficiently touched and affected by the awareness of his lowly state until he has compared himself with God's majesty."[6]

Such an awareness of ourselves is spiritually healthy. Few things block our growth of fearing God as do feelings of self-righteousness and self-sufficiency. When we're pleased with our goodness and confident of our abilities, we tend not to stand in awe of God. But when we're shorn of our self-righteousness and stripped of sinful self-sufficiency, we're in position to fear Him.

Then not only do we fear God, but we bring Him pleasure: "His pleasure is not in the strength of the horse, nor his delight in the legs of a man; the LORD delights in those who fear him, who put their hope in his unfailing love" (Psalm 147:10–11). The strength of the horse and the legs of a man are pictures of the natural or human means we tend to rely on—they perhaps refer to military strength in both cavalry and infantry. But God does not take pleasure in those objects of our trust. Rather He delights in us when we fear Him and hope in His love and faithfulness. He wants us to stand in awe of Him and therefore to trust Him. We can do this only as we learn to think great thoughts about God. And when we do, we'll enjoy fearing Him.

Before leaving this chapter, let's quickly review the suggestions I've made for growing in the fear of God. I've mentioned prayer, then exposure of our minds to the Word of God through hearing it taught and reading and studying it ourselves. I recommended some good books that direct our thoughts toward God, then encouraged you to develop the habit of thinking great thoughts about God.

How will you apply these suggestions? Perhaps you're already well underway in all of them, or possibly there's an area or two where you can improve. If so, start now to develop a plan of action. A valuable asset at a time such as this is a friend with whom you can be a mutual stimulus:

> Two are better than one,
>> because they have a good return for their work:
> If one falls down,
>> his friend can help him up.
> But pity the man who falls
>> and has no one to help him up! (Ecclesiastes 4:9–10)

We all need someone to encourage us and keep us going, and it should be a mutual relationship. By ourselves most of us will fail to progress, but with another's help we'll have a good return for our work.

Notes

1. The context of Jeremiah 32:38–41 may cause some readers to think these promises are restricted to the restoration of the exiled Jews back to the land of Israel. However, the writer of Hebrews applies similar promises from Jeremiah 31:31–34 to the new covenant time in which we live. Additionally the phrase "everlasting covenant" in Jeremiah 32:40 looks beyond the return of the exiles to God's eternal relationship with us.

2. John Bunyan, "A Treatise on the Fear of God," *The Works of John Bunyan,* vol. 1 (1875, reprint, Grand Rapids: Baker, 1977), 460. I have taken the liberty of modernizing Bunyan's writing for today's reader.

3. Bunyan, "Fear of God," 461.

4. Norval Geldenhuys, *The Gospel of Luke, The New International Commentary on the New Testament* (Grand Rapids: Eerdmans, 1977), 306–7.

5. Bunyan, "Fear of God," 460.

6. John Calvin, *Institutes of the Christian Religion,* Book One, *The Knowledge of God the Creator,* ed. John T. McNeill, trans. Ford Lewis Battles, 2 vols. (Philadelphia: Westminster, 1960), 1:39.

9

HE IS LORD

All of Life Under All His Authority

WE LIVE IN A DAY of bumper-sticker slogans. Some are amusing and elicit a chuckle from us; others are repugnant and disgusting. Some are downright dangerous, such as "Question Authority." Of course all of us have trouble with authority at times. But now questioning and even resisting it seems to have been raised to a national virtue. It is spreading like a virus throughout our society.

The fact is, however, God has built authority into the entire fabric of our moral universe. Society, even on a purely human plane, could not function without it. The opposite is anarchy: a state of lawlessness or disorder due to lack of authority.

Beginning with this chapter we're going to consider fundamental characteristics of a person who fears God. By _fundamental_ I mean essential foundation stones upon which a God-fearing life is built—if we give attention to them, we'll make progress in fearing God. _Foremost among these fundamental traits is the commitment to live all of life under God's authority._

God established His authority over mankind with Adam in the Garden of Eden: "And the LORD God commanded the man, 'You are free to eat from any tree in the garden; but you must not eat from the tree of the knowledge of good and evil, for when you eat of it you will surely die'" (Genesis 2:16–17). The effect of this single prohibition was to confront Adam head-on with God's absolute authority and thus to face him with the demand for clear-cut obedience. Of course, Adam and Eve did not obey, and authority has been a problem for us ever since, both in resisting it and abusing it. As people who want to fear God we must therefore learn what it means both to submit to authority and to exercise it properly in all our various relationships to authority structures.

It should go without saying that those who fear God submit to His authority gladly and willingly. We see God insisting on His authority (in its most basic meaning of "the right to command") from Genesis to Revelation. The Ten Commandments (Exodus 20:1–17) are an expression of God's authority. Moses speaks of God's "commands, decrees and laws," which the Israelites were to obey (Deuteronomy 6:1). The psalmist said, "You have laid down precepts that are *to be fully obeyed*" (Psalm 119:4). God's people are clearly reminded of this in Jeremiah 7:22–23—"For when I brought your forefathers out of Egypt and spoke to them . . . I gave them this command: *Obey me*, and I will be your God and you will be my people. Walk in all the ways I command you, that it may go well with you." Jesus said, "If you love me, you will *obey* what I command" (John 14:15; see also verses 21, 23). All these references assume divine authority to issue commands and to call everyone to account for obedience to them at the final judgment (Revelation 20:12).

Clearly the issue of God's authority over His creatures is one of the most basic principles of Scripture. It underlies everything else. We know that the Bible, overall, is the revelation of God's plan of redemption of sinners through Jesus Christ. But that plan of redemption is basically the re-establishment of His authority over rebellious human beings whom He calls out of darkness into the kingdom of His Son (Acts 26:18, Colossians 1:13). The whole purpose of Jesus' death was to "redeem us from all wickedness [that is, from rebellion against His authority], and to purify for himself a people that are his very own, eager to do what is good [to live under his authority]" (Titus 2:14).

THE AUTHORITY OF CHRIST

Bringing people everywhere under the authority of Jesus Christ is the essence of His Great Commission to the church. Jesus said, "All authority in heaven and on earth has been given to me. Therefore go and make disciples of all nations" (Matthew 28:18–19). I first learned this passage from the King James Version, which reads "all power" instead of "all authority." Since *power* connotes ability, I originally understood Jesus' statement to be what I called the "enabling clause"—that He was saying, "Since I have all power, you will be successful in carrying out My commission."

Authority, however, speaks primarily of the right to command, although it carries with it the idea of corresponding power to enforce that command. *To make disciples, then, is to bring people under the sway of Christ's authority.* It is to teach them to obey everything He has commanded us.

Baptist commentator John Broadus wrote this about Jesus' words:

> To disciple a person to Christ is to bring him into the relation of pupil
> to teacher, "taking his yoke" of *authoritative* instruction, accepting
> what he says as true because he says it, and submitting to his
> requirements as right because he makes them. . . . We see then that
> Christ's intimated *authority* is not only the basis of our duty to disciple
> others, but the basis of all true discipleship.[1] (emphasis added)

Everything Jesus teaches us to do is of course wise and good, and the more we grow in the Christian life the more we see this to be true. But we obey Him not because we judge His commands to be wise and good, but because He is God and has a perfect right to be believed and obeyed. We do not, to use a popular expression, "make Christ Lord of our lives."

He *is* Lord. Our duty is to acknowledge His Lordship and submit to His authority.

THE AUTHORITY OF SCRIPTURE

To live under Christ's authority necessarily means to live under the authority of His Word. I read a sermon in which the speaker said we're to live in obedience to Jesus Christ, not to Scripture. This, however, is drawing a false and unwarranted distinction between Christ and His Word.

How can I obey anyone in authority over me if I do not have that person's instructions or commands? In the matter of authority we cannot separate a person from his or her words. Christ has spoken to us through the Bible. The only way I can live in obedience to Him is to live in obedience to His Word as given to us in Scripture.

It is not "bibliolatry" to place the authority of Scripture on a par with the authority of Christ. It is true that all authority rests in the *person* of Christ, but it is equally true that He expresses His authority through His written Word. To separate the authority of Christ from the authority of His Word, as some seek to do, is a subtle ploy to undermine the authority of Scripture.

And when we speak of Jesus' words, we mean *all* Scripture, not just His spoken words recorded in the four gospels, Acts, and Revelation. "All Scripture is God-breathed" (2 Timothy 3:16a). As Peter explained it, "Men spoke from God as they were carried along by the Holy Spirit" (2 Peter 1:21). In the realm of spiritual authority, Scripture's words from Paul or James or Peter are as authoritative as those from Jesus, because it was the Spirit of Jesus who inspired those men, leading them to say exactly what He wanted.

We must do more, however, than agree that all Scripture is authoritative for our lives. To be God-fearing people, we must submit to it as our rule of faith and duty, believing what it says and doing what it commands. As

John Bunyan said, "It is not the knowledge of the will of God, but our sincere complying therewith, that proves we fear the Lord."[2]

This compliance with His will includes letting the Bible mold our opinions and values. It is common today to hear someone in a Sunday school class or Bible study discussion group saying, "I think so and so," simply giving his or her opinion on an issue. No appeal is made to Scripture. To fear God, however, we must constantly ask ourselves, "What does the Bible say on this issue?"

Some years ago when I was working in the business and financial affairs of the Navigators, my boss called me into his office to discuss a major problem. Another staff member had verbally committed the organization to accepting a piece of real estate in return for a lifetime income to the donor (a common practice among nonprofit organizations). My boss had gone to look over the property and discovered to his dismay that the property, an old estate, was in a sad state of repair and fraught with problems. He concluded it would be unwise to accept the property; yet a verbal commitment had been made.

He called me in to discuss what we should do. Since no contract had been signed, he was trying to determine if we could back out of the deal with integrity. "Can you think of any Scripture that will give us guidance?" he asked. I suggested Psalm 15, which says, "LORD, who may dwell in your sanctuary? Who may live on your holy hill? He . . . who keeps his oath even when it hurts" (verses 1,4). My boss said, "That's our answer." He concluded we must keep our verbal commitment.

That's an example of what it means to live under the Bible's authority. We could have sat for hours and discussed our opinions on what to do. Most likely we would have been seeking justification for backing out of the deal. And we probably would have found one if we had avoided the Bible and sought the answer in our own opinions.

Not every decision we face has a Scripture passage speaking so directly to it as Psalm 15 spoke to our real estate deal. We might be surprised, however, to find how clearly God's Word addresses our issues if we're familiar enough with Scripture to find the appropriate passages. When no specific passage comes to mind, we should always ask, "What *principles* in the Bible give guidance in this instance?"

Paul used this method when discussing the right of Christian workers to be supported by those who benefit from their ministry:

> Who serves as a soldier at his own expense? Who plants a vineyard and does not eat of its grapes? Who tends a flock and does not drink of the milk? Do I say this merely from a human point of view? Doesn't the Law say the same thing? For it is written in the Law of Moses: "Do not muzzle an ox while it is treading out the grain." Is it about oxen that God is concerned? Surely he says this for us, doesn't he? Yes, this was written for us, because when the plowman plows and the thresher threshes, they ought to do so in the hope of sharing in the harvest.
> (1 Corinthians 9:7–10)

Paul appealed to a command in the Old Testament that had nothing to do with the subject at hand. He looked beneath the Old Testament application to a specific farming situation and found the underlying principle. He then applied the principle to a contemporary situation and found scriptural guidance. Note that he appealed to the *authority* of Scripture to establish the right of Christian workers to be supported in the ministry. Too often today we spend hours in a committee meeting discussing an issue without once asking ourselves, "What does the Bible say on this subject?"

The person who fears God realizes that life cannot be compartmentalized into spiritual and secular but must all be lived as God directs us in His Word. This person consistently and habitually reads and studies the Bible to determine what he should believe and how he should live. The God-fearing person seeks after "the knowledge of the truth that leads to godliness" (Titus 1:1). He or she wants to know the truth, not just intellectually but in a way that promotes growth in godliness.

HUMAN AUTHORITY

Living under God's authority also means we willingly live under the human authority structures He has established. Here we immediately encounter sensitive issues. It seems to be one thing to acknowledge God's authority but quite something else to submit to human authority structures, especially when we have a choice. The "Question Authority" bumper sticker may express it quite blatantly, but to some degree that attitude lurks in every one of our hearts as one expression of our fallen sinful nature.

To guide us into this discussion I want to make three general observations about human authority. First, the Bible clearly teaches that certain human authority relationships have been established by God. To resent these relationships is to resent God's authority.

Second, human authority is not a status or privilege to be exploited for personal goals, but a responsibility to be borne for the benefit of others.

Third, your place in an authority structure (whether exercising authority or submitting to it) does not determine your personal significance. This is especially true among Christians, who "are all one in Christ Jesus" (Galatians 3:28).

There has never been a time in my life when I wasn't subject to some authority, even beyond that of government. Until I was an adult, I was subject to my parents and to various teachers and coaches. As an officer in the navy I was both under authority and exercised authority. The same was true during my brief stint in secular employment. It has been true for more than forty years' service with the Navigators. During all these years, despite a few difficult experiences, I simply accepted the fact that this is the way God ordained life. I've never felt submission to authority made me less of a person.

With that introduction, let's turn to specific areas of authority.

GOVERNMENTAL AUTHORITY

The classic Scripture passage regarding governmental authority is Romans 13:1–7. Notice especially the purposes for which God established this authority.

> Everyone must submit himself to the governing authorities, for there is no authority except that which God has established. The authorities that exist have been established by God. Consequently, he who rebels against the authority is rebelling against what God has instituted, and those who do so will bring judgment on themselves. For rulers hold no terror for those who do right, but for those who do wrong. Do you want to be free from fear of the one in authority? Then do what is right and he will commend you. For he is God's servant to do you good. But if you do wrong, be afraid, for he does not bear the sword for nothing. He is God's servant, an agent of wrath to bring punishment on the wrongdoer. Therefore, it is necessary to submit to the authorities, not only because of possible punishment but also because of conscience.
>
> This is also why you pay taxes, for the authorities are God's servants, who give their full time to governing. Give everyone what you owe him: If you owe taxes, pay taxes; if revenue, then revenue; if respect, then respect; if honor, then honor.[3]

Governmental authority has been established by God for our good. This is true in the most primitive societies with their tribal chiefs as well as in the complex cultures of large nations. Moreover, God in His providence has established the *particular* governmental authority under which we live. Paul no doubt had in mind both the general concept and the specific application of the Roman government. Paul was never theoretical; he was always thinking of concrete situations. So he was telling Roman believers to submit to the Roman authorities under which they lived.

Note also that governmental authority is part of God's plan for society. Paul even refers to those in authority as "God's servants." They are His agents to execute punishment on those who do wrong. This speaks to the most elemental function of government—the preservation of law and order for the public good.

In our time government has become more complex. We have speed limits, zoning regulations, food and drug laws, environmental laws, and on and on. We often consider them excessive or unfair. I spent twenty-five years overseeing the Navigators' compliance with all those laws, regulations, and ordinances, so I understand why we bristle at them. Remember, however, that though Roman law was not as extensive as ours, it was also excessive and unfair at times. Nevertheless, Paul said we must submit, because government has been instituted by God.

This word *submit* goes deeper in its meaning than simple adherence to specific laws or ordinances. It indicates recognition of our subordinate state in the whole realm of governmental authority and consequently our willing subservience to that authority. If we rebel against it we are rebelling against what God has instituted.

Of course our situation is noticeably different from Paul's day. Under our representative form of government it's at least theoretically possible for us to address issues through the legislative or judicial processes. Apart from such lawful means of change, however, our responsibility is to submit to the authority of government.

There are two ways we can rebel: in our actions and in our attitudes. The word *submit* speaks to both. You and I don't usually rebel in our actions because of possible consequences. What we have to watch more often is a rebellious attitude.

The one exception to our submission is when authorities clearly seek to stop our obedience to God. At that point our response should be, to use Peter's words, "We must obey God rather than men!" (Acts 5:29; see also 4:19–20).

We must be careful, however, in applying that scriptural principle. In our city a church of about a hundred people was meeting in a private home, creating parking problems in the neighborhood. The pastor bitterly resisted the city's efforts to enforce its zoning laws, claiming abridgment of the church's religious freedom. In my opinion this was not the case. God in His Word had not told the church to meet at that house. Instead it seems the church was disobeying God by resisting the city's legitimate authority to establish zoning regulations. We can easily become confused in applying the principle of obeying God rather than man.

If the government forbids believers to meet together at all, that's a different issue. This of course is happening in many countries today, and we support believers' efforts there to obey God rather than human authority.

AUTHORITY IN THE CHURCH

I was shocked the first time I heard a message from Hebrews 13:17— "Obey your leaders and submit to their authority. They keep watch over you as men who must give an account. Obey them so that their work will be a joy, not a burden, for that would be of no advantage to you." It had never occurred to me that I should submit to those in leadership in our church. I had to do a lot of hard thinking on that message before I came to the conclusion I had the wrong attitude toward spiritual authority.

Leadership in the church is serious business. God holds church leaders accountable for the spiritual welfare of their people. They are to watch over us "as men who must give an account."

Paul said to the Ephesian elders, "Keep watch over yourselves and all the flock of which the Holy Spirit has made you overseers. Be shepherds of the church of God, which he bought with his own blood" (Acts 20:28). Paul pointed out that it was the Holy Spirit who made these men elders. We may vote on our elders and deacons or the calling of a pastor, but we should do so in utter submission of our minds and hearts to the Holy Spirit's guidance. He is the One to appoint overseers, and He is the One to whom they're accountable. Our responsibility is to submit to their leadership. We're also commanded to "respect" them and to "hold them in the highest regard in love because of their work" (1 Thessalonians 5:12–13).

Balancing our responsibility to submit to church leaders is their responsibility to govern in a biblical manner. They must first remember they're responsible to God and will one day have to give an account to Him for their leadership. Then they're to serve as examples to those entrusted to their care, exercising their authority without being authoritarian (1 Peter 5:3).

I appeal to you to honestly assess your attitude toward those in leadership over you in the church. Is it one of submission or independence?

AUTHORITY IN THE FAMILY

A third authority structure God established is the family. Paul deals with three family relationships—husband and wife, parents and children, and masters and slaves. (Since the master-slave relationship no longer exists in those terms, I'll treat that one later as an employer-employee relationship.)

Ephesians 5:22–6:4 is the classic passage for authority relationships in the family. Here we're confronted with one of the most sensitive and controversial issues among Christians today: What does Paul teach about submission of wives to husbands? Consider the relevant verses carefully:

> Wives, submit to your husbands as to the Lord. For the husband is the head of the wife as Christ is the head of the church, his body, of which he is the Savior. Now as the church submits to Christ, so also wives should submit to their husbands in everything.
>
> Husbands, love your wives, just as Christ loved the church and gave himself up for her to make her holy, cleansing her by the washing with water through the word, and to present her to himself as a radiant church, without stain or wrinkle or any other blemish, but holy and blameless. In this same way, husbands ought to love their wives as their own bodies. He who loves his wife loves himself. (5:22–28)

The basic issue boils down to this: Does a believing wife have an obligation before God to submit to the headship authority of her husband, or does Paul teach a mutual submission of husband and wife to each other? The advocates of the latter view cite Ephesians 5:21, "Submit to one another out of reverence for Christ," in support of their position.

Much has been written on this subject from both points of view, and I don't expect here to say anything new. Let me mention also that this is a subject on which godly, sincere Christians disagree. Whichever side we take, we need to be gracious and loving toward those with whom we disagree. And if you disagree with my position, please don't put the book down at this point.

This book is on the fear of God (not on the husband-and-wife relationship), and this chapter is on living under God's authority (and the authority structures He's established) *as an expression of our fear of Him.* A principle taught by Paul in another relationship—"Slaves, in all things obey those who are your masters . . . with sincerity of heart, *fearing the Lord* (Colossians 3:22, NASB)—should be our governing principle here as well. We need to approach this difficult subject with the desire to fear God in our conclusions and applying those conclusions to everyday life.

Let's look first at the passage exhorting us to mutual submission (Ephesians 5:21). On this I've found the words of New Testament scholar F. F. Bruce to be helpful. He points out this verse's place in introducing a "household code" that represents "a special application of the Christian grace of submission." Bruce writes,

> Christians should not be self-assertive, each insisting on getting his or her own way. As the Philippian believers are told, they should be humble enough to count others better than themselves and put the interests of others before their own, following the example of Christ, who "emptied himself," "humbled himself," and "became obedient," even when the path of obedience led to death on the cross. . . . Even those who fill positions of responsibility and honor in the Christian

community, to whom their fellow-believers are urged to render submission and loving respect, earn such recognition by being servants, not lords. . . .

Bruce then examines the verses that follow the mutual submission command:

While the household code is introduced by a plea for mutual submissiveness, the submissiveness enjoined in the code itself is not mutual. As in the parallel code in Colossians 3:18–4:1, wives are directed to be subject to their husbands, children to be obedient to their parents, and slaves to their masters, but the submissiveness is not reciprocated: husbands are told to love their wives, parents to bring up their children wisely, and masters to treat their slaves considerately.[4]

When we read in Ephesians 5:24 that wives should submit to their husbands *as the church submits to Christ,* it seems clear that Paul doesn't intend a mutual submission relationship between husbands and wives, since a mutual submissiveness between Christ and the church is unthinkable. Similarly, no one would interpret the mutual submission principle to mean parents and children should be mutually submissive to each other. Therefore, I conclude that Paul means for wives to submit to their husbands, just as a simple reading of the text would lead us to think he means, however unpalatable it may seem to some.

But the passage doesn't indicate an absolute surrender of the wife's will. It doesn't say she exists merely to serve her husband. Nor does it forbid her from partnering with her husband in managing the home and family. It *does* teach that she cultivate a willingness to yield to her husband's authority and to follow his leadership. Above all it means she should not try to compete with him as the head of the home.

Does this submission mean the wife is inferior to the husband, or that she's a second-class citizen in the marriage? Not at all. We've already observed that believers are all one in Christ (Galatians 3:28). The fact that I'm to submit to a person in governmental authority does not make me inferior to that individual. It's simply a recognition of his God-ordained role in an authority structure God has established. The same should be true in the home.

That this is Paul's teaching seems to be clear from his repetition of this principle in Colossians 3:18, "Wives, submit to your husbands, as is fitting in the Lord," and in Titus 2:3–5, "Older women . . . can train the younger women . . . to be subject to their husbands." The same principle is taught in 1 Peter 3:1–7, applying even to wives with unbelieving husbands.

As for the husband, he is not to exercise his leadership in an authoritarian or self-serving manner, requiring blind and absolute submission to his will or insisting that he always be served. Rather he's to love his wife as Christ loved the church and gave Himself up for her (Ephesians 5:25). This obviously denotes a sacrificial, self-giving love that seeks to promote the spiritual, emotional, and physical well-being of his wife. It means the husband should be considerate and thoughtful about the needs of his wife and any impositions he might make upon her.

Perhaps the best insight on the attitude a husband should have toward his authority role comes from words Jesus spoke to His disciples: "You know that the rulers of the Gentiles lord it over them, and their high officials exercise authority over them. Not so with you. Instead, whoever wants to become great among you must be your servant, and whoever wants to be first must be your slave—just as the Son of Man did not come to be served, but to serve, and to give his life as a ransom for many" (Matthew 20:25–28). This is how the mutual submission principle (Ephesians 5:21) is worked out in daily life.

PARENTAL AUTHORITY

Paul's teaching that children should obey their parents (Ephesians 6:1–3) is straightforward enough. I want to point out, however, that we parents have a duty to train our children to obey. Our responsibility in our God-given role as parents is to see that our children submit to our authority. It's especially important that a father teach his children to submit to their mother's authority as much as to his. Teaching our children to respect and obey those in authority over them—beginning with Mom and Dad—is one of the ways we help them learn to fear the Lord (Deuteronomy 6:1–2). The lack of this teaching is one of the most serious problems in Christian families today.

As is his custom, Paul here again turns from addressing those under authority to those exercising it—in this case, from children to fathers. His instruction is, "Do not exasperate your children" (Ephesians 6:4; see also Colossians 3:21). This is another warning against authoritarianism. The father's authority should be exercised for the spiritual and moral benefit of all the children. That's essentially the meaning of Paul's next words: "Instead, bring them up in the training and instruction of the Lord."

Paul is always even-handed in his treatment of authority structures within the family, always balancing both sides of the equation. The wife's duty to submit to her husband is balanced by the husband's duty to love his wife. The children's duty to obey their parents is balanced by the father's duty not to be overly demanding and authoritarian. The slave's duty to serve his master wholeheartedly is balanced by the master's duty to treat his slaves kindly and fairly.

We see this same balance in what Scripture says about authority in the church. The believers' duty to obey those in authority in the church is balanced by Peter's warning to elders not to lord it over God's people. The only place where we don't find this balancing principle is in the realm of governmental authority. Obviously Paul or Peter could not exhort unbelieving Roman officials to govern in a Christian manner. The principle of exercising authority for the benefit of others should, however, be a guiding rule for Christians in positions of governmental authority today.

AUTHORITY IN THE WORKPLACE

The principles underlying the master-slave relationship apply in today's employer-employee situations. The classic passage addressing this is Colossians 3:22–25. Notice once again how submission to an authority structure God has ordained is a concrete expression of our fear of the Lord.

> Slaves, obey your earthly masters in everything; and do it, not only when their eye is on you and to win their favor, but with sincerity of heart and reverence for the Lord. Whatever you do, work at it with all your heart, as working for the Lord, not for men, since you know that you will receive an inheritance from the Lord as a reward. It is the Lord Christ you are serving. Anyone who does wrong will be repaid for his wrong, and there is no favoritism.

If we substitute employees for slaves and employers (owners, managers, supervisors) for masters, the passage is straightforward enough. We're to work at our jobs or professions as working for the Lord. God is our ultimate employer, and we're to serve Him with reverence ("fearing the Lord," NASB).

Paul's instruction to masters (and to whoever has authority in the workplace) is to provide those under their authority "with what is right and fair, because you know that you also have a Master in heaven" (Colossians 4:1). The employer's authority is not absolute. He also is under the authority of God Himself, and God will hold him accountable for how he treats his employees. In the Old Testament, God's people were warned not to treat hired workers ruthlessly, but instead to "fear your God" (Leviticus 25:43). This should be the attitude of Christian employers today—treating employees fairly out of the fear of the Lord.

Our problem is not in understanding these principles but in applying them. When I was a young officer in the navy, I served on a small ship under a commanding officer who was very difficult to work with. The man had almost no people skills, and none of the officers (including me) respected him. Then one day in the course of Bible study I encountered 1 Timothy 6:1—"All who are under the yoke of slavery should consider their masters worthy of full respect, so that God's name and our teaching may not be slandered."

I wasn't exactly under a yoke of slavery, though sometimes I felt I was. In any event the principle of respecting one in authority over me was impressed upon me by the Holy Spirit applying His Word to my heart. I was convicted of my sinful attitude and immediately began taking steps to correct it. I said nothing to our captain or to the other officers, none of whom were Christians. Yet somehow the captain sensed something had changed in our relationship. Months later I was transferred from that ship. As I was about to leave, the captain called me into his stateroom and said, "Bridges, I really hate to see you go."

It isn't easy to submit to the authority of those who do not exercise it in a sensitive manner. But our submission should not hinge on their manner, as slaves are told in 1 Peter 2:18–19—"Submit yourselves to your masters with all respect, not only to those who are good and considerate, but also to those who are harsh. For it is commendable if a man bears up under the pain of unjust suffering because he is conscious of God." Note that last phrase. "Because he is conscious of God" probably means "because he is aware of God's all-seeing eye and desires to please Him." This is consistent with Paul's instructions for slaves to obey "in the fear of the Lord."

ALL OF MY LIFE

This brings us back to our major theme in this chapter: A fundamental trait of a God-fearing person is to live all of life under God's authority. We're to live under the authority of His Word and under the authority of those God has placed over us in government, in the church, in the family, and in the workplace.

Before leaving this chapter, take time to pray over each of these authority relationships. Is any one of them troublesome to you? Ask yourself these questions:

- Do I wholeheartedly acknowledge God's authority, both in His precepts and His providences, in my life? Do I resent or question any of His providential circumstances in my life?
- Do I seek to live all of life under the authority of God's Word, believing what it says and seeking to apply its teachings to *every* area of my life?
- Am I chafing—either openly or secretly in my heart—under any God-ordained human authorities? Are there any relationships here in which I need to change my attitude or actions?

Don't answer with a simple yes or no. Be specific about situations that may be troublesome to you, either as one under authority, or as the one exercising authority. What steps do you need to take to establish God-fearing, biblical relationships in those situations? Don't just say, "I need to be more submissive to my husband," or "I need to be more loving to my wife." Where exactly do you need to be more submissive or more loving? Only by dealing with particulars will we make progress toward living in the fear of God.

As you consider God's authority and the authority structures He has established, keep in mind that He exercises His authority in love. As I was concluding the writing of this chapter, my mind was drawn to Galatians 2:20 where Paul writes of "the Son of God, who loved me and gave himself for me." It is the Son of God who loves *me* and gave Himself for *me* who now claims all authority over me. How can I resist the authority that springs from such a heart of love?

Notes

1. John A. Broadus, *Commentary on Matthew* (1886, reprint, Grand Rapids: Kregel, 1990), 593.

2. John Bunyan, "A Treatise on the Fear of God," *The Works of John Bunyan,* Volume 1 (1875, reprint, Grand Rapids: Baker, 1977), 458.

3. Other Scriptures addressing the issue of our relationships to those in authority are 1 Timothy 2:1–2, Titus 3:1–2, and 1 Peter 2:13–17.

4. F. F. Bruce, *The Epistle to the Colossians, to Philemon, and to the Ephesians,* The New International Commentary on the New Testament series (Grand Rapids: Eerdmans, 1984), 382–3.

10

THE FRUIT OF THE TREE

The Delight of Right Obedience

A RECENT ISSUE of a national news magazine featured a cover story titled, "The Trouble with Premarital Sex."[1] Amidst all the discussion of pros and cons, I looked in vain for any reference to what the Bible and God might have to say on the subject. A high church official and the executive director of the Christian Coalition were quoted as stating that premarital sex is morally wrong, but at least according to the article, their assertions included no backing from the Bible.

The truth is, neither the Bible nor God are considered in most moral issue discussions anymore. A large denomination recently made a major moral decision based on "the historical tradition of our church." No mention was made of God's will or the Bible's teaching on the issue.

In contrast to the direction of our society, *a major characteristic of one who fears God is obedience to Him.* When I began studying the fear of God several years ago, the first thing I did was use my computer Bible program to print out all the Scripture texts on the subject. Scanning over those several pages of verses I was struck by the frequency with which the fear of God is linked to obeying Him. More than one-fourth of all the verses on my printout made such a connection.

For example, when the Israelites were about to enter the Promised Land, Moses said to them,

These are the commands, decrees and laws the LORD your God directed me to teach you to observe in the land that you are crossing the Jordan to possess, so that you, your children and their children after them may fear the LORD your God as long as you live by keeping all his decrees and commands that I give you, and so that you may enjoy long life. (Deuteronomy 6:1–2)

Note the words, "so that you . . . may fear the LORD your God . . . by keeping all his decrees and commands." We fear the Lord by obeying Him. And it is a conscious obedience to *God's commands* as given in His Word that constitutes this godly fear.

The linkage of obedience to godly fear is continued throughout the Old Testament. Two sample passages will serve to show both sides of this obedience. Proverbs 8:13 says, "To fear the LORD is to hate evil," while Psalm 112:1 says, "Blessed is the man who fears the LORD, who finds great delight in his commands." Hating evil on one hand and delighting in God's commands on the other are both concrete expressions of the fear of God.

Scripture also draws a frequent connection between wickedness and the absence of fearing God. The first time the expression *fear of God* is used in the Bible, it's in this negative sense, when Abraham said, "There is surely no fear of God in this place" (Genesis 20:11). Later we read of the Amalekites who "had no fear of God" and therefore attacked the Israelites when they were weary and worn out (Deuteronomy 25:17–18). Quite obviously the same statements could be made about our society today. All the moral decadence we see is because people have no fear of God. God is seldom in their thoughts.

Perhaps the best-known Scripture linking the fear of God with obedience is Ecclesiastes 12:13 —"Now all has been heard; here is the conclusion of the matter: Fear God and keep his commandments, for this is the whole duty of man."

The book of Ecclesiastes essentially teaches us how to live amid life's tensions, frustrations, and disappointments. Having covered a vast range of instructions, the "Teacher" (1:1, 12:9), sums up his findings: "Fear God and keep his commandments." Charles Bridges, a nineteenth-century Church of England minister, pointed out a contrast here between a "legal principle" —the fear of the consequences of disobeying God—and a spirit of "filial love" springing from an assured forgiveness of our sins through Christ:

> Two short sentences sum up the whole— *Fear God, and keep his commandments.* The sentences are in their right order. *The fear of God* is the hidden principle of obedience. . . . It is the work of the Spirit in the heart of the regenerate. . . . It is not a legal principle of terror or bondage, but the genuine spirit of confidence—the delicate expression of filial love in the heart of the child of God—the holy fruit of forgiveness. Here we walk with our Father, humbly, acceptably, securely—looking not at an offended God with terror—but at a reconciled God with reverential love. All the gracious influences on the soul—cherished under the power of the Spirit—all flow out in godly *fear* towards him.[2]

Though the fear of God does include a certain fear of incurring God's displeasure, the dominant element should be the filial love about which Charles Bridges speaks.

Yet we must not lose sight of the connection the Teacher draws between fearing God and keeping His commandments. Obedience is the fruit of the tree of which the fear of God is the root. We cannot rightly obey God if we do not fear Him—if we do not honor, reverence, and love Him.

OBEDIENCE OR MORALITY?

At this point we need to distinguish between obedience springing from the fear of God and mere human morality. There are many morally upright, decent people in our society who do not fear God. Their morality grows out of such things as family upbringing and perhaps church attendance where they hear sermons urging them to be good and do their duty. Let me give you an example of this kind of morality. Here are three verses from an unknown author's poem that I clipped from a local business newspaper a few weeks ago.

> When you get what you want in your struggle for self
>   And the world makes you a king for a day,
> Just go to the mirror and look at yourself,
>   And see what THAT man has to say.
>
> For it isn't your father or mother or wife
>   Whose judgment upon you must pass;
> The fellow whose verdict counts most in your life
>   Is the one staring back from the glass. . . .
>
> He's the fellow to please, never mind all the rest,
>   For he's with you clear up to the end,
> And you've passed your most dangerous, difficult test
>   If the man in the glass is your friend.

The overall sentiment of the poem—the importance of personal integrity—is commendable. But it isn't an integrity that springs from the fear of God. In fact it's the "man in the glass"—not God—whom the author tells us we must satisfy. There's nothing about our obligation to God. It is mere human morality.

Sad to say, we Christians can lapse into this kind of morality: an obedience to a certain moral lifestyle that has little to do with the fear of God. But morality does not qualify as biblical obedience unless it springs from the fear of God—from a reverential awe of who He is and what He has done for us.

EXPRESSING OUR LOVE FOR GOD

The Bible also draws a close connection between love to God and obedience. For example, 1 John 5:3 reads, "This is love for God: to obey his commands." And Jesus said, "Whoever has my commands and obeys them, he is the one who loves me" (John 14:21). This connection is also brought out frequently in the Old Testament. One of many instances is Deuteronomy 6:5—"Love the LORD your God with all your heart and with all your soul and with all your strength." This verse occurs in the middle of a longer section having to do with obedience to God. Words such as *commands, decrees,* and *laws* fill the passage (verses 1–9). Israel is to "be careful to obey" (verse 3). The commands were to be constantly on the hearts and minds of the people (verses 6–9). It's in this context of obedience that God's people are instructed to love Him with all their hearts. To love God, then, is to obey Him.

The nation of Israel related to God on the basis of His covenant with them. In ancient Middle Eastern cultures the word *love* is used in treaties, or covenants, to denote the faithful adherence to the directives of the overlord. Meredith Kline, who has studied extensively the ancient Near East covenants, writes, "When swearing allegiance to the suzerain [a superior feudal lord or overlord] the vassals at times declared: 'Our lord we will love.' And a vassal wishing to clear himself of suspicion of infidelity protests that he is the king's great servant and 'friend' (literally, one who loves the suzerain)." Then Kline points out that "to love the suzerain meant precisely to serve him by obeying the particular demands stipulated in his treaty."[3] Israel was to love God, then, by obeying the commands and decrees of His covenantal law given to them at Mount Sinai.

Since we find a direct connection between fearing God and obedience to Him, plus a direct connection between loving God and obedience to Him, we can conclude that fearing God and loving God are also closely connected. Deuteronomy 10:12–13 draws all these attitudes and actions together in a single sentence:

> And now, O Israel, what does the LORD your God ask of you but to *fear* the LORD your God, to *walk* in all his ways, to *love* him, to *serve* the LORD your God with all your heart and with all your soul, and to *observe* the LORD's commands and decrees that I am giving you today for your own good?

The words *walk, serve,* and *observe* are three different ways of expressing the same thought: Obey God. Israel was to fear God, love God, and obey Him. The commandments, then, provided a framework within which the Israelites could express both their reverence for God and their love of Him. The same is true for us today. Our obedience to God's moral will found throughout Scripture is an expression of *our* love for God and our reverence of Him.

In the previous chapter we saw that the fear of God expresses itself fundamentally in submission to the authority of God and His Word. Without meaning to detract from that concept, we can also acknowledge that submission to authority, even in its most positive sense, may often be cold and impersonal. We can submit to someone in authority over us without either liking or loving the person, or even getting to know the person. We submit because it's the appropriate thing to do. We must go further than that with God, however.

Yes, we must acknowledge His authority in its most basic sense—His right to command. God's instructions in Scripture are not merely guidelines or advice for better living. They are *commands,* and they're to be *fully* obeyed (Psalm 119:4). Furthermore, apart from faith in Christ and His atoning work, all who fail to obey the entire law are under a curse (Galatians 3:10). So we must not in any way temper or water down submission to God's authority as an expression of our fear of Him. But we should submit out of love to Him and reverence for Him. That is, we should obey Him with our whole heart.

And our submission should not be with a slavish fear, but with a fear of reverential awe. Keep in mind the tension between the way we should view God in His transcendent majesty and the way we behold Him as our Father. Both sides of this tension work together to produce the right motive and the effective motivation to obey God.

OBEDIENCE IN RELATIONSHIPS

To fear God by obeying Him means that we seek to follow all of His commands for us. We must not pick and choose or seek to reinterpret some of the them. We may willingly obey such commandments as "You shall not murder," "You shall not commit adultery," "You shall not steal." But are we as quick to obey "You shall not covet . . . anything that belongs to your neighbor" (Exodus 20:13–17)? Similarly, do we truly believe Jesus' words that anger fits under the prohibition against murder, and lust in the category of adultery (Matthew 5:21–22, 27–28)?

Too often we define sin in terms of those actions that may be least troublesome to us: drunkenness, dishonesty, sexual immorality, abortion, homosexuality. We see the sinfulness of society around us but not the sin in our own hearts: critical and judgmental attitudes (which are actually evidences of pride), selfishness, gossip, back-biting, insisting on our own way, and seeking to manipulate or intimidate others.

The one place where Paul warns us not to grieve the Holy Spirit is not in Scriptures dealing with dishonesty or immorality, but in a section dealing with our speech and other interpersonal relationships (Ephesians 4:29–32). He says, for example, "Do not let any unwholesome talk come out of your mouths, but only what is helpful for building others up according to their needs, that it may benefit those who listen" (4:29).

Unwholesome speech includes not only vulgar language (which Paul addresses in Ephesians 5:4), but any kind of speech that tends to tear down the persons addressed or those spoken about: complaining, gossip, slander, critical words, harsh and impatient words. This prohibition is absolute: "Do not let *any* unwholesome talk come out of your mouths but *only* what is helpful for building others up." Immediately after this Paul says, "And do not grieve the Holy Spirit." We grieve the Holy Spirit not only with dishonesty or immorality, but also by our gossip, complaining, and sharp words.

If we express our fear of God by keeping *all* His decrees and commands as Moses said (Deuteronomy 6:2), then we must give attention to our interpersonal relationships. Consider, for example, the following list from Romans 12.

- Love sincerely (verse 9).
- Be devoted to one another in brotherly love (10).
- Honor others above yourself (10).
- Share with others in need (13).
- Practice hospitality (13).
- Bless those who persecute you (14).
- Rejoice with those who rejoice (15).
- Mourn with those who mourn (15).
- Live in harmony with one another (16).
- Do not be proud or conceited (16).
- Do not repay evil for evil (17).
- Seek to live at peace with everyone (18).
- Do not seek revenge (19).
- Overcome evil with good (21).

These instructions may sound like a laundry list of moralisms, something we might hear at a service club luncheon. We agree with them. We give lip service to them. But do we honestly seek to practice them?

These words are not just moralisms from the pen of the apostle Paul; they are the words of God. If we accept the authority of Scripture, then we must view every one of these relational actions as God's commands to be carried out in the fear of God. We honor one another above ourselves *in the fear of the Lord.* We practice hospitality *in the fear of the Lord.* We overcome evil with good *in the fear of the Lord.*

THE GREAT COMMANDMENT, AT GREAT COST

I don't want to appear indifferent to the more flagrant sins in society around us. They are serious, and, what is more distressing, they are creeping into our churches. But in our focus on other people's sins we tend to forget that Jesus said the first commandment is to "love the Lord your God with all your heart and with all your soul and with all your mind. . . . And the second is like it: Love your neighbor as yourself" (Matthew 22:37–39). All the Law and the Prophets hang on those two commandments (verse 40).

Notice how Paul picks up on this priority of love in two of his letters.

The commandments, "Do not commit adultery," "Do not murder," "Do not steal," "Do not covet," and whatever other commandment there may be, are summed up in this one rule: "Love your neighbor as yourself." Love does no harm to its neighbor. Therefore love is the fulfillment of the law. (Romans 13:9–10)

You, my brothers, were called to be free. But do not use your freedom to indulge the sinful nature; rather, serve one another in love. The entire law is summed up in a single command: "Love your neighbor as yourself." (Galatians 5:13–14)

In both instances Paul says that the command "Love your neighbor as yourself" sums up the law, a similar statement to that which Jesus made. Likewise James refers to the commandment "Love your neighbor as yourself" as the "royal law" (James 2:8).

I fear we do not take these words seriously enough. We don't embrace the fact that our first and highest duty in the Christian life (apart from love to God) is to love one another. We focus on "manageable sins" that we seldom commit, and neglect the greatest commandment, though God brings it before us again and again in His Word. The command to love one another appears in some form in all but four books of the New Testament. (And even in those four it is present indirectly; see Acts 4:32–35 and 20:35, 3 John 6, Jude 21–23, and Revelation 2:19).

Some fifty passages in the New Testament command us to love one another. Consider the comprehensiveness and intensity of this command as seen in these representative samples:

"And live a life of love, just as Christ loved us and gave himself up for us as a fragrant offering and sacrifice to God" (Ephesians 5:2).

"And over all these virtues put on love, which binds them all together in perfect unity" (Colossians 3:14).

"The goal of this command is love, which comes from a pure heart and a good conscience and a sincere faith" (1 Timothy 1:5).

"Keep on loving each other as brothers" (Hebrews 13:1).

"Above all, love each other deeply, because love covers over a multitude of sins" (1 Peter 4:8).

How can we miss it? How can we seem to focus on everything else but love?

I think the answer is that love is costly. To forgive in love costs us our sense of justice. To serve in love costs us time. To share in love costs us money. Every act of love costs us in some way, just as it cost God to love us. But we are to live a life of love just as Christ loved us, and gave Himself for us, at great cost to Himself.

NEVER LESS THAN THE GOLDEN RULE

How can we get a handle on such an immense subject as love? What does it mean, for example, to love your neighbor as yourself?

In that familiar verse known as the Golden Rule, Jesus says, "So in everything, do to others what you would have them do to you, for this sums up the Law and the Prophets" (Matthew 7:12). To treat others as we would like to be treated "sums up the Law and the Prophets." This is exactly what Paul said about loving your neighbor as yourself. Therefore to love your neighbor as yourself means to treat your neighbor as you would like to be treated. Love may sometimes mean more than that, but it certainly never means less.

Of course your neighbor isn't just the person next door. It is your spouse, your children, your parents, your in-laws, your roommate, co-workers, fellow church members, even other drivers on the freeway. Your neighbor is anyone you come in contact with and interact with in some way.

To treat these "neighbors" as you would like to be treated sounds simple enough, but it has wide-ranging implications. If you don't like to be gossiped about, you shouldn't gossip about others. If you like others to be patient and forbearing with you, be patient and forbearing with others. If a husband wouldn't want his wife to admire other men in a sexual way, he shouldn't look that way at other women.

Consider love's description in 1 Corinthians 13:4–5: "Love is patient, love is kind. It does not envy, it does not boast, it is not proud. It is not rude, it is not self-seeking, it is not easily angered, it keeps no record of wrongs." Doesn't every one of these expressions describe the way you want other people to treat you? Then this is the way you must treat others if you want to be obedient to God. Obedience is more than not committing adultery; it is being patient with your spouse. Obedience is more than not murdering someone; it is not being easily angered with him or keeping record of his wrongs against you.

The statement "Love your neighbor as yourself" is only the last half of a sentence in its original occurrence in Scripture. The full sentence reads, "Do not seek revenge or bear a grudge against one of your people, but love your neighbor as yourself. I am the LORD" (Leviticus 19:18). Note that it's in the context of bearing a grudge or seeking revenge that we're told to love our neighbor as ourselves. *This means love always forgives.* "Since God so loved us, we also ought to love one another" (1 John

4:11). God loved us and forgave us at great cost to Himself, the cost of His own dear Son. We in turn are to love others, even at great cost to ourselves. Sometimes the cost is tangible—for example, in damage to our reputation if we've been slandered. At other times the cost may be a willingness to not see justice done as a condition of forgiveness.

So we both fear God and love Him by obeying His law. And we obey His law by loving others, by treating them as we want to be treated. Living the Christian life is difficult but not complicated. Yes, at times we may agonize over the right course of action. But if we seriously seek to follow this royal law, "Love your neighbor as yourself," we'll usually know what to do.

But once we know what to do, we may not want to do it. The cost seems too high. We might have to humble ourselves, inconvenience ourselves, forego our sense of justice. So we may evade those issues by rationalizing.

My wife is involved in a number of activities outside the home, each of them at her own choosing. Within the last ten days almost all of them have converged on her at once, leaving little time for domestic duties. Love on my part means I should step in and help out with more of the household chores. But I'm busy too. I have a deadline for this book staring me in the face. What am I to do?

I have three choices. I can do nothing, with the rationalization that all these activities are optional for her, whereas writing this book is part of my job. Or, with the same rationalization, I can step in and help out but resent every moment of it. The third option is to come to her rescue out of love, treating her as I would like to be treated if I were in a similar tight situation, even if it costs me time when I feel I have none to spare. Only this option is acceptable to God.

FULLY RESPONSIBLE, FULLY DEPENDENT

There are other times, many in fact, when we want to obey but can't seem to do it. We identify with Paul when he said, "I have the desire to do what is good, but I cannot carry it out. For what I do is not the good I want to do; no, the evil I do not want to do—this I keep on doing" (Romans 7:18–19).

Through all these instances we learn that we're unable to live the Christian life in our own moral strength and will power. We learn the truth of Jesus' statement, "Apart from me you can do nothing" (John 15:5). But God also intends that we learn the converse truth: "I can do everything through him who gives me strength" (Philippians 4:13). God wants us to learn both the necessity and the positive results of depending upon the Holy Spirit to enable us to live the Christian life.

One of the most fundamental truths we must learn in Christian growth is that we are responsible, yet dependent. That is, we are responsible to obey God's commands. We are responsible for our sin. We cannot blame the devil or other people. We sin because we choose to sin. We do not obey because we choose not to obey. Yet at the same time we do not have the resources within ourselves to obey. We are completely dependent upon the Holy Spirit.

Notice how this principle is taught by Paul in Philippians 2:12–13.

Therefore, my dear friends, as you have always obeyed—not only in my presence, but now much more in my absence—continue to work out your salvation with fear and trembling, for it is God who works in you to will and to act according to his good purpose.

First, Paul urges them to apply themselves diligently to working out their salvation—displaying daily the evidence of their new life through obedience to God's commands. And of course what Paul wrote to the Philippian believers is applicable to us today; we, too, are responsible to work out our salvation.

This is no secondary endeavor to be attended to after we've fulfilled all our other responsibilities. Rather it should be our highest priority. As Jesus said, we're to seek *first* His kingdom and His righteousness. Our salvation is to be worked out in how we carry out our daily activities. This is no easy task to be accomplished on the back stroke. According to

New Testament commentator William Hendriksen, the meaning and tense of the verb *work out* indicate "continuous, sustained, strenuous effort."[4]

But Paul's exhortation does not suggest that we have the ability to do this by our own power. Rather the Philippians are told to work out their salvation *with fear and trembling*—"conscious of their own insignificance and weakness and sinfulness and fallibility," as New Testament Professor Jan J. Müller writes, "and full of trembling and holy fear before God whose will is to be done, and for whose honour they have to work, and to whom an account will have to be given."[5]

It is an awesome thought to realize the extent of our responsibility before God and yet to be painfully aware that we do not have within ourselves the ability to carry out the least of His commandments. That's why Paul hastens to add those encouraging words of verse 13—"for it is God who works in you to will and to act according to his good purpose."

Obedience to God is very much our responsibility—but a responsibility that must be carried out in utter dependence on the Holy Spirit. We work as He enables us to work. We cannot make one inch of progress in obeying God apart from His working in us to enable us.

To work hard, but only in dependence on the Holy Spirit, is a difficult lesson to learn. We know we must work hard, but in that very work we can easily slip into reliance on our own human will power instead of depending on the Holy Spirit to work in and through our wills. Yet this dependence on the Holy Spirit is absolutely essential to fearing God by obeying Him.

ALWAYS UNDER THE GOSPEL

We need to also keep in mind that our obedience is never the means of earning any merit or blessing from God. Though we're to make every effort to obey, our best works always fall short of that perfection which

God's law demands. We never obey God with *all* our heart and soul and mind, and we never perfectly love our neighbor as ourselves. Yet, "whoever keeps the whole law and yet stumbles at just one point is guilty of breaking all of it" (James 2:10).

This is why we must learn to live *under the gospel* every day. The gospel is not just for unbelievers; it is for believers also, because we are still sinners. Every day we need the reassurance that all our sins are forgiven (Colossians 2:13) because Christ paid for them all on the cross. Furthermore, we need to realize that only "through Jesus Christ" are even our very best deeds "acceptable to God" (1 Peter 2:5). In themselves they are never good enough to merit God's approval. As one old Puritan is reputed to have said, "Even our tears of repentance need to be washed in the blood of the Lamb."

The great theologian B. B. Warfield expressed it this way:

> We must always be accepted for Christ's sake, or we cannot ever be accepted at all. This is not true of us only "when we believe." It is just as true after we have believed. It will continue to be true as long as we live. Our need of Christ does not cease with our believing; nor does the nature of our relation to Him or to God through Him ever alter, no matter what our attainments in Christian graces or our achievements in Christian behavior may be. It is always on His "blood and righteousness" alone that we can rest. There is never anything that we are or have or do that can take His place, or that can take a place along with Him. We are always unworthy, and all that we have or do of good is always of pure grace.[6]

Note Dr. Warfield's emphasis on our continuing need to be accepted "for Christ's sake"; that it is always on "His 'blood and righteousness' alone that we can rest." The good news, however, is that we *are* accepted for Christ's sake, and our works are accepted on the same basis.

This is what Paul was saying when he wrote, "The life I live in the body, I live by faith in the Son of God, who loved me and gave himself for me" (Galatians 2:20). Paul knew his best attainments were never good enough, either to merit salvation in eternity or blessings in this life. For both he relied on Christ and Christ alone.

Paul was no sluggard. He neither preached nor practiced "easy believism," the erroneous contention that because we're saved by grace, Christian discipleship is merely optional.

Remember what Paul wrote in Philippians 3:12–14.

> Not that I have already obtained all this, or have already been made
> perfect, but I press on to take hold of that for which Christ Jesus took
> hold of me. Brothers, I do not consider myself yet to have taken hold
> of it. But one thing I do: Forgetting what is behind and straining
> toward what is ahead, I press on toward the goal to win the prize for
> which God has called me heavenward in Christ Jesus.

Paul pressed on; he strained forward. The imagery in his words is that of a runner pushing and striving with everything in him to break the tape, to cross the finish line first. Yet for all this effort, Paul lived by faith in Christ and His righteousness for acceptance by a holy God.

If you and I are to fear God by keeping His commandments, we also must learn to live by faith in Jesus Christ. Otherwise our obedience will degenerate into a works-righteousness, and our fear of God into a slavish fear. Only as we realize that we're "sons of God through faith in Christ Jesus" (Galatians 3:26), and that God the Father accepts us through Christ, can we fear God in filial fear, the loving fear of a child toward his father.

TEACHING OUR CHILDREN

Not only must we learn to fear God by keeping His commandments; we must also teach our children to do likewise. We must not only teach them to obey; *we must teach them to obey in the fear of the Lord.* Ours is the same purpose Moses set forth in Deuteronomy 6:2—"so that you, your *children* and their children after them may fear the LORD your God as long as you live by keeping all his decrees and commands that I give you, and so that you may enjoy long life."

I fear we aren't following through on the teaching pattern Moses goes on to give us in verses 6 and 7:

> These commandments that I give you today are to be upon your hearts. Impress them on your children. Talk about them when you sit at home and when you walk along the road, when you lie down and when you get up.

Consider this sobering quote from a recent edition of a Christian magazine:

> The failure to teach God's law in our churches has had devastating consequences. Not only is gross sin being flaunted in the public square but also the moral conduct of our church children has degenerated to alarming proportions. Josh McDowell has recently published the results of his study of young people who are actively involved in evangelical churches. He discovered that within the previous three months:
> - 66% had lied to their parents.
> - 36% had cheated on an exam.
> - 55% had engaged in sexual activity.
> - 20% had tried to hurt someone physically.
>
> Most of these teenagers profess to believe the gospel for salvation. Yet most are not obeying God's law. Something is gravely wrong.[7]

Though the writer ascribes this serious condition to the failure to teach God's law in our churches, it is also due to a failure to teach the fear of God in Christian homes. God holds us as parents responsible for teaching our children to obey Him. We cannot pass this off to Sunday school teachers or the Christian school. Those agencies may supplement our efforts, but the primary responsibility lies with us.

Even the instruction given in Christian homes is too often mere moralism. Parents want their children to be good, to stay out of trouble, to not get drunk or smoke pot. Little effort is made to teach them to fear God and obey Him out of reverence for Him. Because of this, many young people do not come to see themselves as sinners desperately in need of a Savior. Many of them go through the motions of "accepting Christ" without ever being convicted of their personal need of Him. I realize conviction of sin is the work of the Holy Spirit, but He does use human agencies, and His primary design is to use parents.

Everything I've written in this chapter about obedience as a mark of those who fear God should be passed on to our children. They need to be taught what it means to fear God, to love Him and obey Him. They need to be taught the primacy of loving their neighbor as themselves and how this is worked out in treating others as they want to be treated. They need to understand that obedience is possible only through the enabling power of the Holy Spirit. Above all, they need to see that their only hope of acceptance by a holy God, both in this life and eternity, is through faith in the shed blood and righteous life of our Lord Jesus Christ.

That God holds parents responsible for teaching their children is a truth that predates the Mosaic Law. Concerning Abraham, God said, "For I have chosen him, so that he will direct his children and his household after him to keep the way of the LORD by doing what is right and just, so that the LORD will bring about for Abraham what he has promised him" (Genesis 18:19).

May we who are parents accept our responsibility, as Abraham did, to teach our children to fear the Lord by obeying Him. Only then are we ourselves obeying God.

OUR RESPONSE

On a subject as broad as obedience, there are so many points of possible application that they could become overwhelming. I have identified six areas below, each framed as a personal question. I suggest you read slowly over these questions and select one you feel is most helpful to you at this time. Reread the section of this chapter dealing with that issue (section titles are given), and determine what you need to do to apply that particular teaching in your life.

1. Is my obedience little more than human morality, or is it done in the fear of God? ("Obedience or Morality?")

2. Do I obey God only out of a sense of duty, or because I love Him and fear Him? ("Expressing Our Love for God")

3. Do I define sin primarily in terms of the gross sins of society, or do I first recognize my own personal sins of pride, selfishness, judgmental attitude, gossip, discontent, and so on? ("Obedience in Relationships")

4. As I review the list of interpersonal relationship actions from Romans 12:9–21, what is my greatest need from among them at this time? ("Obedience in Relationships")

5. Is there some person in day-to-day contact with me whom I am not treating as I would like to be treated? ("The Great Commandment, at Great Cost" and "Never Less than the Golden Rule")

6. As a parent, am I seeking to teach my children what it means to obey in the fear of the Lord, or am I simply instilling human morality in them? ("Teaching Our Children")

Notes

1. David Whiteman: "The Trouble with Premarital Sex: Was It Good for Us?" *U.S. News & World Report,* May 19, 1997, 57–64.

2. Charles Bridges, *An Exposition of Ecclesiastes* (1860, reprint, Edinburgh: Banner of Truth Trust, 1960), 309.

3. Meredith G. Kline, *Kingdom Prologue* (self-published, 1993), 41.

4. William Hendriksen, *New Testament Commentary, Exposition of Philippians* (Grand Rapids: Baker, 1962), 120.

5. Jan J. Müller, *The Epistles of Paul to the Philippians and Philemon, The New International Commentary on the New Testament* (Grand Rapids, Eerdmans, 1955), 91.

6. Benjamin B. Warfield, *The Works of Benjamin B. Warfield,* vol. 7, *Perfectionism,* Part 1 (1931, reprint, Grand Rapids: Baker, 1991), 113.

7. Thomas Ascol, "A Neglected Topic for Needy Times," *The Founders Journal,* Issue 28, Spring 1997, 2.

11

HE IS HERE

All of Life in His Conscious Presence

SEVERAL YEARS AGO a Christian magazine published an anonymous article by a Christian leader recounting his fall into pornography. It all began when, alone in a hotel room in a distant city, he saw an advertisement for an exotic dancer at a local night club. Rationalizing to himself that to be an effective Christian leader he had to experience all of life, he was soon on his way to the show.

But it didn't stop there. He was hooked, and for the next five years fought a desperate battle with extreme sexual lust.

Suppose that instead of his being alone, the man's wife or perhaps an elder from his church had been with him that night. Would he have gone to the show? Of course not.

The fact is, though, *God* was with him. God was there looking with indignation on that performance designed to excite men's lust. God was there looking with grief on His erring child. As He says of His people in Jeremiah 16:17, "My eyes are on all their ways; they are not hidden from me, nor is their sin concealed from my eyes."

"YOU ARE THERE"

We have been studying some of the fundamental characteristics of a person who fears God, characteristics so foundational that they significantly influence every other aspect of life. We've seen first that this person submits to God's authority, and second that he or she seeks to obey God in every area of life.

A third characteristic is that a God-fearing person lives all of life in the conscious presence of God. I use the phrase *conscious presence* deliberately. The truth is, we live at all times in the presence of God whether we're aware of it or not. We can say with David,

> Where can I go from your Spirit?
>> Where can I flee from your presence?
> If I go up to the heavens, you are there;
>> if I make my bed in the depths, you are there.
> If I rise on the wings of the dawn,
>> if I settle on the far side of the sea,
> even there your hand will guide me,
>> your right hand will hold me fast. (Psalm 139:7–10)

As a God-fearing man, David was keenly aware of never being absent from God's all-pervasive presence. Neither the height of the heavens nor the depth of the earth nor the farthest boundaries of the sea could provide an escape from God. Wherever David went, God was there beholding all he did.

To help us understand this, the Bible teaches both the *immensity* and the *omnipresence* of God. These two descriptive terms are related but distinct, as theologian A. A. Hodge points out:

> The immensity of God is the phrase used to express the fact that God
> is infinite in his relation to space, i.e., that the entire indivisible essence
> of God is at every moment of time contemporaneously present to
> every point of infinite space. . . .

Omnipresence characterizes the relation of God to his creatures as they severally occupy their several positions in space.[1]

Perhaps the two terms are best understood by use of human analogy. As I write, I'm sitting behind my desk. By reaching forward with my arm I can barely touch the front of it. But I can't be both behind and in front of my desk at the same time. God, however, is both behind my desk and in front of it at all times, not by extension of His "arms," so to speak, but with His entire being. He is in fact everywhere present in my study, in our house, and in the entire universe. Even on the most distant star in the universe, God is there in His indivisible essence just as much as He is in my study. That is God's immensity.

Solomon acknowledged God's immensity in his dedication prayer for the temple: "But will God really dwell on earth? The heavens, even the highest heaven, cannot contain you. How much less this temple I have built!" (1 Kings 8:27).

God's omnipresence arises obviously from His immensity and refers to His continuous presence *with each of us*. This is what David was acknowledging to God in Psalm 139. Wherever we are, "You are there." God is with me in my study and with my wife in the kitchen at the same time. When I travel to a distant city, God is just as much with my wife back home as He is with me on my trip. He is present with my Chinese Christian brother on the other side of the world just as much as He's with me in Colorado. Even if we could travel in a spaceship to that most distant star, God would be there with us.

Jeremiah 23:23–24 speaks to both God's immensity and His omnipresence:

> "Am I only a God nearby," declares the LORD,
>> "and not a God far away?
> Can anyone hide in secret places
>> so that I cannot see him?" declares the LORD.
> "Do not I fill heaven and earth?" declares the LORD.

In His Sight and Company

It is the omnipresence of God that is most applicable to us. It means that we are never out of His presence and His all-seeing eye. We can hide from one another—or we can hide our activities from each other —but never from God. As Proverbs 15:3 says, "The eyes of the LORD are everywhere, keeping watch on the wicked and the good."

One characteristic, then, of a God-fearing person is the continual awareness that wherever he or she goes, God is there. Such a consciousness of God's presence should obviously affect our conduct. As J. I. Packer has written, "Living becomes an awesome business when you realize that you spend every moment of your life in the sight and company of an omniscient, omnipresent Creator."[2]

The man referred to at the beginning of the chapter went to that lustful show because he did not practice the conscious awareness of God's presence. Even if the fact of God's presence occurred to him, he either ignored it or pushed it aside.

We may cluck our tongues disapprovingly at such obvious sin, but which of us isn't guilty sometimes of disregarding God's constant presence? If you've ever slowed down to the speed limit at the sight of a highway patrol car, you were driving without the conscious presence of God. God, not the state trooper, should be our highway patrolman, because God is always with us. A God-fearing person should be the same at all times, knowing we live every moment of our lives in His presence. We need to establish the habit, though, of constantly being aware of this fact.

David was keenly aware of God's constant presence. "You know when I sit and when I rise," he acknowledged. "You discern my going out and my lying down; you are familiar with all my ways" (Psalm 139:2–3). The God who created the universe and keeps the stars in their courses takes note of every move we make. He observes our slightest sideward glance and hears our every whispered word.

The person who fears God is conscious that God is aware of every minute detail, every mundane activity in his or her life. Such awareness serves as a check on temptation to sin. This doesn't mean living in constant fear that God is going to "get us." It does mean that because we're aware of His all-seeing eye and all-hearing ear, we live in a way that pleases Him as He sees what we do and hears what we say.

Because of God's continuous presence with us, all our activities should be done in the fear of the Lord. Among the Israelites, even ordinary real estate transactions were to be done in the fear of God (Leviticus 25:14–17). They were also told to fear God rather than charging interest to the poor (Leviticus 25:36), and to fear God rather than ruling ruthlessly over their fellow Jews (Leviticus 25:43). From these ordinary marketplace and worka-day examples we see that all of life, even in its most mundane affairs, is to be lived in the fear of God, conscious of His all-pervasive presence and all-seeing eye.

Paul's instruction to slaves in Colossians 3:22–25 was to obey whether or not they were under the eye of their master. The reality is that God is present whether the master is there or not. Applying this principle to today's working world, we see that the Christian is always to work not just to win his or her employer's favor, but as if working for the Lord and under His watchful eye. This means we don't steal time, for example, in extra-long coffee or lunch breaks, or do shoddy work because no supervisor is there to observe us. It means we accurately report business expenses, because it is God, not just the controller's department, who audits our reports.

In the same manner, Paul's instructions to masters to provide their slaves "with what is right and fair" was based on the fact that masters also "have a Master in heaven" (Colossians 4:1). God was watching over their treatment of slaves with His all-seeing eye.

The truth, then, is that every interaction we have with another person is performed in the presence of God.

In Leviticus 19:14 is a rather intriguing warning regarding physically disabled people: "Do not curse the deaf or put a stumbling block in front of the blind, but fear your God. I am the LORD." I can't imagine the necessity for such a warning in the respectful Jewish culture, but obviously God knew it was needed. In our society today I can imagine some mischievous and immature teenagers gleefully cursing or insulting a deaf person, or even deliberately setting up an obstacle for a blind person to stumble over.

In both cases the biblical warning is couched in terms of the fear of God. The deaf person can't hear himself being cursed, but God hears. The blind person can see neither the stumbling block nor whoever put it in his way, but God sees. Undoubtedly in this context, the most prominent aspect of the fear of God is actual fear of His retributive justice.

Implied in all these instructions and warnings is an underlying principle of integrity. We should never take advantage of anyone: the poor, the disabled, the buyer or seller, our employer or employees. Rather in all our affairs of life and our interactions with other people we should always be conscious of His all-pervasive presence, His all-seeing eye, and His all-hearing ear. This is where integrity actually begins—living all of life in the conscious awareness of God's constant presence. And this should be a fundamental characteristic of the person who fears God.

OUR EVERY THOUGHT IN EXACT DETAIL

God not only sees and hears all we do or say; He even knows our thoughts. "You perceive my thoughts from afar," David said. "Before a word is on my tongue you know it completely, O LORD" (Psalm 139:2,4). Psalm 44:21 also tells us that God "knows the secrets of the heart." And in Jeremiah 17:10, God says, "I the LORD search the heart and examine the mind."

Therefore to live in God's conscious presence means that we also live in the awareness that God knows our every thought. All of us have thoughts that we would be ashamed for other people to know. We entertain thoughts of jealousy, covetousness, envy, resentment, and lust. We have critical thoughts about another person's dress or speech or mannerisms. We mentally argue with people, or in our minds tell off someone in a way we wouldn't dare verbalize. As someone has humorously said, if all our thoughts for the past week were projected on a screen for others to see, we'd have to leave town.

But our thoughts are no joking matter to God. Thoughts that we would be ashamed to share with our spouse or deepest friend are all fully known to God. He knows them in the exact same detail that we think them. As Hebrews 4:13 so forcefully states, "Nothing in all creation is hidden from God's sight. Everything is uncovered and laid bare before the eyes of him *to whom we must give account.*" This passage suggests that we'll have to give account for every sinful thought.

Jesus said, "I tell you that men will have to give account on the day of judgment for every careless word they have spoken" (Matthew 12:36). It is sobering to realize that this same accountability holds true not only for our words and deeds, but even for our thoughts.

Since God knows our every thought in exact detail, the person who fears God seeks to control his or her thought life in the same way we regulate our conduct. If we wouldn't go to the nightclub to see the exotic dancer, we don't allow thoughts of that nature to lodge in our minds. If we wouldn't murder, then we don't harbor thoughts of anger and resentment toward another person. It's true that anger is not as serious as murder, nor lustful thoughts as serious as adultery, but Jesus makes it clear that our thoughts and heart attitudes are judged by God just as much as our actions (see Matthew 5:21–22,27–28).

Solomon warned us, "Above all else, guard your heart, for it is the wellspring of life" (Proverbs 4:23). The Hebrew word translated as *heart* generally refers to our entire conscious person—our reasoning, understanding, emotions, conscience, and will. You can readily see, however, that all those internal activities are carried out in the realm of our thoughts. So basically Solomon was warning us to guard our thoughts.

Paul said, "We take captive every thought to make it obedient to Christ" (2 Corinthians 10:5). Although the context indicates he was referring to the thoughts of his opponents at Corinth, it still is a worthy objective for us regarding our own thought lives. We need to be as obedient in our thoughts as in our actions.

Controlling our thought life has two sides to it. We must both deal with negative, sinful thoughts and seek to fill our minds with positive, godly thoughts. Paul's description of godly thought patterns in Philippians 4:8 is a good model: "Finally, brothers, whatever is true, whatever is noble, whatever is right, whatever is pure, whatever is lovely, whatever is admirable —if anything is excellent or praiseworthy—think about such things."

Using Paul's list we can ask the following questions to evaluate our thoughts:

- *Is it true?* Are my thoughts about a person or a situation really accurate? Am I ascribing a sinful motive to someone without actually knowing the person's motive?
- *Is it noble?* Does this thought express the highest Christian ideals? Does it put another person in the best possible light?
- *Is it right?* Is it just and fair toward other people? Or does it tend to injure or defraud (even in our minds) another person's reputation?
- *Is it pure?* Is it morally and sexually pure?
- *Is it lovely?* Is it attractive and amiable? Do our thought patterns make us easy for others to deal with?
- *Is it admirable?* Would this thought receive the esteem of others if it were known?
- *Is it excellent or praiseworthy?* Is it commendable even to my own conscience?

Paul is obviously setting before us the highest standard for our thought life. I confess to squirming a bit even as I wrote out those questions. My thought patterns, I'm afraid, often fall short of Paul's ideal.

But dare we settle for any lower standard when we think all our thoughts in the presence of God? Even though we'll continually fall short, we must seek to make every thought obedient to Christ. And because we need the Lord's help, we do well to pray with David, "May the words of my mouth and the meditation of my heart be pleasing in your sight, O LORD, my Rock and my Redeemer" (Psalm 19:14).

HE KNOWS ALL OUR MOTIVES

God's knowledge of us penetrates even deeper than our thoughts. It reaches to our motives, to why we do what we do. "The LORD searches every heart and understands every motive behind the thoughts" (1 Chronicles 28:9). We sometimes do the right thing for the wrong reason, or perhaps a combination of right and wrong reasons. We sincerely want to help someone or contribute to some worthy objective, but we also want to look good in the process.

Sometimes we're not even aware of our mixed motives, but God sees motives that we don't. Paul wrote,

> My conscience is clear, but that does not make me innocent. It is the Lord who judges me. Therefore judge nothing before the appointed time; wait till the Lord comes. He will bring to light what is hidden in darkness and will expose the motives of men's hearts. At that time each will receive his praise from God. (1 Corinthians 4:4–5)

Paul's conscience was clear, but he recognized that he might have hidden motives of which even he was not aware. This fact shouldn't make us introspective, always questioning whether our motives are right and pure. But it should cause us to recognize that our motives often are mixed at best. When we recognize a wrong motive we should confess it, claiming the cleansing blood of Christ (1 John 1:7). And we should ask God to make us aware of wrong motives we don't see.

The important thing to realize is that everything about us—not only every word and action, but also every thought and motive—lies before God as an open book. To fear God means living in this continual awareness of His presence and knowledge.

HE ALWAYS HOLDS OUR HAND

The fact that we live in the constant presence of God should be not only sobering but also encouraging to us. Note the transition David makes in Psalm 139. In verse 7 he acknowledges that he cannot *flee* from God's presence. In verse 10 he speaks of God's right hand holding him fast, like a parent tightly gripping the hand of a small child both to guide him and to protect him from danger. David has moved from God's *watchful presence* to consideration of His *protecting presence.*

When our children were small and we were in a crowd or crossing a busy street, I wasn't satisfied for them to hold my hand. I wanted to hold theirs. This was reinforced when I once had the frightening experience of losing our three-year-old daughter in the supermarket. I knew that in the jostling of a crowd my son or daughter could easily lose my hand, or while crossing a street they might let go to run across. So I held on tightly. Of course it was most often a mutual thing. They were insecure enough to cling as tightly to my hand as I gripped theirs.

That's a picture of God's way with us. He is pleased when we cling to His hand, so to speak, in dependence upon Him. But whether we cling to Him or not, He grips our hand. As David said, "Your right hand will hold me fast."

We see this picture again in Psalm 73, where Asaph wrote, "Yet I am always with you; you hold me by my right hand" (verse 23). The context of that verse is worth noting to fully appreciate what Asaph was saying. Early in the psalm Asaph is struggling with an apparent injustice of God: The wicked always seemed to be prospering. "This is what the wicked are like," Asaph concludes—"always carefree, they increase in wealth" (verse 12).

In contrast Asaph looks at himself: "Surely in vain have I kept my heart pure; in vain have I washed my hands in innocence" (verse 13). It seemed to him that the godly were worse off than the wicked. Then Asaph came to his senses and confessed, "When my heart was grieved and my spirit embittered, I was senseless and ignorant; I was a brute beast before you" (verses 21–22).

Immediately after this confession, Asaph acknowledges God's faithfulness and His constant care. He realized God always held him by his right hand even when circumstances tempted him to think otherwise.

If we truly fear God in the fullest meaning of that term we, too, will confess with Asaph that God always holds us by our hand—even when it seems He is not.

The truth of God's continuous protecting presence is taught throughout Scripture. As Moses was preparing to turn over to Joshua his role of leading Israel, he said to Joshua and the people, "The LORD himself goes before you and will be with you; he will never leave you nor forsake you. Do not be afraid; do not be discouraged" (Deuteronomy 31:8). The Lord would go before them and be with them. He would never leave them nor forsake them.

This same promise is repeated in one form or another in several places in the Old Testament. (See Genesis 28:15; Deuteronomy 31:6,8; Joshua 1:5; and 1 Chronicles 28:20.) The writer of Hebrews also picks it up when he says, "Keep your lives free from the love of money and be content with what you have, because God has said, 'Never will I leave you; never will I forsake you'" (13:5).

OUR REASON FOR NOT BEING AFRAID

Closely associated with this promise of God's continuous protective presence is His command of encouragement, "Don't be afraid." I was amazed when I pulled up on my computer screen verses with the phrase "don't [or "do not"] be afraid." This refrain occurs throughout the Bible from Genesis 15:1 to Revelation 2:10. It is of course because God is always with us that we should not be afraid. For example, in 1 Chronicles 28:20, David said to Solomon, "Do not be afraid or discouraged, for the LORD God, my God, is with you." The little child is not afraid as long as his mommy or daddy grips his hand. It's when he somehow gets separated from them that he becomes afraid.

God, however, is always with us. It's impossible for one of His children to become separated from Him, whatever our perception may be. David apparently felt separated from God on numerous occasions. In Psalm 10:1 he complains that God hides Himself in times of trouble. In Psalm 13:1 he asks, "How long, O LORD? Will you forget me forever?" In Psalm 31:22 he exclaims, "I am cut off from your sight!" But then he adds, "Yet you heard my cry for mercy when I called to you for help." God is always with us, holding our hand and saying "Don't be afraid," even when we don't perceive His presence.

My wife and I signed up for a study program in Israel, the fulfillment of a twenty-year dream of mine. We were to fly from Denver to Atlanta, where we would meet the others of our party, then travel as a group to Tel Aviv. There we would be met by our study leader and a bus to take us to our first destination in southern Israel.

I carefully arranged our flight schedule so we would arrive in Atlanta four hours before our transatlantic flight departed—plenty of time, I thought, to allow for any delay in the Denver-to-Atlanta flight. I was wrong. The airplane in Denver had a mechanical problem. We tried to get on another flight but were unsuccessful. There was nothing to do but wait for the plane's repair. We finally taxied out to the runway and started to take off, only to develop another mechanical problem. By the time this too was repaired, we had lost our four hours.

During that time of waiting in Denver two passages of Scripture kept going through my mind. The first was Ecclesiastes 7:13, "Consider what God has done: Who can straighten what he has made crooked?" I knew God was sovereignly in control of our schedule, and it was becoming apparent to me that He was thwarting or "making crooked" our plan to be on the flight to Israel with our group.

The second passages of Scripture was the promise we looked at earlier, "Never will I leave you; never will I forsake you." It seemed as if God was saying to me through those Scriptures, "I'm not going to let you make that flight in Atlanta, however hard you try. You cannot straighten what I have made crooked. But don't be afraid; I will not forsake you. Even though you'll arrive in Israel long after your group does, I will not leave you stranded."

I needed that reassurance. As it turned out, God did thwart our plans. We missed our flight to Israel and had to wait twenty-four hours for the next one. It was a disappointment to realize we would miss the first day of our study program, but my main concern was what we would do when we landed in Israel by ourselves. We would arrive about 6:00 P.M.; where would we stay that first night? How would we locate our group, and how would we get to where they were? I know these are not earth-shaking concerns, but I'm not the adventuresome type. To say the least, I was struggling with anxiety.

Through the airline I sent a message ahead to Tel Aviv telling of our delay, but I had no assurance it would get through (especially since a previous message from Denver to Atlanta had not).

We finally landed in Israel and walked out of the Tel Aviv airport into a huge crowd of people waiting to meet other passengers. What do we do? At that moment my wife spotted a man holding a sign that read, "Mr. and Mrs. Bridges." He loaded us into a Volkswagen van and drove us about four or five hours into the desert to where our study group was spending the night. It was midnight and everyone was in bed, but we managed to find our assigned room. At last we had arrived. God had not left us stranded in Tel Aviv. He had not forsaken us.

I realize our little episode pales in comparison with the major crises others face, such as losing your job when you're the primary or only source of family income. It pales in comparison with the death of my first wife after a seventeen-month bout with cancer. But whether we're facing a major or minor crisis in our lives, God's promise is the same. He will never leave us; He will never forsake us. This is the assurance we can have as we learn to live in the protective presence of God.

SEEING ALL, HE STILL LOVES US

There's still more good news about God's constant presence with us and His knowledge of us. Despite all He sees and knows of our sin, He still loves us. When He chose us in Christ even before the creation of the world (Ephesians 1:4), he knew even then about all our sinful ways, all our unholy thoughts, all our unkind words and self-centered motives. He chose us not because He foresaw that we would be good, but because of His own sovereign love to us.

When God the Father sent His Son to be the atoning sacrifice for our sins, He laid on Him the iniquity of us all (Isaiah 53:6). Christ bore all our sins on the cross. Because of that, the apostle Paul could write, "He forgave us all our sins" (Colossians 2:13), and "Blessed is the man whose sin the Lord will never count against him" (Romans 4:8). Despite all the sin God sees in our lives, He has cleansed us with the blood of Christ and clothed us with His righteousness. We are still sinners, but we are forgiven sinners.

Because of this we can be absolutely honest before God. We should be, because He knows all about us anyway. But too often, because of a sense of guilt, we try in some way to hide our sin from God by rationalizing about it or seeking in some way to justify or excuse it. We're like the little boy protesting, "But he hit me first!"

We can also be brutally honest with ourselves. However ugly our sin may be, we know that it is covered by the blood of Christ. If we have spoken critically or slanderously about someone, we can admit it, calling it exactly what it is. If we have "padded" our expense account report, we can face up to the fact that we have effectively stolen from our employer.

David had learned the freedom of knowing how God knew all about him and still loved him. Because of this he willingly asked God to search his heart for any offensive ways in him (Psalm 139:23–24). If you and I learn this freedom, we too can ask God to search our hearts. We can ask Him to reveal sin that we aren't even aware of, sins such as selfishness, pride, and stubbornness. It's painful to have such sins brought to light, but we must see them before we can repent of them and deal with them.

People who fear God live their lives in the conscious presence of God. They act, speak, and think in the continual awareness that God sees all their actions, hears all their words, and knows all their thoughts. On the one hand, this has a sobering and restraining influence on them to keep them from sin, even in their thoughts. On the other hand, they have the joy of knowing that even though God knows all about their sin, He has forgiven them through Christ and accepts them through His merit.

They're grateful for both the restraining influence and the assurance of forgiveness that comes from knowing they live constantly in His presence. And in this they experience joy in fearing Him.

PRACTICING HIS PRESENCE

How consistently do you practice the conscious awareness of God's presence? Can you think of situations where you would have acted differently if you had been practicing the presence of God?

Are there recurring events or activities in your life in which you need to make a special effort to practice the awareness of His presence, either as a restraint against temptation or as an encouragement that God's protective presence is with you?

Review Paul's description of a positive thought life in Philippians 4:8. Has the Holy Spirit specifically spoken to you about one of those qualities? If so, what do you need to do to change?

What steps do you intend to take to grow in your practice of the conscious presence of God?

Notes

1. A. A. Hodge, *Outlines of Theology* (1879, reprint, Edinburgh: Banner of Truth Trust, 1972), 140–1.

2. J. I. Packer, *Knowing God* (Downers Grove, Ill.: InterVarsity, 1973), 76.

12

FOR LIFE AND BREATH AND EVERYTHING

Depending on God

INDEPENDENCE AND self-sufficiency are hallmarks of our civilization. Children are trained from infancy to make it on their own. The childhood story of the little train engine that chugged up the mountain saying, "I think I can, I think I can" is one illustration of how we seek to develop self-reliance and determination even in preschoolers. Later on, high school athletes are urged to reach deep within themselves to find the courage and fortitude to win their games. Adults are told that if we simply believe in ourselves, we can become whatever we want to be. Even in the spiritual realm, a prominent physician said, "I have great belief in spiritual strength, but spiritual strength, to me, comes from within."

This independence is to some extent inbred in human nature. I remember one of our children, still in the high-chair stage, refusing to be helped by stubbornly asserting, "Me can do it." Of course we want children to grow up with a reasonable degree of self-confidence and a realization that they can develop the necessary skills and maturity to make it on their own in life. At the same time, however, we should realize that God wants us to learn the truth of our absolute dependence on Him.

In the last chapter we saw that a person who fears God lives all of life in the conscious presence of God. Another characteristic of such a person is that *he or she lives all of life in conscious dependence on God.* Again I use that word *conscious* deliberately, because whether we realize it or not, we're actually dependent upon God every moment of our lives.

John Murray has well said that "the fear of God means that God is constantly in the center of our thought and apprehension, and life is characterized by the all-pervasive consciousness of dependence upon him and responsibility to him."[1] This attitude of absolute dependence on God is not one to be temporarily assumed, as in a time of crisis, but is to be sustained through all the routine activities of life, both spiritual and temporal. We need to cultivate a spirit of dependence on God just as much in driving to church as in teaching a Sunday school class once we get there.

FOR LIFE ITSELF

This absolute dependence upon God for everything is taught clearly in Acts 17:25—"And he is not served by human hands, as if he needed anything, because he himself gives all men life and breath and everything else."

We're dependent upon God for life itself. David recognized this when he said, "My times are in your hands" (Psalm 31:15). When Daniel rebuked King Belshazzar for his pride and arrogance he said, "But you did not honor the God who holds in his hand your life and all your ways" (Daniel 5:23). What was true for David and Belshazzar is just as true of us today. We have only to look around us to recognize it: Life is uncertain and unpredictable. "You do not know what a day may bring forth" (Proverbs 27:1).

Every breath we breathe is a gift from God. Most of the time we're not even aware of breathing; it's involuntary and unconscious. Yet both the air we breathe and the autonomic nervous system that regulates our breathing are God's gifts. Admittedly it's difficult to cultivate a sense of dependence on God for something we do unconsciously and automatically. But we can make it a point to periodically throughout the day pause to acknowledge our dependence on God just for life itself.

FOR DAILY SUSTENANCE

Paul told his Athenian audience that God gives not only life and breath but *everything else.* Through His providential rule over His creation, God sustains, feeds, and nourishes us. When Jesus taught us to pray, "Give us today our daily bread" (Matthew 6:11), He was teaching us to acknowledge our dependence upon our heavenly Father for the food we eat.

It's true that God has ordained our work as His usual way of supplying our food. As He said to Adam, "By the sweat of your brow you will eat your food" (Genesis 3:19). And even before Adam's sin and the consequent curse, God had "put him in the Garden of Eden to *work* it and take care of it" (Genesis 2:15). From the very beginning God ordained that we work for our food; yet at the same time Scripture says He gives it to us.

God gives us our food and other necessities of life by blessing our labors and making them productive. The Scriptures consistently affirm this truth. For example, Psalm 104:14–15 reads:

> He makes grass grow for the cattle,
>> and plants for man to cultivate—
>> bringing forth food from the earth:
> wine that gladdens the heart of man,
>> oil to make his face shine,
>> and bread that sustains his heart.

Some people believe that such Scriptures mean only that God established the laws of nature and that these laws now operate quite apart from any divine intervention. The Scriptures, however, affirm God's direct and immediate control over nature. Consider the following passage:

> He unleashes his lightning beneath the whole heaven
>> and sends it to the ends of the earth. . . .
> He says to the snow, "Fall on the earth,"
>> and to the rain shower, "Be a mighty downpour." . . .
> The breath of God produces ice,
>> and the broad waters become frozen.
> He loads the clouds with moisture;
>> he scatters his lightning through them.
> At his direction they swirl around
>> over the face of the whole earth
>> to do whatever he commands them.
> He brings the clouds to punish men,
>> or to water his earth and show his love. (Job 37:3,6,10–13)

It could be argued that the descriptions of God's actions in this passage are simply metaphorical expressions to denote the laws of nature. But note in the final verse God's twofold motive: to punish or to show His love (verse 13). Such discriminating motives cannot be ascribed simply to laws of nature that God has left to run their course.

God again confirms His direct control over our food and water supply in Amos 4:6–9.

> "I gave you empty stomachs in every city
>> and lack of bread in every town,
>> yet you have not returned to me,"
>>> declares the LORD.
> "I also withheld rain from you
>> when the harvest was still three months away.
> I sent rain on one town,
>> but withheld it from another.

One field had rain;

   another had none and dried up.

People staggered from town to town for water

   but did not get enough to drink,

   yet you have not returned to me,"

      declares the LORD.

"Many times I struck your gardens and vineyards,

   I struck them with blight and mildew.

Locusts devoured your fig and olive trees,

   yet you have not returned to me,"

      declares the LORD.

Note God's direct, immediate control over the so-called acts of nature. "I gave you empty stomachs." "I also withheld rain from you." "I sent rain on one town but withheld it from another." "I struck your gardens and vineyards." Nothing could be more clear than that the Jews were utterly dependent upon God for their food and water supply. When the Jews became rebellious and forgot this, God criticized them for what was missing in their thoughts: "They do not say to themselves, 'Let us fear the LORD our God, who gives autumn and spring rains in season, who assures us of the regular weeks of harvest'"(Jeremiah 5:24).

What was true for the Jews in the days of Amos is just as true for us. Jesus reminded us that His Father "causes his sun to rise on the evil and the good, and sends rain on the righteous and the unrighteous" (Matthew 5:45).

Though the Amos passage speaks of God's judgment through the *withholding* of food and rain, the Bible just as clearly affirms His blessing through His gracious provision. Just before the Israelites entered Canaan, Moses warned them,

When you have eaten and are satisfied, praise the LORD your God for the good land he has given you. . . . Otherwise, when you eat and are satisfied, when you build fine houses and settle down, and when your herds and flocks grow large and your silver and gold increase and all you have is multiplied, then your heart will become proud and you will forget the LORD your God, who brought you out of Egypt, out of the land of slavery. . . . You may say to yourself, "My power and the strength of my hands have produced this wealth for me." But remember the LORD your God, for *it is he who gives you the ability to produce wealth,* and so confirms his covenant, which he swore to your forefathers, as it is today. (Deuteronomy 8:10–18)

It is God who gives us the ability to work—and then, through His providential circumstances, blesses our work as He chooses.

OUR DANGER

All the Scriptures we've looked at on this subject were of course addressed to people living in an agricultural economy where they could observe firsthand the work of God in providing or withholding their food. It's more difficult for us today when we buy our food in well-stocked supermarkets and when our refrigerators and pantry shelves have a week's supply or more of food.

In fact with the comfortable living standard so many of us enjoy, we're in danger of having the same attitude Moses warned the Israelites about: "*My* power and the strength of *my* hands have produced this wealth for me" (8:17). If we substitute "my ability, education, and experience" for "my power and the strength of my hands," we can apply Moses' warning directly to our Christian culture today.

Complete dependence on God is a hard lesson to learn. We know we must work in order to provide the essentials of daily life, but in that very work we may easily forget that it is God who enables us to work; that it is God who gives us the intellectual and physical skills that qualify us to work and, yes, even provides the job itself. The God-fearing person recognizes this dependence on God and readily acknowledges God as the source of all provision of the necessities and comforts of this life.

John Calvin addressed this relationship of the fear of God and our conscious dependence on Him in his *Institutes*. He wrote:

> Until men recognize that they owe everything to God, that they are nourished by his fatherly care, that he is the Author of their every good, that they should seek nothing beyond him—they will never yield him willing service. Nay, unless they establish their complete happiness in him, they will never give themselves truly and sincerely to him.[2]

In the same paragraph Calvin also speaks of "reverence joined with love of God." This is his description of fearing God. And he says this reverence and love for God are brought about by "the knowledge of His benefits." That is, a conscious awareness of our dependence on God as our Father who supplies our needs will increase our fear of Him. It's equally true that the person who delights to fear God will seek to cultivate an ever-growing sense of dependence upon Him.

DEPENDING ON HIM IN OUR PLANS

Our dependence on God, however, goes far beyond life and breath and the necessities of daily life. We're also dependent upon Him for the successful execution of our plans.

Few things are more common than planning. We plan to do the laundry today, or go shopping tomorrow, or take a vacation next month. Our calendars are full of things we plan to do. Turning to Scripture we find Paul planning to visit the believers at Rome on his way to Spain (Romans 15:24). Then we read in Proverbs that "The plans of the diligent lead to profit," and "Plans fail for lack of counsel" (Proverbs 21:5, 15:22).

Even God has plans. Job acknowledged to God that "no plan of yours can be thwarted" (Job 42:2), and Paul speaks of the "plan of him who works out everything in conformity with the purpose of his will" (Ephesians 1:11). So everyone makes plans, and planning is encouraged in the Bible.

Yet a certain type of planning is condemned in Scripture: planning that does not recognize our dependence on God for the successful execution of those plans.

James speaks to the issue this way:

> Now listen, you who say, "Today or tomorrow we will go to this or that city, spend a year there, carry on business and make money." Why, you do not even know what will happen tomorrow. What is your life? You are a mist that appears for a little while and then vanishes. Instead, you ought to say, *"If it is the Lord's will,* we will live and do this or that." (James 4:13–15)

James speaks to people making ordinary business plans. In a modern-day setting he was addressing business people who might plan to open a new store or introduce a new product line. He does not condemn such planning. He does not even condemn the plans to make money. What he does condemn are plans that don't take into account our dependence on God for their success.

Christians of my grandparents' generation often qualified their statements of intent with the phrase, "Lord willing." They were saying, "I plan to do such and such *if it is the Lord's will."* In their writing they would end a sentence expressing some plan with the initials D.V., standing for the Latin phrase *Deo volente,* or "God willing." They were thereby acknowledging their dependence on God for the success of their plans.

Although the expression "Lord willing" undoubtedly became a meaningless cliché for many people, it's a practice well worth resuming because it forces us back to the realization of our absolute dependence on God. I'm not suggesting we overdo it—"I'm going to have cereal for breakfast, Lord willing." But we ought to use the phrase often enough to remind ourselves that we really are dependent on God for our plans, even for such mundane activities as having cereal for breakfast.

The events leading to my first wife's death (at least those events known to us) actually started on her birthday seventeen months earlier. Our son was home from college for the summer, and the three of us planned to go out to dinner that evening. My wife had what we thought was to be a routine doctor's appointment that morning. It was not routine. She was admitted immediately to the hospital without even the opportunity to go home and collect the personal things she would need for the hospital stay. Plans for an ordinary birthday dinner were squashed. I was again reminded that "Many are the plans in a man's heart, but it is the LORD's purpose that prevails" (Proverbs 19:21).

Someone has observed that our life is like a path having a thick curtain hung across it, a curtain that recedes before us as we advance, but only step by step. None of us can tell what is beyond that curtain. None of us knows what will happen to us tomorrow or even in the next hour. Often things go as planned, but sometimes our plans are thwarted.

Occasionally we hear that some public event has been "canceled due to circumstances beyond our control." The fact is, however, all circumstances are beyond our control. We are absolutely dependent upon God for the carrying out of our plans. The person who fears God not only acknowledges this, but delights to do so. He or she finds great joy in realizing our dependence on the moment-by-moment care of our loving, sovereign heavenly Father.

DEPENDING ON HIM THROUGH OTHERS

One area of life where we're likely to realize our lack of independence and self-sufficiency is in our relationships with other people. All of us regularly encounter situations where we're dependent on the decisions or actions of someone else. These decisions or actions vary from the most routine and ordinary to ones affecting our future career or well-being. I discovered I needed to see my doctor the day before I was to leave on a week's trip. I was totally dependent on the doctor's receptionist to work me into his schedule. It was her call. She easily could have said he had no more room in an already over-crowded day. I was dependent on her decision.

A Ph.D. candidate became a Christian in the midst of his doctoral studies. For that reason, a previously supportive but ungodly professor tried to block the granting of his degree. The student was seemingly at his mercy. Between these two instances—mine very minor, and the graduate student's career-threatening—lies a vast amount of instances in all our lives where we depend on other people.

You may think I deal in trivial matters when I refer to such minor events as a doctor's appointment. One reason I do is because this is where we mostly live. Most of life is commonplace and ordinary. The Ph.D. candidate faced his degree crisis once. But a dozen times in his life he might need a doctor's appointment on short notice. He, along with each of us, needs to learn we're as dependent on God in the mundane events of life as we are in the extraordinary ones.

Furthermore, it's often easier to recognize our dependence on God in the major events than in the minor ones. A potentially life-changing crisis stands out in bold relief and immediately draws our attention to our dependence on Him. The more ordinary experiences tend to slip by without that recognition. Instead we tend to depend on ourselves and other people in these situations.

The person who fears God, however, rejoices in the fact that we actually are *not* dependent on other people. We are dependent on God. The Bible consistently affirms that God is able to and does in fact carry out His plans through the decisions of people.

My favorite passage of Scripture on this subject is one we looked at earlier, Proverbs 21:1—"The king's heart is in the hand of the LORD; he directs it like a watercourse wherever he pleases." If the heart of the most powerful monarch is in God's hand, then surely decisions by doctors' receptionists and graduate school professors are also subject to His control.

This truth does not nullify the freedom people have in their choices, nor does it reduce our responsibility to act prudently and discreetly when we are, humanly speaking, dependent on the decisions and actions of others. God works *through* people's wills, not against them, so that they freely make the choices He wants them to make. How God does this is of course a mystery. This is a part of God that He has not revealed to us. Nevertheless, it's a fact that God teaches us over and over in the Bible. (See, for example, Exodus 12:35–36, Ezra 1:1, Isaiah 45:13, Daniel 1:9, and 2 Corinthians 8:16–17.)

What is our responsibility to influence the decisions or actions of others? We can act presumptuously here in either of two opposite directions. One is to assume God is *not* in control, so that we rely totally on our efforts and ability to influence others. The other extreme is to think that since God is in control, we need do nothing. But the wise course is to take all the steps we can take in a biblical manner, then to trust God for whatever the outcome. The extent to which we fear God will largely determine how well we're able to steer the proper course between the two extremes.

ACTIVE, ACTUAL RELIANCE

This brings us to the application of our conscious dependence on God. It isn't enough to passively believe we're dependent upon God for every aspect of our lives. We must *actively* rely on Him.

The primary way we do this is through prayer. J. I. Packer has written:

> The prayer of a Christian is not an attempt to force God's hand, but a humble acknowledgment of helplessness and dependence. When we are on our knees, we know that it is not we who control the world; it is not in our power, therefore, to supply our needs by our own independent efforts; every good thing that we desire for ourselves and

for others must be sought from God, and will come, if it comes at all, as a gift from His hands.[3]

By *praying* we recognize our helplessness and dependence. By *praying* we recognize that we are not in control of our lives, our health, our plans, or the decisions other people make respecting us. We recognize, as Dr. Packer said, that we must seek God for every good thing we desire for ourselves and others.

As people who fear God, we also recognize that God is not a divine bellhop, on call to respond to our every desire. We cannot use God simply to accomplish our aims. Rather we come expressing our need, committing it to Him and leaving the outcome in His hands, knowing He is our infinitely wise and loving heavenly Father.

At the same time when we pray we should recognize God's power and His ability to do anything He chooses to do. When we study the prayers in the Bible we notice how frequently God is addressed as the sovereign, all-powerful One who is able to answer their prayers. Asa, king of Judah, prayed:

LORD, *there is no one like you* to help the powerless against the mighty. Help us, O LORD our God, for *we rely on you,* and in your name we have come against this vast army. O LORD, *you are our God;* do not let man prevail against you. (2 Chronicles 14:11)

Years later, Asa's son Jehoshaphat faced another military crisis. He prayed:

O LORD, God of our fathers, *are you not the God who is in heaven?* You rule over all the kingdoms of the nations. *Power and might are in your hand,* and no one can withstand you . . . O our God, will you not judge them? For we have no power to face this vast army that is attacking us. We do not know what to do, but *our eyes are upon you.* (2 Chronicles 20:6,12)

Note how both Asa and Jehoshaphat acknowledged both their helplessness and God's power.

We see this again in the prayers of the believers in the infant church of Acts 4. When faced with the threats from the Jewish Sanhedrin they prayed:

Sovereign Lord, . . . you made the heaven and the earth and the sea, and everything in them. You spoke by the Holy Spirit through the mouth of your servant, our father David:

"Why do the nations rage
and the peoples plot in vain?
The kings of the earth take their stand
and the rulers gather together
against the Lord
and against his Anointed One."

Indeed Herod and Pontius Pilate met together with the Gentiles and the people of Israel in this city to conspire against your holy servant Jesus, whom you anointed. They did what your power and will had decided beforehand should happen. Now, Lord, consider their threats and enable your servants to speak your word with great boldness. Stretch out your hand to heal and perform miraculous signs and wonders through the name of your holy servant Jesus. (Acts 4:24–30)

Consider how those early disciples acknowledged God's power and ability to answer their prayer. They addressed Him as "Sovereign Lord." They reminded God that the people responsible for the crucifixion of Jesus did "what your power and will had decided beforehand should happen"—they had simply been instruments to execute God's plan. Only when the disciples had acknowledged God's ability to answer their prayer did they make their request for personal boldness and for God's powerful working on their behalf.

BEYOND WHAT WE CAN ANTICIPATE

We saw earlier that one of the major aspects of fearing God is the admiration of God's greatness. This is not just passive admiration, however, such as the way we might admire a superb athlete in action. It is admiration at work—admiration that causes us to trust in God and in His power to answer our prayers.

Unfortunately our degree of trust in God often lies more in our ability to foresee a way in which He might answer our prayers than in our belief in His power. If we can't see *how* He can answer, we tend to doubt that He *will* answer. We pray, but if we were really honest with God and expressed our thoughts, this is how it would come out: "You know, Lord, that it's just a long shot. I don't see how You can possibly accomplish it, but I'm going to pray for it and see if something just might happen."

In 2 Kings 6 and 7, Israel's northern kingdom was besieged by the Aramean army. The food shortage became so critical that two women agreed to boil their children and eat them. When the king of Israel heard of this, in desperation he approached the prophet Elisha. Elisha announced that the siege would be lifted the next day and that food would be so plentiful that it would be on sale at bargain prices (2 Kings 7:1).

An officer who was with the king responded doubtfully, "Look, even if the LORD should open the floodgates of the heavens, could this happen?" (7:2). He didn't see how this could possibly occur, and therefore he didn't believe it.

To this Elisha responded, "You will see it with your own eyes, . . . but you will not eat any of it!" (7:2). He prophesied for the officer the humbling experience of seeing this blessing without being able to partake of it.

The next day four lepers sitting at the city gate reasoned with one another along these lines: "Let's go out to the enemy camp. If they kill us, we were only going to die anyway. On the other hand, they have food and they might give us some." When the lepers went out they found the Aramean camp deserted; some supernatural noise-making from God had caused the entire army to flee in fear, leaving behind their plentiful provisions.

After these four lepers had eaten and had stashed away a supply of treasure, they decided, "It isn't right for us to be out here enjoying all this alone. We ought to go back to the city and tell the good news." So they went back and told the people, who then rushed out to gather up the food. Just as Elisha had prophesied, barley and wheat were on sale at bargain prices.

And what happened to the doubtful officer? The king ordered him to stand in the city gate and take charge of the operation. After the officer posted himself there, he was trampled to death by the masses of people going out for food. Elisha's entire prophecy was fulfilled.

Just after my thirtieth birthday, when I was still single, the Navigators asked me to take a three-year assignment overseas. One of the issues I had to work through was the fact that, as far as marriage prospects were concerned, I would be "out of circulation" for those three years and would have to "start from scratch" once I returned. As events turned out, the day I arrived back in the States I had my first date with the young lady who would become my wife. We were married seven months later. There was no way I could have predicted how God would so arrange providential circumstances to bring that about.

As the account from 2 Kings and my own experience illustrate, God is not limited to our ability to see how He can answer our prayers or work on our behalf. Therefore we fear God by depending on Him even when we can't see how He might bring something to pass.

So our prayers should be both an acknowledgment of our own helplessness and dependence, and an expression of our confidence that God can meet our needs in ways we could never anticipate. This is the way we actively rely on God, and so fear Him by consciously depending on Him.

CONTINUAL DEPENDENCE MEANS CONTINUAL PRAYER

I mentioned earlier that a conscious dependence on God is not only for times of crisis but is to be sustained through all the events and activities of life. Obviously this practice has to be developed, since we are so accustomed to depending on ourselves most of the time. I also said the primary way we actively rely on God is through prayer. We can now see why the apostle Paul told us to "pray continually" (1 Thessalonians 5:17). *To depend on God continually is to pray continually.* We should seek to make it a practice to send up short, silent words of prayer throughout the day.

We should pray that we will display the fruit of the Spirit as we interact with other people throughout the day. We should pray for safety as we drive. We should pray for wisdom as we make decisions or do our work.

We should also send up prayers of thanksgiving during the day. We should be "always giving thanks to God the Father for everything, in the name of our Lord Jesus Christ" (Ephesians 5:20).

So we should always be praying and always giving thanks. This is how we live in conscious dependence on God. Just as we express our fear of God through our obedience, so we also express it through our prayers and thanksgivings.

ACCEPTING EVERY CIRCUMSTANCE

If we truly acknowledge our dependence on God, we will also accept His providential workings in our lives, even those circumstances that are difficult for us and which we don't understand.

In the last chapter we saw in Psalm 139 how David practiced the conscious presence of God. We also see in that psalm how he trusted in God's sovereign providence in all his life:

> For you created my inmost being;
>> you knit me together in my mother's womb. . . .
> All the days ordained for me
>> were written in your book
>> before one of them came to be. (139:13,16)

The Hebrew word for "inmost being" is literally "kidneys," a word used in Hebrew idiom for the center of emotions and moral sensitivity.

David was essentially saying, "You created my personality." David ascribed to God not only the creation of his physical body, but also the makeup of his personality or temperament. David was not aware of the genetic code we know about today. But he was writing under the inspiration of the Holy Spirit, who designed the genetic code in the first place. Without being aware of how all this takes place, David was telling us how thoroughly God superintends the genetic code and the biological process. God is fully and directly involved in fashioning each of us into the person—both physically and in temperament—that He wants us to be.

I don't know how many generations back we have to go to determine our genetic makeup, but however far it is, God was overseeing the entire process. We are who we are (apart from sin, of course) because God made us that way.

Not only did God create us the way we are, He also ordained life's path for us. Look again at verse 16: "All the days ordained for me were written in your book before one of them came to be." All the experiences of David's life were written down in God's book before he was even born. This refers not simply to God's prior knowledge of our lives, but to His unique plan for each of us. It includes the family into which we were born, the opportunities we have throughout life, all our successes as well as our failures and disappointments. It includes the circumstances we welcome and those we would just as soon avoid. All the events of our lives were written in God's book before we were born.

God is causing all these events—both what we call "good" and what we would call "bad"—to work together for our good, that is, to make us more and more like Christ. That's why we're told to "give thanks in all circumstances, for this is God's will for you in Christ Jesus" (1 Thessalonians 5:18). Note that this instruction immediately follows Paul's exhortation to "pray continually" (verse 17). We should then cultivate the practice of praying continually and always giving thanks, and doing both in all circumstances because we know that even those difficult trials we shrink from are designed for our ultimate good.

This expression of conscious dependence on God is both a characteristic of those who fear God and a means of growing in that fear. We will come to recognize more each day that not only is God the Creator of our world and all that is in it, but He is also its faithful sustainer and the sovereign ruler of all events. And in that knowledge we will bow in awe before Him.

THE SPIRITUAL DIMENSION

The focus of this chapter has been our dependence on God in the temporal areas of life: daily provision of our needs, successful execution of our plans, the decisions and actions of other people that affect us, the providential circumstances that come our way, and even life itself. One obvious major area we haven't touched on is the spiritual dimension of life.

I have reserved this section until last, not because it's the least important, or even the most important, but because this is the dimension of our lives where we're most apt to recognize our dependence on God. Most of us are quite familiar with Jesus' words, "Apart from me you can do nothing" (John 15:5). We readily acknowledge the truth of Jesus' statement, though we apply it imperfectly.

We do pray, however, over the messages we prepare, the Sunday school lessons we teach, the evangelism opportunities we have, and most other activities that are clearly "spiritual" in our eyes. Even in this realm, though, the more trained and experienced we become in these so-called spiritual activities, the more we are tempted to rely on our training and experience rather than on God.

I was meeting with a man in a one-to-one discipling relationship. One day he said he would like to discuss a particular topic the next week. I thought to myself, "I'm so familiar with that topic I could discuss it now without any preparation." So I didn't prepare. Worse, I didn't pray about it. I was depending completely on my knowledge and experience. As I was driving to our appointment, it dawned on me how totally dependent on myself I was that day. I repented of my self-sufficient attitude and acknowledged to God that only He could make our time fruitful.

Have you ever done anything similar? Each of us should examine ourselves to see how much of our spiritual dependence is really in ourselves rather than in God.

Another reason I reserved this section for the end of the chapter is because I want to point out that there really should be no sharp distinction between the spiritual and the temporal. All of life should be spiritual in the sense that all of life should be lived in the fear of God and to the glory of God.

GROWING IN DEPENDENCE ON GOD

Conscious dependence on God is a spiritual habit that must be developed. Before we leave this chapter, take time to consider how you might grow more in this area of your life. Here are some suggestions:

- Take time at the beginning of each day to acknowledge your dependence on God for life and breath and everything else. During this time thank Him for specific blessings, both spiritual and material.
- Think ahead through your day. Acknowledge your dependence on God for all your foreseen activities of the day, asking for His direction and enablement in each of them.
- Commit to Him the *unforeseen* events of the day, again asking for His ability to respond to each in a way pleasing to Him.
- Seek to develop the habit of continually offering throughout the day those short, silent prayers that recognize your powerlessness and His power. Use whatever reminder strategies will help you develop this habit, such as sticky notes in strategic places or the

hourly chime on your wristwatch alarm. Don't consider such methods too childish or "unspiritual" to help you learn this important habit.

- Most of all, pray regularly that God will help you and make you more and more aware that you are in fact dependent on Him for life and breath and everything else.

Finally, don't be discouraged by failure. We have all been too much shaped by our culture of independence, so developing this attitude of dependence on God does take time. It's worth the effort, though, because as you grow in your conscious dependence on Him you'll increasingly experience the joy of fearing God.

Notes

1. John Murray, *The Epistle to the Romans,* vol. 1 of *The New International Commentary on the New Testament* (Grand Rapids: Eerdmans, 1994), 105.

2. John Calvin, *Institutes of the Christian Religion,* ed. John T. McNeill; trans. Ford Lewis Battles, 2 vols. (Philadelphia: Westminster, 1960), 1:41.

3. J. I. Packer, *Evangelism and the Sovereignty of God* (London, InterVarsity, 1961), 11.

13

HIS EXCELLENCE
SHINING FORTH

Bringing Glory to God

THE WESTMINSTER Shorter Catechism rightly answers the question, "What is the chief end of man?" by saying, "Man's chief end is to glorify God, and enjoy him forever." As we continue our studies of the fundamental characteristics of a person who fears God we come now to the summum bonum of them all: *The person who fears God seeks to live all of life to the glory of God.* "Do it all for the glory of God," Paul aptly stated—"whether you eat or drink or whatever you do" (1 Corinthians 10:31).

We cannot truly fear God without seeking His glory. If we recall John Murray's description of the fear of God as consisting of "awe, reverence, honor, and worship," then we see that by definition the fear of God focuses on God's glory.

This connection of the fear of God with the glory of God is brought out clearly in the song of Moses and the Lamb, as the victorious saints sing, "Who will not *fear you,* O Lord, and *bring glory to your name?* For you alone are holy" (Revelation 15:4). We fear the Lord, or reverence Him, by bringing glory to His name. To bring glory to His name involves first of all a *response* to Him, and second a *reflection* of Him to others.

The glory of God is the sum of all His infinite excellence and praise-worthiness set forth in display. To glorify God is first of all to respond properly to this display by ascribing to Him the honor and adoration due Him because of His excellence. We call this *worship* (the subject of our next chapter).

The second way we glorify God is by reflecting His glory to those around us in the way we live our daily lives. Jesus said, "Let your light shine before men in such a way that they may see your good works, and *glorify* your Father who is in heaven" (Matthew 5:16, NASB).[1] And R. C. H. Lenski wrote, "We do all things for 'God's glory' when the excellence of God's attributes is made to shine forth by our actions so that men may see it."[2]

OUR FIRST AIM, OUR TRUE AIM

What is your aim in life? Is it to be successful, or happy, or prosperous in whatever you pursue? Is it to be well thought of as a parent, or as a professional person, or even as a Christian? Does your aim terminate on yourself or your family?

What is your true aim?

If we're to glorify God in the way we live, we must make God's glory our primary aim. All other goals in life, both temporal and spiritual, must be secondary. We must seek first His kingdom and His righteousness before everything else. For example, the Christian student should aim at God's glory ahead of academic excellence or popularity or athletic achievement. That doesn't mean he or she should not strive to be a good student or athlete, or be well thought of by other students. But the student should seek those things with the aim of glorifying God, and only in such ways that God is glorified.

When our son was a junior in a Christian high school, his basketball team went to the state tournament for the first time in the school's history. They lost their first game by one point to the team that eventually won the state championship. The sports editor of our local newspaper, who often comes across as rather hard-bitten and cynical, wrote his next editorial about the game. The thrust of his column was about the outstanding sportsmanship of the Christian team. After commenting on several specific instances of this, he wrote, "This is how basketball was meant to be played."

Did the boys play hard to win? Absolutely. Were they disappointed to lose by one point? Sure they were. Was God glorified in the way they played? Yes. When a crusty sports editor recognizes the difference in sportsmanship between believers and unbelievers, God is glorified. To me as a parent, that article was more valuable than if the boys had brought home the state championship trophy.

What is true of the Christian student should also be true of those of us who are adults. All the activities of life should be pursued with the aim of glorifying God. Note again the all-encompassing breadth of Paul's words in 1 Corinthians 10:31: *"Whatever* you do, do it *all* for the glory of God."* Nothing in life is too ordinary or insignificant to be excluded. Even our eating and drinking is to be done for God's glory. Nothing is so important that we can say it supersedes the pursuit of God's glory.

Are you about to close a lucrative business deal, or make a major career decision, or launch into some other major endeavor? If you fear God, His glory should be your first consideration in your business or your career. All of life is to be lived for the glory of God.

GETTING DOWN TO DETAILS

Again, though, let's get down to those nitty-gritty details of everyday life. In your driving, is your first priority to glorify God or to get where you're going as quickly as possible? When you go shopping, do you treat salespeople in such a way that if they knew you were a Christian, they would see God glorified in you?

Some months ago my wife and I stopped at a bakery with what we thought was a "two for the price of one" coupon. It's a small specialty bakery where a salesclerk waits on each customer. My wife selected two loaves of bread and handed the young lady our coupon. "I'm sorry," the clerk said, "but this coupon is good only at the new store we just opened." The coupon didn't state this limitation, but that's what the bakery intended, and they stuck to it (not good customer relations in my opinion, but that's beside the point of the story). My wife said, "Well, just give me one loaf," and she paid for it. As the clerk entered the transaction in her cash register she said to us, "You people are so nice to me."

"What do you mean?" I asked

"People have been angry at me all day over this coupon deal," she replied, "and you didn't get angry."

Later my wife and I talked about how we could have used that brief conversation as a means of witness, which we had failed to do. But the lesson I learned from that minor shopping event is this: As a Christian I am never "off duty." Even in such an ordinary event as buying a loaf of bread I have an opportunity to either glorify God or shame Him by the way I conduct myself.

So what should be my aim in such a situation? Should it be to glorify God or to vent my disappointment and displeasure at the bakery because of their promotional mistake? I'm not dealing in trivialities here. Events like these make up most of our existence. Life is largely a mosaic of little things: routine events, everyday duties, and ordinary conversations. How we conduct ourselves in these circumstances determines largely whether we glorify God in our lives.

SO OTHERS CAN SEE GOD

It's so easy to let a statement such as "Man's chief end is to glorify God" roll off our tongues without really knowing what we're saying. So a couple of years ago I decided to do a Bible study on the subject of glorifying God. I wanted to find out what the Bible says about it. How do we glorify God? I found a number of answers, some of which we'll consider later in this chapter, but what caught my attention was how our actions toward other people determine whether we glorify God or shame Him.

In Titus 2:4–5, Paul gives a list of what older women should train the younger women to do: "to love their husbands and children, to be self-controlled and pure, to be busy at home, to be kind, and to be subject to their husbands, *so that no one will malign the word of God.*" This last phrase is a remarkable statement. There's nothing extraordinary about any of the items on that list. They're all part of the routine of daily living. Yet Paul implies that failure in any of those areas brings discredit to God and His Word, while a life lived as Paul described will glorify God.

A couple of paragraphs later, Paul says a similar thing about slaves: "Teach slaves to be subject to their masters in everything, to try to please them, not to talk back to them, and not to steal from them, but to show that they can be fully trusted, *so that in every way they will make the teaching about God our Savior attractive*" (Titus 2:9–10).

Have you ever thought about the fact that the way you fulfill your duties at work or the way you perform your professional services can make the teaching about God attractive? Why isn't the gospel more attractive to unbelievers today? Isn't one primary reason the fact that in the everyday affairs of life, we Christians are no different from the general mass of unbelievers? Sure, we don't get drunk or commit adultery, but do we buy and sell, work at our jobs, play at our various sports, or drive on the road in such a way as to glorify God and make His gospel attractive to those who see us?

Paul asked the religious Jews of his day, "You who brag about the law, do you dishonor God by breaking the law? As it is written: 'God's name is blasphemed among the Gentiles because of you'" (Romans 2:23–24). Isn't this true to some degree today? A person with a Christian fish symbol on his car drives in a discourteous or reckless manner and causes God's name to be ridiculed by unbelievers. I read an article in which the son of a prominent minister was quoted as saying, "If God is like my father, I want nothing to do with Him." The father undoubtedly thought he was glorifying God in the pulpit, but he must have been blaspheming Him in the home.

"Nothing in our conduct," wrote New Testament theologian Simon J. Kistemaker,

> should obstruct God's glory from being reflected in us. That is, in everything we do and say, no matter how insignificant, the world should be able to see that we are God's people. Exalting God's glory ought to be our chief purpose in this earthly life.[3]

RECURRING STRUGGLES

For many of us, certain recurring struggles pose a special challenge for us in glorifying God. It may be a tough work environment where there's the temptation to join a crowd of complaining and negative employees. It could be the hassle of a long daily commute to work where you're competing with other drivers for the faster lane. Perhaps it's a difficult home situation because of an unsupportive spouse or children resisting parental authority. One young couple I know have had to deal with a landlord who causes them repeated distress.

Can you think of a recurring situation in your own life where you need to make a special effort to glorify God? For me it's airplane trips. Since a large part of my work and ministry is conference speaking, I make about twenty-five trips a year. Our city has few direct flights to other cities, so I usually take two or more connecting flights going and again returning. That means I have about a hundred airplane boardings every year. With that much exposure and the crowded flights of today, there's ample opportunity to think only of myself. I want to board early enough to make sure I get my carry-on luggage into the overhead compartment before the "inconsiderate" people (with the big bags) take up all the space.

Or if a flight is canceled, I want to be near the front of the line at the airline service counter to get rebooked. After all, I do have to be at my destination by a certain time. At least that's the way I tend to think.

My first priority, though, is not to get to my destination on time, or to get my carry-on bag into the overhead compartment. My first priority is that in all those activities I will glorify God by my behavior.

Recently I was reminded of the bakery incident I referred to a few pages ago, when a flight attendant thanked me for being so nice. Actually I hadn't done anything. What I had *not* done was complain as other passengers around me had because the coffeemaker in the airplane galley wasn't working. This time I was obviously a Christian because I was reading my Bible, so it was a clear opportunity to honor or dishonor God by my behavior.

There's another lesson to be learned from the bakery and airplane incidents. Life is a hassle for most people today. That means abundant opportunities to glorify God in how we treat others or in how we respond to their treatment of us.

In the last chapter I suggested that, as part of expressing your dependence on God, you think through your day, asking God for His direction and enablement in each foreseen activity. Here is where you can make a specific application of that suggestion. If you have a recurring routine where you face the temptation not to glorify God in your behavior, pray over that event beforehand—daily, if it's a daily event—asking God to help you remember that your aim is to glorify Him in that situation. And even for nonrecurring events, if you know of them beforehand, pray about them. Remember that though we are responsible to glorify God in all we do, we are dependent upon the power of the Holy Spirit to work in us and enable us.

GOD'S GLORY AND MY NEIGHBOR'S WELL-BEING

Paul's exhortation to do *everything* to the glory of God was a response to a specific situation in the Corinthian church—namely, whether it was permissible for believers to eat meat previously offered as a sacrifice to an idol. Some of the Corinthians recognized that an idol was nothing, so they had perfect freedom in their consciences to eat the meat.

Others were still so accustomed to idols that when they ate the meat, they associated it with idolatry, and their weak or overly scrupulous consciences were defiled. They felt guilty as if they had sinned, which indeed they had if they had acted against their consciences (see Romans 14:22–23).

Paul agreed with those who felt free to eat the meat, but he wanted them to be considerate of their "weaker" brothers and sisters in Christ. (See 1 Corinthians 8:1–13 and 10:23–33 for Paul's treatment of this problem.) Specifically he said, "Be careful, however, that the exercise of your freedom does not become a stumbling block to the weak" (1 Corinthians 8:9).

Keep this context in mind as we read how Paul concluded his response to this problem:

> So whether you eat or drink or whatever you do, do it all for the glory of God. Do not cause anyone to stumble, whether Jews, Greeks or the church of God—even as I try to please everybody in every way. For I am not seeking my own good but the good of many, so that they may be saved. (1 Corinthians 10:31–33)

Paul here sets forth two broad principles by which we may gauge our conduct and activities: the glory of God and the well-being, especially the spiritual well-being, of our neighbor. "This is the fundamental principle of practical godliness," wrote Matthew Henry, in commenting on this Scripture. "The great end of all practical religion must direct us where particular and express rules are wanting. Nothing must be done against the glory of God and the good of our neighbors."[4]

Charles Hodge wrote in a similar manner: "The first great principle of Christian conduct is to promote the glory of God; the second is to avoid giving offense, or causing men to sin. In other words, love to God and love to men should govern all our conduct."[5] The truth to especially note here is that the glory of God is closely linked with the well-being of our neighbor. We glorify God when we seek our neighbor's well-being.

Who is my neighbor? In the broad sense it is anyone we come in contact with and who we have opportunity to treat as we would like to be treated. Paul, though, was referring specifically to a weaker brother or sister who might be tempted to sin because of our exercise of freedom. What's in view here is not a critical, legalistic Christian whose list of don'ts we might have violated, but rather someone who might himself sin because of our example.

A friend of mine had a fairly serious alcohol problem before he became a Christian. Fortunately the Lord enabled him to overcome it, but as you may know, such people are always one drink away from slipping back into their problem. Once while he was on a business trip with some fellow believers, his friends ordered a beer or a glass of wine with their meal. As I understand the Scriptures regarding the use of alcohol, this was within the bounds of their freedom in Christ. However, they did this in full knowledge of the fact that my friend had an alcohol problem. So what happened? He ordered a beer also. He later told me he had a serious struggle not to return to his old ways. His friends failed to glorify God in that situation because they did not consider his need.

THE COST

Should another person's sin problem or weak conscience deprive me of the enjoyment of my freedom in Christ? To answer that question, we need only go back to our aim in life. Is my aim to glorify God or to exercise my freedom?

Glorifying God will often cost us something. It may cost our freedom in Christ in some situations. It may cost us time, or inconvenience, or not finding space for our carry-on bag on the airplane. It might even cost a lucrative business deal or an opportunity for career advancement. But Jesus said, "Whoever loses his life for me will save it" (Luke 9:24).

We don't lose our lives all at once, however. We lose them over a lifetime, in individual decisions as we choose whether to glorify God or to satisfy our own desires.

Listen again to Jesus: "Truly, truly, I say to you, unless a grain of wheat falls into the earth and dies, it remains by itself alone; but if it dies, it bears much fruit" (John 12:24, NASB). Jesus later said that we glorify God by bearing "much fruit" (John 15:8). But in John 12 He says we bear "much fruit" by falling into the ground and dying—by losing our lives. If we want to glorify God by bearing fruit we must realize it will often cost us something. In some way or other, we will often have to "fall into the earth and die." For this we were created: to glorify God by bearing much fruit, which often means having to fall into the earth and die.

ONLY BY DEPENDING ON CHRIST

This leads us to another essential aspect of glorifying God in our lives: dependence on Christ. It isn't just good conduct or impeccable character that glorifies God. We all know unbelievers who are morally decent, upright, and generous. Sometimes they put us Christians to shame with their superior behavior. Obviously, though, they do not glorify God. If anything they may, even unintentionally, glorify themselves or their reputations. Others praise them for being gracious or generous or kind. Believers should also desire to be known as gracious, generous, and kind, but we should want the praise or glory directed to God and not to us.

How can we exhibit Christian character and conduct that brings glory to God instead of ourselves? It cannot be done unless we're first depending on Christ. Let me show you why.

Jesus said, "If a man remains in me and I in him, he will bear much fruit" (John 15:5). To *remain* in Christ is what we commonly call *abiding* in Christ. How do we abide? By relying or depending on Him for both our righteousness and our spiritual strength (see Philippians 3:9 and 4:13).

The unbeliever who is gracious and generous and kind relies on himself, perhaps influenced by his own moral upbringing, to exhibit those qualities. Sometimes we as Christians do the same, but in this self-reliance we do not bring glory to God. We can bring God glory—what Jesus called bearing fruit—only when we rely on Him for the enabling power to do so.

Paul taught this principle when he prayed that the Philippians would be "filled with the fruit of righteousness that comes through Jesus Christ—to the glory and praise of God" (Philippians 1:11). The only fruit of character that brings glory and praise to God is that which comes through Jesus Christ as we look to Him to work in our lives and enable us to glorify Him.

Peter taught the same principle:

If anyone speaks, he should do it as one speaking the very words of God. If anyone serves, he should do it with the strength God provides, so that in all things God may be praised through Jesus Christ. To him be the glory and the power for ever and ever. Amen. (1 Peter 4:11)

Note what Peter said. If anyone serves, *he should do it with the strength God provides,* so that God—not the person, but God—will be praised or glorified. God is glorified not just by gracious and kind behavior, but by behavior that results from a reliance upon Christ.

God is not glorified by self-generated righteousness or human will power. He is glorified only when we both make it our aim to glorify Him and depend on Christ through His Spirit to enable us to do so. It is God who must bless our intentions and our efforts to glorify Him, and He blesses when we rely on Christ, not ourselves.

NOT SEEKING GLORY FOR OURSELVES

We must not only make it our aim to glorify God; we should also aim *not* to seek glory or praise for ourselves. In Isaiah 42:8, God says, "I am the LORD; that is my name! I will not give my glory to another or my praise to idols." God is jealous for His glory, and He will not share it with us. This speaks not only to our actions but to our motives, which lie totally open before God.

Our problem is that too often we desire—very subtly and perhaps even unconsciously—to share in God's glory. As one of my pastor friends said about his sermons, "I want people to leave the service saying, 'Isn't God great!' but in my heart I hope they also say, 'Isn't Bill great!'" All of us, if we're honest, can identify with my friend Bill. All of us want to look good to others. We enjoy being commended for our Christian character and good behavior.

What should we do, then, when we are commended; when, for example, the flight attendant says, "Thank you for being so nice"? Certainly we should not respond with a self-disparaging remark such as, "Oh, it wasn't me. It was the Lord." Such a statement only draws attention to ourselves. Rather we should simply say "Thank you" to the other person, and in our hearts say "Thank you" to God. God, who knows our hearts and sees our desires to glorify Him, will then use our efforts as He sees fit.

THE STEWARDSHIP OF PAIN

Jesus said we're to let our light shine before men that they may glorify our Father in heaven. We've seen that how we behave before other people is the way we let our light shine. There are also other ways, and one of the most prominent is by our trusting God in times of adversity.

In an earlier book, *Trusting God*, I wrote, "It often seems more difficult to trust God than to obey Him. The moral will of God given to us in the Bible is rational and reasonable. The circumstances in which we trust God often appear irrational and inexplicable."[6] I wrote those words ten years ago, and I still believe them today.

The thrust of *Trusting God* is probably best summed up in the statement that God is infinite in His sovereignty, wisdom, and love. Because of that, we can be sure that whatever adversity we may encounter, God is causing it to work out for our good. With that in mind, I have believed and taught for many years that we are to "give thanks in all circumstances" (1 Thessalonians 5:18), even the difficult ones. We glorify God, then, when we trust Him even when we don't understand what He is doing through the difficult circumstances we encounter. We glorify God when we can say with Job, "Though he slay me, yet will I trust in him" (Job 13:15, KJV).

When we encounter deep heartache or adversity, we may want to deny that God had anything to do with it. This is a common response today and seems to protect God's character, but it does so at the cost of His sovereignty. Another response is to get angry at God, which of course means we question both His love and His justice. Or we may simply try to endure the pain, heroically perhaps, but not in a way honoring to God. Or we can trust Him because we believe that He is sovereign, wise, and loving.

Several years ago I came across another option that builds upon the foundation of trusting God. This option is called the "stewardship of pain," and I'm indebted to the pastor of my long-ago college days for this concept.[7]

We usually think of Christian stewardship in terms of money. Some churches have "stewardship campaigns" during which they seek to get their membership to pledge toward the annual church budget. Then the concept of stewardship was broadened to include our time and talents—or as one slogan puts it, "Be a good steward of your time, talents, and treasure." The idea behind these concepts is that whatever resources God has given us, He has entrusted them to us as stewards to use for His glory.

Now apply that idea to pain, either physical or emotional. If we believe God is sovereignly in control of all circumstances of our lives, then our pain is something He has given to us just as much as our time or talents or treasure. He has entrusted the pain to us as stewards to be used for His glory.

How can we be good stewards of the pain God gives us? One way I've already mentioned is to trust Him even though we don't understand the purpose of the pain. Another way is to ask for and experience the sufficiency of His sustaining grace, as Paul did with his thorn in the flesh, to the extent that we can actually rejoice in our weaknesses so that Christ's power may rest on us (2 Corinthians 12:7–10). We can then, as God gives opportunity, testify to the sufficiency of His sustaining grace. In doing so, however, we want to seek the glory of His grace, not the glory of our ability to endure.

We can also ask God to bring to our attention any opportunities of ministry that our pain may open up. I think immediately of the international ministry that quadriplegic Joni Eareckson Tada has with disabled people and their relatives. I think also of a friend, a woman whose husband divorced her many years ago. Though she went through heartbreaking years as a single parent, today she has a fruitful ministry among other divorced women. She became a steward of her pain.

In one of His postresurrection appearances to the disciples, Jesus said to Peter,

> "I tell you the truth, when you were younger you dressed yourself and went where you wanted; but when you are old you will stretch out your hands, and someone else will dress you and lead you where you do not want to go." Jesus said this to indicate the kind of death by which Peter would glorify God. Then he said to him, "Follow me!" (John 21:18–19)

Apparently Peter died as a martyr. Tradition tells us he was crucified.[8] Whether that is true or not, Jesus said that by his martyrdom Peter would glorify God. He would bring glory to God in his pain. God wants us to do the same thing with whatever pain He has given us.

GLORIFYING GOD BY TRUSTING IN HIS PROMISES

Closely akin to trusting God in our pain is trusting Him to fulfill His promises, even when we can't imagine how He can fulfill them. We all know the story of how God promised a son to Abraham, a promise He did not fulfill for twenty-five years. Although Abraham struggled with doubt (see Genesis 15:2; 16:1–4; 17:17–18), he ultimately believed God. Paul said of him,

> Against all hope, Abraham in hope believed and so became the father of many nations, just as it had been said to him, "So shall your offspring be." Without weakening in his faith, he faced the fact that his body was as good as dead—since he was about a hundred years old—and that Sarah's womb was also dead. Yet he did not waver through unbelief regarding the promise of God, but was strengthened in his faith and *gave glory to God,* being fully persuaded that God had power to do what he had promised. (Romans 4:18–21)

By his faith Abraham gave glory to God. He ascribed to God the sovereign power to do whatever He purposed and to fulfill all the promises He had made. In that way he gave glory to God.

Today you and I have the same privilege to glorify God by believing His promises. In 2 Corinthians 1:20, Paul wrote:

> For no matter how many promises God has made, they are "Yes" in Christ. And so through him the "Amen" is spoken by us *to the glory of God.*

Every promise God has made is "Yes" in Christ. They will all be fulfilled in Him and through Him. So what is our response to be? It is to say "Amen" to the glory of God. The word *amen* means "it is true." When we say "Amen" to God's promises we are saying we believe they will be fulfilled, and in that we glorify God.

It isn't easy to believe His promises that are so long outstanding. After two thousand years we're still awaiting Christ's return. Even in the first century, scoffers were ridiculing that promise (2 Peter 3:1–4).

A promise that has been outstanding for some four thousand years is God's word to Abraham in Genesis 22:18, "And through your offspring all nations on earth will be blessed, because you have obeyed me." I understand that promise to mean that from every nation a significant number of people (as opposed to a token few) will be brought into Christ's kingdom. Yet today we see huge blocks of people—the Muslims, Hindus, and Buddhists being the largest—that seem almost impervious to the gospel. Will we believe God's promise to Abraham despite these long centuries of delay? Will we continue to plead that promise before Him even if we do not see it fulfilled in our lifetimes? Will we say, "Amen, it is true" and so bring glory to God by believing His promise?

As we conclude this chapter, let us again acknowledge this fulfilling and life-stretching truth: To fear God is by definition to aim for His glory. If we're to be God-fearing people then we must make it our aim to glorify Him in all that we are and all that we do.

Notes

1. Sometimes the NIV translation uses the word *praise* instead of *glorify*. When this occurs I have quoted from the NASB to keep the word *glorify* as consistent usage.

2. R. C. H. Lenski, *The Interpretation of St. Paul's First and Second Epistles to the Corinthians* (Minneapolis: Augsburg, 1963), 425.

3. Simon J. Kistemaker, *New Testament Commentary, Exposition of the First Epistle to the Corinthians* (Grand Rapids: Baker, 1993), 358.

4. Matthew Henry, *A Commentary on the Whole Bible* (Old Tappan, N. J.: Revell, n.d.), 6:559.

5. Charles Hodge, *An Exposition of the First Epistle to the Corinthians* (London: Banner of Truth Trust, 1959), pages 202–3.

6. Jerry Bridges, *Trusting God* (Colorado Springs: NavPress, 1988), 17.

7. E. F. Hallock, *Preacher Hallock* (Los Angeles, Acton House, 1976), 101.

8. D. A. Carson gives a helpful discussion of this tradition. D. A. Carson, *The Gospel According to John* (Grand Rapids: Eerdmans, 1991), 679–80.

14

HE IS WORTHY

Fearing God in Worship

ACCORDING TO a recent news magazine article, just 2.8 percent of Brazil's population owns 57 percent of the land—an area greater than Spain, France, Germany, and England combined.[1] Much of this land is unused. Tenant farmers customarily owe one-third of their crops to the landowners, and many of them live in abject poverty. A growing number of them are joining a squatters' movement to wrest some of the unused land for themselves.

Compare the state of affairs in Brazil with David's recognition that God is the owner of the whole earth. He said in Psalm 24:1, "The earth is the LORD's, and everything in it, the world, and all who live in it." In reality, all of us—even the wealthiest people in the world—are all like the tenant farmers in Brazil. God owns everything; we own nothing.

In fact, according to David, we don't even own ourselves. Not only does *everything* in the world belong to God, but also *all who live in it.* This is doubly true for the Christian, for as Paul says in 1 Corinthians 6:19–20, "You are not your own; you were bought at a price." God owns us first by creation and again by redemption.

The recognition that God is the ultimate owner of everything, and that we are only stewards of that which He has given to us, lies at the heart of the fear of God. It is a recognition of our dependence upon Him and our responsibility to Him, and thus provides the basis for our worship of Him.

Job was a man who, according to the testimony of God Himself, feared God (Job 1:8). He was also a very wealthy man, "the greatest man among all the people of the East" (Job 1:2–3). We know how God allowed Satan to attack Job so that he lost all of his children and all of his possessions in a single day. How did Job respond?

> Job got up and tore his robe and shaved his head. Then he fell to the ground in worship and said:
> "Naked I came from my mother's womb,
> > and naked I will depart.
> The LORD gave and the LORD has taken away;
> > may the name of the LORD be praised."
> In all this, Job did not sin by charging God with wrongdoing.
> (Job 1:20–22)

Job's response was to worship God by acknowledging that God was really the owner of all that he possessed and that God had a right both to give and to take away. Consequently, Job did not become angry at God and charge Him with wrongdoing. Instead he *worshiped* God because he feared Him.

What is worship? In Scripture the word *worship* is used to denote both an overall way of life and a specific activity. When the prophet Jonah said, "I am a Hebrew and I worship the LORD, the God of heaven, who made the sea and the land" (Jonah 1:9), he was speaking of his whole manner of life. In contrast, Psalm 100:2 says, "Worship the LORD with gladness; come before him with joyful songs." The psalmist there speaks of a specific activity of praising God. This is the sense in which we normally use the word *worship* today.

These two concepts of worship—a broad one and a more narrow, specific one—correspond to the two ways by which we glorify God that I mentioned in the previous chapter. We glorify God by ascribing to Him the honor and adoration due Him—the narrow concept of worship. We also glorify God by reflecting His glory to others—the broader, way-of-life manner of worship.

WORSHIP AS A WAY OF LIFE

Look at how this broader concept is taught in a familiar verse from Paul: "Therefore, I urge you, brothers, in view of God's mercy, to offer your bodies as living sacrifices, holy and pleasing to God—this is your spiritual act of worship" (Romans 12:1). To offer our bodies as living sacrifices is to worship God. That Paul intended not just the physical body, but one's entire being, is implied from Romans 6:13, where he speaks of offering ourselves to God and the parts of our bodies to Him as instruments of righteousness.

To offer your body to God necessarily involves offering your mind, emotions, and will to Him also. It is the wholehearted dedication to God of heart, mind, will, words, and deeds—in fact all that you are, have, and do. It is a total way of life. Paul called that our spiritual act of worship.

To attempt to worship God in only the narrow sense of praising Him without seeking to worship Him in our whole way of life is hypocrisy. Jesus rebuked the Pharisees because they were going through outward motions of worship, but their hearts were not committed to God. "You hypocrites!" He said. "Isaiah was right when he prophesied about you: 'These people honor me with their lips, but their hearts are far from me. They worship me in vain; their teachings are but rules taught by men'" (Matthew 15:7–9).

I cannot judge the hearts of people, but it seems many of our churches today are full of this kind of hypocrite: people who appear to worship God on Sunday but live for themselves the rest of the week. I'm not suggesting they are living a lifestyle of gross sin. On the contrary, most of them live highly respectable lives; otherwise they wouldn't be in church on Sunday morning. But they do not live to the glory of God during the week. They live for the fulfillment of themselves and their goals.

John Calvin had this comprehensive sense of worship in mind when he described the worship of God as "the beginning and foundation of righteousness."[2] In the paragraph where he says this, Calvin uses *worship* and *the fear of God* almost interchangeably. In that broad sense, this entire book is about worship. When we fear God we will worship Him, both as a way of life and in the more narrow sense of praising and adoring Him.

From here on in this chapter we'll focus on the more limited definition of worship, but it's important to understand that a lifestyle of worship is the necessary foundation for all our praise and adoration, both privately and corporately.

WORSHIP AS PRAISE AND ADORATION

What really is this worship, in the sense of praise and adoration? The Puritan Stephen Charnock called it "nothing else but a rendering to God the *honor* that is due him."[3] John MacArthur defined it as *"honor* and *adoration* directed to God."[4] A. W. Tozer gave a more expanded meaning. He said that God "wants to cultivate within us the *adoration* and *admiration* of which He is worthy. He wants us to be *astonished* at the inconceivable elevation and magnitude and splendor of Almighty God!"[5] Note the words I emphasized in these quotations: *honor, adoration, admiration,* and *astonishment.* These are also words we use to describe the fear of God.

One of the best biblical descriptions of worship is Psalm 29:1–2.

> Ascribe to the LORD, O mighty ones,
>> ascribe to the LORD glory and strength.
> Ascribe to the LORD the glory due his name;
>> worship the LORD in the splendor of his holiness.

This is the essence of worship: *Ascribe to the Lord the glory due His name.* Before we can do that, however, we have to understand something of the glory that is *due* Him. We have to begin grasping His greatness, sovereignty, holiness, wisdom, and love. We have to meditate on and pray over passages such as Isaiah 6:1-8, Isaiah 40, Daniel 4:34-35, Psalm 104, and 1 John 4:8–10.

In the Daniel passage, notice how Nebuchadnezzar worshiped God after his seven years of animal-like insanity:

> At the end of that time, I, Nebuchadnezzar, raised my eyes toward
> heaven, and my sanity was restored. Then I praised the Most High;
> I honored and glorified him who lives forever.
>> His dominion is an eternal dominion;
>>> his kingdom endures from generation to generation.
>> All the peoples of the earth
>>> are regarded as nothing.
>> He does as he pleases
>>> with the powers of heaven
>>> and the peoples of the earth.
>> No one can hold back his hand
>>> or say to him: "What have you done?" (Daniel 4:34–35)

Nebuchadnezzar praised and honored and glorified God. He acknowledged the eternalness of His person, His dominion or rulership, and His absolute sovereignty. He then goes on to exalt God's righteousness and justice:

> Now I, Nebuchadnezzar, praise and exalt and glorify the King of
> heaven, because everything he does is right and all his ways are just.
> And those who walk in pride he is able to humble. (4:37)

Nebuchadnezzar didn't quibble with God over the severe chastening he had received at God's hand. Rather he praised God's justice. He knew he had received what he justly deserved. At the same time we can reasonably infer that he praised God for His mercy, which he had experienced in being restored to his kingdom and very likely in being brought into a genuine conversion encounter with the living God.

The lesson here is that in order to render heartfelt worship to God, we must be gripped in the depth of our being by His majesty, holiness, and love; otherwise our praise and adoration may be no more than empty words.

Isn't this one reason why much of our worship today is so anemic and heartless? We aren't likely to have the kind of encounter experienced by Nebuchadnezzar, or even by Isaiah or Jacob or Peter or John. But we can encounter God in His Word as we meditate on it and pray over it, asking the Holy Spirit to reveal to our hearts the glory of God as seen in His infinite attributes. We must do this if we're to worship God in a manner of which He is worthy.

HEARTFELT THANKSGIVING

It has been said that we praise God for who He *is* and thank Him for what He *does* for us. Such a precise distinction between praise and thanksgiving probably isn't wise, but the statement does call our attention to the fact that thanksgiving is an important aspect of worship.

In Romans 1:18, Paul speaks of "all the godlessness and wickedness of men" which has called forth God's wrath. Then he tells us how all this ungodliness and wickedness began: These people "neither glorified him as God *nor gave thanks to him*" (1:21). Their wickedness was a result of their failure to worship God—their failure to give God the glory and thanksgiving due to Him.

Luke's account of ten lepers who cried out to Jesus to heal them is an insightful story that helps us see how important thanksgiving is to our worship. Jesus told them, "Go show yourselves to the priests." As they went on their way they were healed.

One of them, when he saw he was healed, came back, praising God in a loud voice. He threw himself at Jesus' feet and thanked him—and he was a Samaritan.

Jesus asked, "Were not all ten cleansed? Where are the other nine? Was no one found to return and give praise to God except this foreigner?" (Luke 17:15–18)

Ten were cleansed; only one returned to give thanks. Jesus emphasized the uncalled-for disparity between the many and the one: *Where were the other nine?* The lesson is obvious. God does note when we take time to thank Him and when we don't.

I believe God also takes note of the sincerity and depth of meaning we put into giving thanks to Him. The expression "Thank you" covers a vast range of situations, from the most ordinary spur-of-the-moment kind to those with eternal significance. I might say "Thank you" to a friend for lending me his pen for a moment. I use the same words to thank God for my salvation, which is of eternal consequence. How can I distinguish between these two infinitely different deeds of kindness when I must use the same words to express my thanks in both situations?

The answer lies in the depth of meaning we put into those words. To say with deep feeling to my friend who lends me his pen, "Thank you with all my heart" would be effusive and inappropriate. He would probably think I was a bit strange. But to say those words to God with deep feeling is not only appropriate but the very minimum we should do.

Being healed of leprosy—or of cancer in our time—lies in between the lending of a pen and the gift of eternal life. Obviously it is much more significant than borrowing a pen. At the same time it is vastly *less* significant than having eternal life. If we had to choose between being healed of cancer and receiving eternal life, the decision for any Christian would be easy. Yet how often do we express our thanksgiving to God for the gift of eternal life with as much depth of feeling as the one leper who "came back, praising God in a loud voice" and who "threw himself at Jesus' feet and thanked him"?

Before we leave this story, I call your attention again to the close relationship between praise and thanksgiving. Look back at the verses quoted above, and notice how the healed leper praised God—*and* thanked Jesus.

David also combined praise and thanksgiving in his beautiful prayer of worship as recorded in 1 Chronicles 29:10–14.

> David praised the LORD in the presence of the whole assembly, saying,
>> "Praise be to you, O LORD,
>>> God of our father Israel,
>>> from everlasting to everlasting.
>> Yours, O LORD, is the greatness and the power
>>> and the glory and the majesty and the splendor,
>>> for everything in heaven and earth is yours.
>> Yours, O LORD, is the kingdom;
>>> you are exalted as head over all.
>> Wealth and honor come from you;
>>> you are the ruler of all things.
>> In your hands are strength and power
>>> to exalt and give strength to all.
>> Now, our God, we give you thanks,
>>> and praise your glorious name.
> "But who am I, and who are my people, that we should be able to give as generously as this? Everything comes from you, and we have given you only what comes from your hand."

David began by praising God for His surpassing glory. Note how he heaps up words of praise and adulation: *greatness, power, glory, majesty,* and *splendor.* David was not simply being eloquent. He was pouring forth heartfelt praise. He acknowledged here what we've already seen in Psalm 24:1—everything in heaven and earth belongs to God. He recognized God's sovereignty: "You are exalted as head over all." And he confessed that all wealth and honor come from God. Then he thanked God for the ability to be so generous. In fact he explicitly affirmed that everything he and his officials had given toward building the temple was only a returning to God what had first come from His hand.

It's difficult to separate thanksgiving from praise in our worship of God. A better practice is to join them, as we see in Psalm 100:

> Enter his gates with thanksgiving
> and his courts with praise;
> give thanks to him and praise his name.
> For the LORD is good and his love endures forever;
> his faithfulness continues through all generations. (100:4–5)

PRIVATE WORSHIP

Both private and corporate worship—that which we do individually and that which we do with other believers—are taught in Scripture. For example, David says in Psalm 69:30, "I will praise God's name in song and glorify him with thanksgiving." Here David refers to his own personal worship.

Again in Psalm 86:12, he says, "I will praise you, O Lord my God, with all my heart; I will glorify your name forever." This particular example of David's private worship follows immediately after his prayer that God would give him an undivided heart to fear His name (verse 11). Once again we see the connection between the fear of God and the worship of God.

Actually the fear of God and the worship of Him feed each other. The more we fear God—bowing before Him in reverential awe—the more we'll be compelled to worship Him. But it's also true that spending time worshiping Him will stimulate and increase our fear of God.

The vitality and genuineness of corporate worship is to a large degree dependent upon the vitality of our individual private worship.

If we aren't spending time daily worshiping God, we're not apt to contribute to the corporate experience of worship. If we aren't worshiping God during the week, how can we expect to genuinely participate in it on Sunday morning? We may indeed go through the motions and think we have worshiped, but how can we honor and adore One on Sunday whom we have not taken time to praise and give thanks to during the week?

I agree with John MacArthur who wrote,

> Music and liturgy can assist or express a worshiping heart, but they cannot make a non-worshiping heart into a worshiping one. The danger is that they can give a non-worshiping heart the sense of having worshiped.
>
> So the crucial factor in worship in the church is not the form of worship, but the state of the hearts of the saints. If our corporate worship isn't the expression of our individual worshiping lives, it is unacceptable. If you think you can live anyway you want and then go to church on Sunday morning and turn on worship with the saints, you're wrong.[6]

In contrast to the once-a-week worshiper (and that term itself is an oxymoron), David worshiped God continually. "I will extol the LORD at *all* times," he said; "his praise will *always* be on my lips" (Psalm 34:1).

Again in Psalm 145:1–2 he told God,

> I will exalt you, my God the King;
> I will praise your name for ever and ever.
> *Every day* I will praise you
> and extol your name for ever and ever.

He goes on to say, "Great is the LORD and most worthy of praise; his greatness no one can fathom" (verse 3). In these words we sense the depth of his feeling, an emotion that could not be "pumped up" with a once-a-week visit to the house of God.

ESSENTIALS OF WORSHIP

Jesus spelled out the first essential of worship when He said to the Samaritan woman, "God is spirit, and his worshipers must worship in spirit and in truth" (John 4:24).

The "spirit" in which Jesus says we must worship God is the human spirit. It is what Paul often refers to as the heart. Worship is not just an external act. True worship must come from the heart and reflect a sincere attitude and desire.

"Without the heart," Stephen Charnock wrote,

> it is no worship; it is a stage play, an acting a part without being that person really which is acted by us: a hypocrite, in the notion of the word, is a stage player. . . . We may be truly said to worship God, though we [lack] perfection; but we cannot be said to worship him if we [lack] sincerity.[7]

Jesus said we must also worship "in truth." Our worship must be in harmony with what God has revealed about Himself in His Word. It is possible to have zeal without knowledge (Romans 10:2). For example, if we stress only one side of God's attributes—say, His mercy and love—without also stressing His sovereignty and holiness, we're not worshiping in truth.

A second essential in worship is that we must always come to God through Christ. Paul is explicit about this: "*In him* and *through faith in him* we may approach God with freedom and confidence" (Ephesians 3:12); "For *through him* we both [Jews and Gentiles alike] have access to the Father by one Spirit" (2:18). And having come through Christ, we can approach God with confidence: "We have confidence to enter the Most Holy Place by the blood of Jesus" (Hebrews 10:19).

In our earlier discussion of God's holiness we saw that in the Old Testament era there were three restrictions on entering God's Most Holy Place in the temple: *Only* the high priest could enter, and *only* once a year, and *only* with the blood of atonement (Hebrews 9:5). But now, says the writer to the Hebrews, all believers may enter. In fact we have *confidence* to enter, implying free and continuous access.

So two restrictions have been removed, while one remains: *We still must come by the blood.* Only now it is not the blood of a goat, but the blood of Jesus. Though we have been born again, and though our sins—past, present, and future—have been forgiven, we must still approach God through the merit of Jesus Christ. We are never of ourselves worthy to come before a holy God.

Nineteenth-century theologian Archibald Alexander composed a devotional exercise, apparently for his own private use, that included these words:

> I am deeply convinced that my best duties have fallen
> far short of the perfection of Thy law, and have been
> so mingled with sin in the performance, that I might
> justly be condemned for the most fervent prayer I
> ever made.[8]

Dr. Alexander's observation about himself is true of every one of us. Because of the continued presence of indwelling sin in our hearts and our consequent lack of perfect obedience, we are never, of ourselves, worthy to come into the presence of God and worship. We must always come through Christ. Our "spiritual sacrifices," as Peter said, are "acceptable to God *through Jesus Christ*" (1 Peter 2:5).

The writer of Hebrews taught this same truth: *"Through Jesus,* therefore, let us continually offer to God a sacrifice of praise—the fruit of lips that confess his name" (Hebrews 13:15). It is always through Jesus that we offer to God a sacrifice of praise. Our most fervent expressions of worship, either in prayer or song, are unacceptable to God if they are not offered through His Son.

A third essential to worship is a heart free from cherished sin. David said, "If I had cherished sin in my heart, the Lord would not have listened" (Psalm 66:18). To cherish a sin is to hold on to some sinful disposition or course of action we know is wrong. Perhaps you have been wronged by someone and you know you should forgive as the Lord forgave you. Yet you are unwilling to let go of that unforgiving spirit. Instead you cherish it and nourish it. You cannot truly worship God when you are in that state.

Perhaps you are involved in some unethical business practice that may be barely legal but does not meet the test of love, of treating others as you would like to be treated. In your innermost heart you know the practice is wrong but you're unwilling to give it up because of the financial cost. Or perhaps you love to gossip. The Holy Spirit has convicted you of it many times, but you enjoy it. You get a perverse delight out of running down other people because it makes you feel good about yourself. If you're resisting the convicting work of the Holy Spirit, you are cherishing sin in your heart, and you cannot truly worship God.

Let me emphasize that there's a difference between struggling with sin and cherishing it. You may genuinely desire to forgive another person. In your mind you have said many times, "I forgive her," yet your own corrupt heart keeps bringing it up. You cry out to God to change *you,* but for some reason He allows you to keep struggling. That is not cherishing sin; that is warring against it. What you need to do in that case is to appropriate the blood of Christ to cleanse your conscience so you may worship freely (see Hebrews 9:14).

HELP IN OUR WORSHIP

Perhaps the idea of private worship is new to you. You have always thought of worship as something to do on Sunday morning at church with other believers. Now you see the importance of private, daily worship, but you don't know how to begin.

Of course the first thing you have to do is select a time. I have my personal worship in conjunction with my daily Bible reading and prayer, which I do each day before breakfast. As I mentioned in chapter 7, I begin my prayer with words designed to capture both the awe and the intimacy with which we should relate to God. I consciously and deliberately enter His presence through the merit of Christ, acknowledging my sinfulness, pleading His cleansing blood, and confessing that only through Christ can I call God my Father.

The joy of realizing my sins are forgiven and that I am accepted by the Father through Christ lifts my soul to praise and thanksgiving. I often use a biblical prayer of praise such as David's in 1 Chronicles 29:10–14. I take time to thank God for my salvation and for the way He has led in my Christian life throughout the years. I consider where I could have been had God not intervened in my life at various points.

I reflect on my humble beginnings as a child growing up during the depression years in a working class family and consider where God has brought me. I think of Jacob's words that describe so accurately my own life's story: "I am unworthy of all the kindness and faithfulness you have shown your servant. I had only my staff when I crossed this Jordan, but now I have become two groups" (Genesis 32:10). I acknowledge my absolute dependence on God for life and daily provision. I thank Him for a godly wife and for children who follow Him.

As I read the Bible, I often come across passages of Scripture that remind me of some truth about God, or perhaps even reveal to me something new. When that happens I pause once again and worship.

Sometimes I use a book titled *The Valley of Vision,* a collection of Puritan prayers and devotions to stimulate my own sense of praise. Here's an example:

> GREAT GOD,
> In public and private, in sanctuary and home,
> may my life be steeped in prayer,

filled with the spirit of grace and supplication,
each prayer perfumed with the incense of atoning blood.
Help me, defend me, until from praying ground
I pass to the realm of unceasing praise.
Urged by my need,
Invited by thy promises,
Called by thy Spirit,
I enter thy presence, worshiping thee with godly fear,
awed by thy majesty, greatness, glory,
but encouraged by thy love.
I am all poverty as well as all guilt,
having nothing of my own with which to repay thee,
But I bring Jesus to thee in the arms of faith,
pleading His righteousness to offset my iniquities,
rejoicing that he will weigh down the scales for me,
and satisfy thy justice.
I bless thee that great sin draws out great grace,
that although the least sin deserves infinite punishment
because done against an infinite God,
yet there is mercy for me,
for where guilt is most terrible,
there thy mercy in Christ is most free and deep.
Bless me by revealing to me more of his saving merits,
by causing thy goodness to pass before me,
by speaking peace to my contrite heart;
Strengthen me to give thee no rest
until Christ shall reign supreme within me,
in every thought, word, and deed,
in a faith that purifies the heart,
overcomes the world, works by love,
fastens me to thee, and ever clings to the cross.[9]

Some people use hymns as a part of their daily worship. A. W. Tozer kept a stack of hymn books in his study for that purpose. Other people use one of many devotional books available. Whatever helps you and is biblical, you should use. The important thing is that you worship God in spirit and truth.

Submission to God is also an important part of worship. We've already seen this demonstrated in the life of Job when he submitted to God's providential dealings. (Although Satan was the agent of Job's trials, their ultimate cause is attributed to God Himself [see Job 1:21 and 42:11]).

After the death of my first wife, a friend passed on to me a little saying by an unknown author that helps me express my submission to God:

> Lord, I am willing
> To receive what You give;
> To lack what You withhold;
> To relinquish what You take;
> To suffer what You inflict;
> To be what You require.

I keep a copy of this in my prayer notebook and pray over it several times a week. I've also added another sentence: "And to do what You send me to do."

Our posture in worship is also important. Old Testament passages that speak of worship often speak of bowing down. For example, Psalm 95:6 says, "Come, let us bow down in worship, let us kneel before the LORD our Maker" (see also Deuteronomy 8:19; 2 Chronicles 20:18 and 29:28; Job 1:20; Daniel 3:5; Ephesians 3:14; Revelation 22:8).

Kneeling or bowing down is a physical expression of reverence and submission. I don't want to imply that you must always bow down to worship effectively, though I think we should do it frequently. The important thing is your attitude of heart. I often do my Bible reading and part of my worship sitting at our dining table. Because of a peculiar deformity in my lower backbone, I'm more comfortable if I slouch down in my chair. When I pause to worship, however, I like to sit up straight with both feet on the floor. Even though this is uncomfortable, I want to do it as a sign of reverence to God.

CORPORATE WORSHIP

As I mentioned earlier, the Scriptures teach both private and corporate worship. David, who said in Psalm 34:1, "I will extol the LORD at all times," also said a few sentences later, "Glorify the LORD with me; let us exalt his name together" (34:3). If you scan a list of Scripture texts with the word *worship* in them, you'll see that a majority refer to corporate worship.

Someone has said that the fear of the Lord ought to control completely worship services of the church. That means our corporate worship services ought to be characterized by awe, reverence, adoration, honor, and love for God. Above all it means that God and His glory should be the focal point of our services.

I asked one person to evaluate the worship services of his church. As he reflected on it, he said, "I think our services are more oriented to the church family than to worship." This was an insightful observation. His church is a very caring community of believers, and a significant part of their Sunday morning service is given to what has been called "body life." Other churches might have evangelism or teaching as the focal point.

It isn't my intent to make a judgment statement about any church service that emphasizes evangelism or body life or teaching. I do believe that such a service should not be called a *worship* service. A worship service should focus on God. This doesn't mean that ministry to members of the body or even to unbelievers will not occur. It does mean that the emphasis is on worship of God, ascribing to Him the praise, adoration, and thanksgiving that are due Him.

I'm not an authority on corporate worship, but the following observations seem self-evident if our services are intended to be times of worship:

- Music should have as its aim the rendering of praise and honor to God, rather than meeting the audience's aesthetic or emotional desires.
- Offerings should be a tangible recognition that all we have comes from God's hand, rather than being simply the way to finance the church budget.
- Corporate prayer should acknowledge God's sovereign power and our own helplessness and dependence on Him, rather than being simply a presentation of various congregational needs.
- Sermons should be given and received as the authoritative Word of God to be submitted to and obeyed, not just a means of stimulating our theological intellects or meeting our felt needs.

To sum it up, every aspect of a worship service ought to in some way exalt and honor God. The benefits to us as worshipers should be secondary.

WORSHIP IN HEAVEN

The book of Revelation includes much that is hard to understand. One thing is clear, however. Worship is a very prominent part of the book. I can think of no better way to understand what worship means than to observe how it is conducted in heaven.

With that in mind let me include four examples from Revelation. Read them slowly, carefully, and prayerfully, asking God to create in you and in your church the same excitement about worship that there is in heaven.

Each of the four living creatures had six wings and was covered with eyes all around, even under his wings. Day and night they never stop saying:

> "Holy, holy, holy
> is the Lord God Almighty,
> who was, and is, and is to come."

Whenever the living creatures give glory, honor and thanks to him who sits on the throne and who lives for ever and ever, the twenty-four elders fall down before him who sits on the throne, and worship him who lives for ever and ever. They lay their crowns before the throne and say:

> "You are worthy, our Lord and God,
> to receive glory and honor and power,
> for you created all things,
> and by your will they were created
> and have their being." (4:8–11)

Then I looked and heard the voice of many angels, numbering thousands upon thousands, and ten thousand times ten thousand. They encircled the throne and the living creatures and the elders. In a loud voice they sang:

> "Worthy is the Lamb, who was slain,
> to receive power and wealth and wisdom and strength
> and honor and glory and praise!"

Then I heard every creature in heaven and on earth and under the earth and on the sea, and all that is in them, singing:

> "To him who sits on the throne and to the Lamb
> be praise and honor and glory and power,
> for ever and ever!"

The four living creatures said, "Amen," and the elders fell down and worshiped. (5:11–14)

All the angels were standing around the throne and around the elders and the four living creatures. They fell down on their faces before the throne and worshiped God, saying:

> "Amen!
> Praise and glory
> and wisdom and thanks and honor
> and power and strength
> be to our God for ever and ever.
> Amen!" (7:11–12)

The twenty-four elders and the four living creatures fell down and worshiped God, who was seated on the throne. And they cried:

> "Amen, Hallelujah!"

Then a voice came from the throne, saying:

> "Praise our God,
>   all you his servants,
> you who fear him,
>   both small and great!" (19:4–5)

Hear again His voice from the throne: *Praise our God, all you His servants, you who fear Him.*

Do you fear God? Then worship Him, both privately and together with other believers. Our chief end is to glorify God and enjoy Him forever. Worship enables us to do both. There is no better way to enjoy the fear of God than to worship Him.

GROWING IN WORSHIP

I've offered a number of suggestions in this chapter for both private and corporate worship. If we're to benefit from them we must ask ourselves some hard questions:

1. Have I presented myself and all that I have to God as a living sacrifice, so that my way of life is a life of worship?
2. Do I practice private worship during the week?
3. Do I take time daily to thank God for all His blessings to me?
4. Is there some "cherished" sin, some practice I'm unwilling to give up, that hinders my worship?
5. Do I seek to enter wholeheartedly and "in spirit and truth" into my church's corporate worship? Or do I simply go through the motions without really worshiping?

None of us will score perfectly on these questions. That is not their intent. Rather they're designed to help us honestly assess ourselves and pinpoint areas of our lives that need improvement. Only then, and as we take steps to improve, will this book be of benefit to us.

Notes

1. Linda Robinson, "Latin Robin Hood," *U.S. News & World Report,* June 23, 1997, 30.

2. John Calvin, *Institutes of the Christian Religion,* ed. John T. McNeill; trans. Ford Lewis Battles, 2 vols. (Philadelphia: Westminster, 1960), 1:377.

3. Stephen Charnock, *The Existence and Attributes of God* (1853, reprint, Grand Rapids: Baker, 1979), 1:212.

4. John MacArthur, *The Ultimate Priority* (Chicago: Moody, 1983), 14.

5. A. W. Tozer, *Whatever Happened to Worship?* (Camp Hill, Pa.: Christian Publications, 1985), 26.

6. MacArthur, *The Ultimate Priority,* 104.

7. Charnock, *The Existence and Attributes of God,* 225–6. I am indebted to MacArthur for calling attention to Charnock's statement by quoting it himself.

8. Quoted by Henry A. Boardman, *The "Higher Life" Doctrine of Sanctification Tried by the Word of God* (1877, reprint, Harrisonburg, Va.: Sprinkle Publications, 1996), 268.

9. Arthur Burnet, ed., *The Valley of Vision: A Collection of Puritan Prayers & Devotions* (Carlisle, Pa.: Banner of Truth Trust, n.d.), 148.

15

SPECIAL BLESSINGS, SPECIAL HONOR

Enjoying Him Now and Forever

WHEN THE WRITERS of the Westminster Shorter Catechism taught us how important it is "to glorify God and enjoy Him forever," they did not say these are mankind's chief *ends,* but our chief *end.* The word is singular. Both glorifying God and enjoying Him together form one aim.

There was a time when I did regard them as two different aims, even assigning different time frames to them. I was expected, so I thought, to glorify God in this life, and then in eternity I would get to enjoy Him.

Perhaps I unconsciously thought of these two parts of our aim in the same way some people think about work and retirement. You *work* for forty or so years, then you get to *enjoy* being retired, but "ne'er the twain shall meet." Don't expect to enjoy your work and avoid all work in your retirement.

The truth is, though, we cannot glorify God—either by our lives or by worship—unless we are enjoying Him. How could you praise someone whom you don't enjoy? How could you genuinely seek to honor someone by your conduct merely out of a sense of obligation?

As we probe these questions, we can see that glorifying God and enjoying Him are really two sides of the same coin.

John Piper even goes a bit further. He says, "The chief end of man is to glorify God *by* enjoying him forever."[1] Piper is fond of saying, "God is most glorified in me when I am most satisfied in Him." That is, to the extent we find our delight in God, to that extent we glorify Him.

GAZING UPON GOD—AND WANTING MORE

David speaks of his delight in God in Psalm 27:4.

> One thing I ask of the LORD,
>   this is what I seek:
> that I may dwell in the house of the LORD
>   all the days of my life,
> to gaze upon the beauty of the LORD
>   and to seek him in his temple.

David asked one thing of the Lord: to enjoy Him. David wanted to *gaze* upon His beauty and *seek* Him in His temple. To gaze is to look intently with wonder or admiration. A young man discovers the girl of his dreams across the aisle at church one Sunday. Before he even begins to initiate a relationship, he seeks inconspicuous opportunities to gaze upon her beauty. This is what David wanted to do, except he was unabashed about it. He wanted to gaze upon the beauty of God's revealed glory, and he wanted everyone to know it.

David says next in Psalm 27:4 that he wanted to *seek* God. To seek is to search for something of value or something greatly desired. David sought a relationship with God. He wanted to enjoy God and gaze upon His beauty.

We might not otherwise think of it this way, but Psalm 27:4 is really a description of the fear of the Lord. Recall Sinclair Ferguson's description of fearing the Lord: "that indefinable mixture of reverence, fear, pleasure, joy, and awe which fills our hearts when we realize who God is and what he has done for us." That is the one thing David wanted. He wanted to enjoy the fear of God in the fullest sense of the term.

Psalm 27:4 is not an isolated text. David wrote in a similar fashion in Psalm 63:1–4.

> O God, you are my God,
>> earnestly I seek you;
> my soul thirsts for you,
>> my body longs for you,
> in a dry and weary land
>> where there is no water.
> I have seen you in the sanctuary
>> and beheld your power and your glory.
> Because your love is better than life,
>> my lips will glorify you.
> I will praise you as long as I live,
>> and in your name I will lift up my hands.

If anything David is even more expressive here than in Psalm 27. He *earnestly* seeks God; his soul *thirsts* for Him, and his body *longs* for Him. Why does he use such intense words? David had beheld God's power and glory and had experienced His love. He had experienced and enjoyed the fear of the Lord. As a result, he wanted even more to enjoy God and praise Him.

Throughout this book I've offered practical suggestions for growing in the fear of God. Let me now give you an underlying principle: You grow in the fear of the Lord by gazing upon the beauty of His attributes and by seeking an ever-deepening relationship with Him. All the practical steps I've suggested are simply the working out of that principle.

To enjoy God is to enjoy the fear of God.

The publisher of this book is WaterBrook Press. That name is taken from Psalm 42:1 (NASB): "As the deer pants for the water brooks, so my soul pants for Thee, O God." The psalmist continues in verse 2, "My soul thirsts for God, for the living God; when shall I come and appear before God?" Once again we see this intense longing for God. We long for God's blessings; the psalmist longed for God Himself. He wanted to experience the reality of a relationship with God. Like the apostle Paul, he wanted to "know Him" (Philippians 3:10).

A similar yearning of God's people is expressed by the prophet Isaiah:

> Yes, LORD, walking in the way of your laws,
>> we wait for you;
> your name and renown
>> are the desire of our hearts.
> My soul yearns for you in the night;
>> in the morning my spirit longs for you.
> When your judgments come upon the earth,
>> the people of the world learn righteousness. (Isaiah 26:8–9)

God's "name and renown" here speaks of His glory; so God's glory was the desire of their hearts. Notice then how Isaiah associates a desire for God's glory with a desire for God Himself. He yearned for Him in the night, and as he awakened in the morning his spirit longed for God.

We cannot long for God's glory to be manifested unless we also long *for Him.*

We cannot glorify God unless we enjoy Him.

At the beginning of this book I wrote that the fear of God is better described than defined. Since then I've tried to paint word pictures of what it means to fear God. We looked at God's glory as He has revealed Himself to us in His greatness, holiness, wisdom, and love. We examined key characteristics of a person who fears God, all of them culminating in the highest of all: glorifying God and enjoying Him forever.

Now we see that the fear of God, the glorifying of God, and the enjoyment of God are so closely intertwined that we cannot separate them. That's why we can speak of *the joy of fearing God* and be both theologically and experientially correct.

Let's be honest, though. Do Scriptures such as Psalm 27:4 describe you? If you're reading this chapter and thinking, "I don't know what he's talking about. I sure don't desire God like David did," I suggest you begin to pray over that verse or similar Scriptures, asking God to make them a reality in your life.

You may need to pray as I sometimes do: "Lord, my sin is more real to me than You are. Help me to know You and desire You as David did." And remember that I'm setting before you the ideal we should aim for. None of us is there yet, but we should keep pursuing it.

PROMISED BLESSINGS

Before we wrap up these studies, let's explore more reasons why we can enjoy the fear of God.

We read in Psalm 112:1, *"Blessed* is the man who fears the LORD, who finds great delight in his commands," and again in Psalm 128:4, "Thus is the man *blessed* who fears the LORD." There is blessing in the fear of the Lord.

To be blessed by God is no small thing. Imagine enjoying the favor of the wealthiest person in the world. Yet all his riches could not buy you good health if you had an incurable disease. Regardless of how wealthy or powerful someone might be, there's always a boundary beyond which he or she cannot go. But God has no boundaries. With Him nothing is impossible (Luke 1:37). And out of His limitless riches, He blesses those who fear Him.

As I've studied the fear of God in the Psalms, I've noticed how often blessing is promised to those who fear Him. In fact there are fifteen or so passages on this subject. I've grouped them under four headings: provision, protection, guidance, and compassion.

ENJOYING HIS PROVISION

Psalm 34:9–10 reads,

> Fear the LORD, you his saints,
>> for those who fear him lack nothing.
> The lions may grow weak and hungry,
>> but those who seek the LORD lack no good thing.

Then in Psalm 111:5 we read, "He provides food for those who fear him; he remembers his covenant forever." God promises to provide for those who fear Him.

Examples of this are found throughout Scripture. One of the most notable is God's provision for the widow at Zarephath (1 Kings 17:7–15). She was gathering a few sticks to cook one last meal for herself and her son to eat—and then die—when the prophet Elijah said to her, "Don't be afraid. Go home and do as you have said. But first make a small cake of bread for me from what you have and bring it to me, and then make something for yourself and your son."

This was a bold request to make. A family is down to its last meager meal, and God's servant tells them to feed him first. But Elijah knew God was going to work a miracle to provide for the widow and her son as well as himself.

This is exactly what happened. "She went away and did as Elijah had told her. So there was food every day for Elijah and for the woman and her family. For the jar of flour was not used up and the jug of oil did not run dry, in keeping with the word of the LORD spoken by Elijah" (17:15–16).

Jesus gave us insight into this incident when He spoke of it in Luke 4:25–26—"I assure you that there were many widows in Israel in Elijah's time, when the sky was shut for three and a half years and there was a severe famine throughout the land. Yet Elijah was not sent to any of them, but to a widow in Zarephath in the region of Sidon."

God sent Elijah to the widow's house not just to provide for him, but to provide also for the widow and her son. God could have provided for Elijah in any number of ways. In fact He had earlier done so through some ravens (1 Kings 17:2–6). God didn't need the widow, but the widow needed Him. God had determined to provide for her, but He did this as she herself provided for Elijah.

Here was a tangible expression of the fear of God. The widow, even though a Gentile and outside of God's covenant nation at the time, through faith obeyed God. She believed God's promise and obeyed His command, both given to her through God's servant.

Hebrews 11:8 tells us that "by faith Abraham . . . obeyed." Obedience—one of those fundamental characteristics of the person who fears God—often requires an act of faith on our part. In fact faith can sometimes be described as "obeying God and trusting Him for the results." This is what the widow did, thereby demonstrating her fear of God.

What God did for the widow, He continues to do today for those who fear Him. It may not be a miraculous provision, but He does order His providences in such a way that He cares for those who fear Him.

Early in my experience in Christian ministry I needed a topcoat, having moved from a mild to a cold climate. I priced a coat in a store but had no money to buy it. One day in the mail I received two letters. One contained a check from a friend for the exact amount of the price of the coat; the other had a request from a mission organization for funds. As I prayed over the funds request I felt prompted to send the entire amount of the check I'd received to the mission. A few days later I received a second check in the mail, again for the price of the coat. God intended to provide the coat I needed, but He also wanted to teach me to trust Him.

God's promise of provision to those who fear Him does raise a question, however. Does He always provide? Aren't there many instances of Christians starving, particularly in parts of Africa and Asia today? I've sometimes struggled with this question myself.

As we seek answers, we must keep in mind that we'll never fully understand the ways of God in a specific situation. As Paul wrote, "How unsearchable His decisions, and how mysterious His methods!" (Romans 11:33, Williams New Testament).

We also need to realize that in God's manner of operating today, He most often supplies the needs of His people who are in dire straits through others of His people. In fact, 2 Corinthians 8 and 9, the Scriptures most often used to teach principles of Christian giving, were written specifically to address this issue: Christians who had plenty meeting the needs of those who had little. Rather than questioning God's faithfulness to His promises, we might better question our own faithfulness as stewards of the resources He has given to us.

ENJOYING HIS PROTECTION

A second promise to those who fear God is protection. A God-fearing person looks to God for protection from harm and danger. Psalm 33:16-18 reads,

> No king is saved by the size of his army;
>> no warrior escapes by his great strength.
> A horse is a vain hope for deliverance;
>> despite all its great strength it cannot save.
> But the eyes of the LORD are on those who fear him,
>> on those whose hope is in his unfailing love.

The contrast here is not between the *use* of human means and reliance upon God, but between *reliance* on human means and on God. The human means in the psalm are all taken from a military setting: the size of an army, the warrior's strength, and the strength of the cavalry horse. David, the author of this psalm, was a warrior himself, so he appreciated the importance of these human means and used them. Yet he turned his hope to God.

I try to be careful when I drive. Yet I know that however careful I may be, only God can protect me from a foolish mistake of my own or another driver. In the fear of God, I must look to Him for protection.

The "eyes of the LORD" in the passage from Psalm 33 refers to His constant watch-care. A contemporary illustration would be the lifeguard at a swimming pool who constantly watches for signs of someone in trouble. But this illustration doesn't do justice to God's watch-care. The lifeguard might be distracted or looking toward the other end of the pool. He or she cannot watch every swimmer every moment. But God's eyes are never distracted, never turned away from us. In His infiniteness He carefully watches over each of His own, every moment of their lives.

Another promise of protection is Psalm 145:19, which reads, "He fulfills the desires of those who fear him; he hears their cry and saves them." God not only watches over us; He listens for our cries for help and saves us. He's like a mother whose ears seem tuned to hear her baby's cry. He even sends His angel to encamp around those who fear Him (Psalm 34:7). None of us knows how many times an angel of God has protected us when we were not even aware of it.

But again the question arises: Does God always save us from harm? Obviously the answer is no. How then do we resolve God's promise with the realities of life? Again we must see God's hand working to bring about His purposes for us, purposes that we often don't understand.

You've probably picked up a recurring theme in this book: the importance of trusting God when we don't understand what He's doing. Although I didn't devote a separate chapter to it, this trait of trusting God in times of adversity is certainly one of the marks of a God-fearing person. And our trust will be rewarded—if not in this life, certainly in the life to come. As William S. Plumer, a nineteenth-century theologian, wrote, "Among all the redeemed in glory there is not one who looks back and sees that on earth there was any mistake in the divine conduct towards him. God does all things well."[2]

ENJOYING HIS GUIDANCE

Psalm 25:12 reads, "Who, then, is the man that fears the LORD? He will instruct him in the way chosen for him."

This instruction "in the way chosen for him" refers to the Lord's guidance in our lives. Christians often talk about "finding" or "knowing" the will of God in regard to a particular decision they must make. The thrust of Scripture, however, is not on our finding God's will, but upon His guiding us. Psalm 23:3, for example, says, "He guides me in paths of righteousness for his name's sake." This is not the place to get into *how* God guides. I just want to point out that guidance is one of the blessings promised to those who fear God.

Not that God's guidance is always easy to discern and follow. Sometimes it *seems* as if He leaves us on our own to determine the best choice or course of action. But in the end, often in ways that surprise us, God guides us in His path for our lives. As we saw earlier in Psalm 139:16, our days were written in His book before one of them came to be, and He will sovereignly fulfill that plan in His own way. As I look back over almost fifty years of being a Christian, I can't think of a single instance where God failed to guide me in some important decision I needed to make.

In all three of these areas of promise—provision, protection, and guidance—I've tried to be realistic about the fact that it often *seems* as if God is not fulfilling one of His promises. Yet we know God cannot lie or be untrue to His Word. As He said to Jeremiah, "I am watching over My word to perform it" (Jeremiah 1:12, NASB).

As those who seek to fear Him, we may *plead* these promises before God, but we have to leave it to Him to fulfill them in the way and time He sees best for us. I emphasize the word *plead* because I prefer that word to the expression "claim the promises of God." The word *claim* suggests an obligation on God's part, of which of course there is none. *Plead*, on the other hand, acknowledges our helplessness and dependence on God, and at the same time recognizes that we have no claim upon Him.

Enjoying His Compassion

One of my favorite passages of Scripture is Psalm 103. This song of praise both begins and ends with the exclamation, "Praise the LORD, O my soul." The entire psalm is a tribute to God's goodness, but I want to direct your attention especially to verses 8–18, which magnify God's compassion.

> [8]The LORD is compassionate and gracious,
>
>> slow to anger, abounding in love.
>
> [9]He will not always accuse,
>
>> nor will he harbor his anger forever;
>
> [10]he does not treat us as our sins deserve
>
>> or repay us according to our iniquities.
>
> [11]For as high as the heavens are above the earth,
>
>> so great is his love for *those who fear him;*
>
> [12]as far as the east is from the west,
>
>> so far has he removed our transgressions from us.
>
> [13]As a father has compassion on his children,
>
>> so the LORD has compassion on *those who fear him;*
>
> [14]for he knows how we are formed,
>
>> he remembers that we are dust.
>
> [15]As for man, his days are like grass,
>
>> he flourishes like a flower of the field;
>
> [16]the wind blows over it and it is gone,
>
>> and its place remembers it no more.
>
> [17]But from everlasting to everlasting
>
>> the LORD's love is with *those who fear him,*
>
>> and his righteousness with their children's children—
>
> [18]with those who keep his covenant
>
>> and remember to obey his precepts.

Note that the psalmist refers three times to God's love or compassion to those who fear Him (verses 11,13,17). Again note the superlatives he uses.

God's love is "as high as the heavens are above the earth" (verse 11). He removes our transgressions from us "as far as the east is from the west" (verse 12). And His love is "from everlasting to everlasting" (verse 17). All three expressions suggest infinity. God's love and compassion are infinite toward those who fear Him.

Today the word *compassion* is used for pity, or for the desire to relieve someone's distress. In Psalm 103, however, it refers to God's patience and forgiveness. He is "compassionate and gracious, slow to anger, abounding in love." "He does not treat us as our sins deserve or repay us according to our iniquities."

The overall message of this portion of Psalm 103 can be summed up in the words of verse 3: It is God "who forgives all your sins." This is the promise to those who fear Him. *He forgives all our sins.* Perhaps this is why Psalm 103 is one of my favorites. The longer I live, the more I see the sinful corruption of my heart; yet the more I see of God's love and compassion toward me. I'm glad the fear of the Lord has more to do with God's character than with mine.

We must never forget, though, why God so freely and completely forgives us. It's only because the penalty for our sins has already been borne by Christ. But the fact that Christ *has* paid our penalty should give us the assurance that God has indeed removed our sins from us as far as the east is from the west. We must always seek our assurance of forgiveness not only in God's compassion toward us, but in Christ's death for us.

So we see the promises of God's blessing to those who fear Him: His provision, protection, guidance, and compassion. Of course all of God's blessings promised throughout the Bible are for those who fear Him. I have selected only a few from the Psalms where the promise is directly connected to the fear of the Lord. All this is to help us understand why there is joy in fearing God.

Before we leave this section, however, there's one more important truth we need to consider. Though these blessings are promised to those who fear God, they do not come to us *because* we fear God. They come to us because of the merit of Christ. He is the One who fully delighted in the fear of the Lord (Isaiah 11:3), and only He has ever perfectly feared God. Our fear of the Lord is always imperfect and inadequate. It could never, on its own merit, earn one iota of the blessings God has promised to those who fear Him. It is only "in Christ" that God's promises to those who fear Him are always "Yes" (2 Corinthians 1:20).

So we do not fear God in order to earn His promised blessings. We fear Him because of who He is and what He has done for us. And then, out of the riches of His own grace in Christ, He fulfills His promises to those who fear Him.

A SCROLL OF REMEMBRANCE

There is still one further reason for joy in fearing God. We read in Malachi 3:16,

> Then those who feared the LORD talked with each other, and the LORD listened and heard. A scroll of remembrance was written in his presence concerning those who feared the LORD and honored his name.

This passage was written in a time of deep spiritual decline among the Jews. They questioned God's love (1:2). They showed contempt for Him (1:6–7). They robbed God of the tithes and offerings due Him (3:8). And they said, "It is futile to serve God" (3:14).

In the midst of this national ungodliness, however, there was a group who feared the Lord, and who talked to one another. Undoubtedly they encouraged each other in the spirit of Hebrews 3:13—"Encourage one another daily, as long as it is called Today, so that none of you may be hardened by sin's deceitfulness."

In commenting on Malachi 3:16, Matthew Henry wrote:

> They spoke often one to another concerning the God they feared, and that name of his which they thought so much of; for out of the

abundance of the heart the mouth will speak, and a good man, out of a good treasure there, will bring forth good things. Those that feared the Lord kept together as those that were company for each other; they spoke kindly and endearingly one to another, for the preserving and promoting of mutual love, that that might not wax cold when iniquity did thus abound. They spoke intelligently and edifyingly to one another, for the increasing and improving of faith and holiness; they spoke one to another in the language of those that fear the Lord and think on his name—the language of Canaan. When profaneness had come to so great a height as to trample upon all that is sacred, then those that feared the Lord spoke often one to another.[3]

And as these faithful, God-fearing people encouraged one another with their words, "the LORD listened and heard." This, of course, is a metaphorical expression, for as we saw earlier, God knows our words before they're even on our tongues. The expression is intended to convey that God took special notice of their words to each other.

Then God had a scroll of remembrance written before Him concerning these people who feared Him and honored His name. God does not need a book of remembrance. Being omniscient, He never forgets. Rather the scroll is an allusion to the "custom of ancient Near Eastern kings to have a record written of the most important events at their court and in their kingdom."[4] (See Esther 6:1–2 for a good example of this.) This was God's way of giving special honor to those who feared Him and who encouraged each other in the fear of the Lord.

We live in a day much like the days of Malachi. Not only has society as a whole become ungodly, but even much of the church of Jesus Christ has lost the fear of God. God is looked upon not as the One to be feared, but as someone to meet our felt needs and help us with our problems. The church today is too much like the Jews of Isaiah's time of whom he wrote:

They say to the seers,
   "See no more visions!"
and to the prophets,
   "Give us no more visions of what is right!
Tell us pleasant things,
   prophesy illusions.
Leave this way,
   get off this path,
and stop confronting us
   with the Holy One of Israel!" (Isaiah 30:10–11)

This is the description of so much of Christianity around us today. "Tell us pleasant things, but above all, stop confronting us with the Holy One of Israel." "Don't speak to us of the fear of God."

God does have His faithful ones, however. Even in these difficult days there are those who delight to fear God and who encourage others to do the same.

Are you one of those? If so you have already discovered the joy of fearing God. But I pray that you and I will continue to grow in this fear until one day we hear those words of ultimate joy:

"Well done, good and faithful servant!
You have been faithful with a few things;
I will put you in charge of many things.
Come and share your Master's happiness!"

Notes

1. John Piper, *Desiring God* (Portland, Ore.: Multnomah, 1986), 73.

2. William S. Plumer, *Psalms* (1867, reprint, Carlisle, Pa.: Banner of Truth Trust, 1975), 419.

3. Matthew Henry, *A Commentary on the Whole Bible* (Old Tappan, N. J.: Revell, n.d.), 4:1499.

4. Pieter A. Verhoef, *The Books of Haggai and Malachi, The New International Commentary on the Old Testament,* (Grand Rapids: Eerdmans, 1987), 321.